Basic Political Writings
of Jean-Jacques Rousseau

Jean-Jacques Rousseau

BASIC POLITICAL WRITINGS

DISCOURSE ON THE SCIENCES AND THE ARTS

DISCOURSE ON THE ORIGIN OF INEQUALITY

DISCOURSE ON POLITICAL ECONOMY

ON THE SOCIAL CONTRACT

Translated and edited by DONALD A. CRESS

Introduced by PETER GAY

HACKETT PUBLISHING COMPANY
INDIANAPOLIS/CAMBRIDGE

JEAN-JACQUES ROUSSEAU: 1712-1778

Cover design by Richard L. Listenberger
Interior design by James N. Rogers

For further information, please address
Hackett Publishing Company, Inc.
P.O. Box 44937
Indianapolis, Indiana 46244–0937

95 94 93 92   4 5 6 7 8 9 10

Library of Congress Cataloging in Publication Data

Rousseau, Jean-Jacques, 1712-1778.
  Basic political writings.

  Bibliography: p.
  Contents: Discourse on the sciences and arts —
Discourse on the origin of inequality — Discourse
on political economy — [etc.]
  1. Political science — Collected works. I. Cress,
Donald A.   II. Title.
JC179.R7   1987b   320'.01   87-23610
ISBN 0-87220-048-5
ISBN 0-87220-047-7 (pbk.)

The paper used in this publication meets the minimum requirements of American National Standard for Information Sciences—Permanence of Paper for Printed Library Materials, ANSI Z39.48-1984.
∞

CONTENTS

TRANSLATOR'S NOTE

The translations contained in this volume are based on the excellent *Oeuvres Complètes de Jean-Jacques Rousseau*, vol. III (Paris: Pléiade, 1964). A comment is in order regarding my translation of "moeurs." No single English word adequately renders "moeurs," a word that denotes both tastes and customs, as well as moral and societal norms. Rather than translate "moeurs" by means of a confusing variety of ever-changing English words or with a long tendentious phrase, I have elected simply to translate "moeurs" as "mores" throughout this volume.

INTRODUCTION

I

Every student of political theory compiling a list, however short, of essential books in his discipline, must include Rousseau's *Social Contract*. All will agree that it is a necessary classic. Yet here agreement ends. The book has been called an encomium to democracy and a blueprint for totalitarianism—or, in an attempt to reconcile the irreconcilable, the design of totalitarian democracy. Individualists, collectivists, anarchists, socialists—all have taken courage from Rousseau's controversial masterpiece.

All these readings cannot be correct at once. There are interpretations of historic texts that vary because they are complementary—they throw light on different aspects or sources of the work. In grasping for larger meanings, such readings can be reconciled in a higher synthesis. But the interpretations that Rousseau's *Social Contract* has endured diverge more sharply than this: they have proffered contradictory conclusions.

How is such a scandal to be explained? It is far from rare in the history of ideas but still startling every time it occurs. For a century after Rousseau's death in 1778, critics assumed that this inconclusive search after his meaning must have been Rousseau's own doing, the inevitable by-product of a disordered mind ruled by extravagant feeling alone. Rousseau, to be sure, explicitly and emphatically disclaimed this perception of his total thought. "I have written on diverse subjects," he said in 1763, defending his great treatise on education, *Emile,* against its condemnation by the archbishop of Paris, "but always on the same principles, always the same morals, the same beliefs, the same maxims, and, if you will, the same opinions." But nearly all of his contemporaries, like many of his later readers, fixated on that stick-figure Rousseau the lachrymose madman, the noble savage, the impious revolutionary; they refused to see, and even look for, that one principle. Whether Rousseau was the prophet of untrammeled reason or untamed irrationality, of anarchic disorder or collective despotism, his claim to the status of a thinker long seemed worse than pretentious. It seemed ludicrous.

Many of these appraisals, which modern research into Rousseau's ideas has made to seem ludicrous in their turn, stemmed from hasty and partisan perusals of his writings. Recalling one phrase or one sentence, readers projected their own wishes or anxieties into the text before them and found in it what they had placed there.

But one must concede that Rousseau, at least to some measure, connived at his fate. He wrote too well for his own good. Coining memorable epigrams, he practically invited his readers to recall his felicitous terse sayings and to neglect the context in which they were embedded and which was essential to their interpretation. "The man who thinks is a depraved animal," he wrote summarily in an early work; and those who stumbled over this stark declaration and read no further, interpreted it as a barbarian's denial of mankind's most distinctive, most civilized quality. No wonder that most of his readers believed—and there are those who still do—that Rousseau championed the "noble savage," even though this notorious phrase does not appear in his writings, and even though the most "primitivist" of his early work, the *Discourse on the Arts and Sciences,* is far from being a defense of savagery, noble or otherwise. The *Social Contract* is strewn with such happy-unhappy epigrams: "Man is born free, and everywhere he is in chains," the ringing antithesis that opens chapter I, seems like a promise of an unmitigated individualism that the rest of his subtle and complex argument cannot, and was not intended to, sustain. And that phrase about forcing men to be free has generated more controversy, more stinging attacks and elaborate apologies, than the rest of the treatise together. Paradoxically, Rousseau would have been less controverted, and less misunderstood, if he had been a little less felicitous and a little more ponderous.

The greatest obstacle to a full comprehension of the *Social Contract* is, however, a failure of method. All too often its students have analyzed it in isolation both from the rest of his writings and from his life. Of these two related failures, the second is obvious, and understandable. The historian of ideas has a justified dread of reducing his texts to mere precipitates of biographical detail. And Rousseau's life is a particularly intractable problem for his interpreter. As malicious critics did not fail to notice in his time, and have noticed since, his life contradicts, point for point, his lofty postures. The temptation is therefore great to take his work as a smokescreen behind which Rousseau the apostle of independence could sponge off the rich, and Rousseau the advocate of family intimacy could hand his children over to an orphanage. But the dialectical interplay of Rousseau's life and work was far richer than this, and only the biographer who escapes patronizing his pathetic subject will throw much light on Rousseau's political thought. The other isolation, that of the *Social Contract* from his "unpolitical" texts, is rather more subtle and even more consequential. Monographs and specialized collections such as C. E. Vaughan's classic edition of *The Political Writings of Jean-Jacques Rousseau* have only sustained that artificial separation. They have encouraged the study of Rousseau's *Social Contract* apart from his writings on education, on music, on the theatre, on love. And such isolated efforts lead to a fragmentary and distorted reading. While, as Rousseau put it, he could not say everything at the same time, everything he wrote still impinged on everything else; the "one principle" that he insisted he always followed informed all his work. And the same holds true of his life: marked by instability, irresponsibility and, at the end, paranoia, it is also, in very complex ways, a clue to his thought.

As so often, Rousseau proves the best guide to his own meaning. "One must study society through men," he set down in *Emile,* "and men through society: those who would treat politics and ethics separately will never understand either." This introduction is intended to serve as a guide to that way of reading the *Social Contract,* and to explore, briefly, its principal dimensions. I want to show that the *Social Contract* was crucially involved in Rousseau's experience, that it was a thoroughly Genevan document; that, read in conjunction with *Emile,* it is one of the most remarkable treatises on education ever written; and that together, summing up all these dimensions, it is at once a most abstruse and a most personal exploration of the question of authority—the place of a son in a world of fathers.

II

Jean-Jacques Rousseau was born in Geneva on June 28, 1712, the son of a footloose, irresponsible, and tearful watchmaker. His mother died in childbirth, nine days after Jean-Jacques' birth, a catastrophe that his father would never let him forget. The conditions and the place of his birth encapsulate some of the decisive forces that were to shape Rousseau's life. They describe the perimeters of his self-confidence and his self-torment. His father, Isaac Rousseau (or so the son recalled the matter many years later) liked to sit down and reminisce with his son about his late wife: "Very well, father," the boy would reply, made precocious by such treatment, "then we're going to cry." Despite all his tears for his family, Isaac Rousseau was often absent, sometimes for long stretches, to ply his watchmaker's trade abroad. While Jean-Jacques Rousseau later chose to remember his childhood as happy and protected, his actual experience, lost in the shadows of time and uncertain family traditions, seems to have been one of affectionate care by his aunts and sentimental but damagingly intermittent attention by his father. Condensing that childhood in his epoch-making if unreliable *Confessions,* he attributed his ineradicable commitment to feeling to this early environment, and his love for classical literature to his sporadic but intense study in his father's scanty library which included, among other tantalizing titles, Plutarch's *Lives* in French. At twelve, he was sent away to be more formally educated by a pastor Lambercier and, it seems, to be paddled by the pastor's sister —an experience which awakened and encouraged masochistic tastes he never overcame. At thirteen, he was both unusually learned and unusually ignorant.

There followed years of apprenticeship, both literal and figurative. Rousseau briefly worked for an engraver, but deserted from what he later described as his intolerable brutalization. At nearly seventeen, he was sent, by an assiduous priest sensing a possible recruit to the Faith, into the house and arms of a recent convert to Roman Catholicism, the Baronne de Warens, at Annecy. It was a fateful encounter. Madame de Warens made an adventurous, somewhat precarious living in a variety of

ways, including serving her new Church by smoothing the path of promis-
ing new adherents. She was young, imaginative, and attractive, only
twelve years Rousseau's senior. And she succeeded: with her help and
that of other agents, Rousseau abjured the Calvinist religion of his fathers.
But his Catholic phase remained, though a long episode, anything but a
profound experience. More lasting was Madame de Warens' success with
Rousseau in the more delicate area of sexual instruction. Living in her
house, he soon called her "Maman," while he was "petit" to her. After
about four years of this cozy intimacy, troubled by the sexual temptations
that seemed to be coming Rousseau's way—he was, after all, over twenty!
—she earnestly invited him to her bed. Rarely has so emotional an en-
gagement had so calculating a prelude.

Rousseau had his doubts and his fears. "In accepting the favours of
'Maman,'" F. C. Green has written in his sensitive treatment of the episode, "Rousseau knew that for some years she had been sexually intimate
with her amanuensis, Claude Anet, a serious, taciturn young man six
years older than Jean-Jacques, who liked and admired him greatly. . . .
For some months, therefore, Jean-Jacques was a reluctant partner in a
ménage à trois."

The fundamental strains that had haunted young Rousseau since his
birth—were birth and death linked? more specifically, was he, Jean-
Jacques, responsible for his mother's death just by being born?—were now
exacerbated as his Maman, with sober deliberation, proposed to confound
the generations. "It was to me," he recalled in his Confessions, "as though
I had committed incest." The impact of such experiences on his political
thought may be obscure, but it was there. The Social Contract is part of a
lifelong campaign for justification, a pursuit of lost innocence.

For some years, Rousseau studied, wrote, took casual posts that inter-
mittently separated him from Madame de Warens, and wrestled with his
conscience. By 1742, he was in Paris, and a new career began for him.
He was no longer in his first youth, but he made up for it. He found interesting and influential connections, and one patron led to another. He
met a number of prominent philosophers, including Voltaire and Diderot,
and read the others; he invented a system of musical notation, wrote
poetry and an opera, and piled up both flattering and humiliating experiences with the nobility. He also burdened himself with a rather unsuitable
mistress, much later his wife, Thérèse Levasseur, with whom he had five
children in rapid succession—children whom he turned over to foundling
homes, still another burden on his already oppressive conscience.

His breakthrough to fame came in 1750, as he had felt impelled to
enter an essay contest of the Academy of Dijon. The academy posed a
question characteristic of such eighteenth-century intellectual lotteries:
has the reestablishment of the arts and sciences contributed to the purification or the corruption of morals? Conventional though it was, the question struck Rousseau like a religious experience. Walking to Vincennes
to visit Diderot, then incarcerated in the fortress there, he read as he
walked, came upon the prize question and was so overcome that, in some-

thing of a trance, he sat down under a tree. At least that is how he chose to recall the genesis of his first important work. "Oh," he wrote in a famous letter a dozen years later, "if I had ever been able to write a quarter of what I saw and felt under that tree, with what clarity I would have shown all the contradictions of the social system! . . . with what simplicity I would have demonstrated that man is naturally good and that it is by his institutions alone that men become evil." The crucial idea of man's original innocence, and his conviction that the modern world rests on contradictions, have already emerged.

Rousseau's decision to take the negative of the proposition was not very novel, if in his own day not precisely popular. But it was his boldness in choosing that side, quite as much as his argumentation, that won him the prize. He was launched. Difficult, embattled, something of an eccentric, Rousseau proved hard to classify, but the defenders of the reigning religious and political establishment found a name for him: he was one of the philosophes, a subversive. It was an identification accurate in many ways, but one that he increasingly resented as the years passed. Rousseau's second discourse, on the origins of inequality, published in 1754, did not win him a prize; its posthumous reputation was far greater than its contemporary fame: socialists would read it as a pioneering modern attack on private property, democrats as a persuasive defense of equality. For Rousseau himself, this second discourse measurably helped him to complicate his ideas about society and politics. He was on his way to his masterpieces of social thought, the *Emile* and the *Social Contract*.

In 1754, definitively estranged from Catholicism, Rousseau, once more the proud "citizen of Geneva," dedicated his second discourse to his native city-state. And a few years later, as he meditated on the political treatise that was to become the *Social Contract,* it was Genevan society, Genevan scenes, Genevan political controversies, as he recalled and reshaped them in the urgency of intellectual creation, that dominated his mind. His celebrated assault on representation in the *Social Contract* is a striking instance of how much Geneva was on his mind as he laid down principles he proclaimed to be universally valid. It was with the pride of a Genevan that he loaded the English political system with contumely: "The English people believes itself to be free. It is greatly mistaken; it is free only during the election of the members of Parliament. Once they are elected, the populace is enslaved; it is nothing." Then a parting shot: "the use the English people makes of that freedom in the brief moments of its liberty certainly warrants its losing it." Certainly its first readers had no difficulty tracing the arguments, the whole tenor of the *Social Contract,* to its Genevan roots. Voltaire, then resident there and passionately meddling in local politics, took it to be a blatant intervention in the domestic constitutional struggles then at a feverish pitch. And when the Genevan Council of Twenty-Five condemned the *Social Contract* in June 1762, its principal reason was the same: in his plaidoyer, Geneva's attorney-general, Jean-Robert Tronchin, cited numerous passages as proof that Rousseau was retailing rebellious notions that had been circulating in his republic since

the beginning of the eighteenth century. Tronchin greatly underrated both
the originality of the *Social Contract* and Rousseau's gift for synthesis.
But in *placing* the governing fantasies of the work he was perceptive and
largely right.

"Geneva," of course, meant more to Rousseau than a political style by
which other political styles could be measured. It was, for him, a place
of cherished recollections, the city where he had first encountered the
Greek and Roman classics and had encountered them—note well—among
his father's books. Plutarch, he was to say years later, "was the first reading of my childhood; it will be the last reading of my old age." His highly
selective and tendentious classicism, as the *Confessions* leave no doubt,
was indeed mingled with his first memories. To him, the best of good
societies would always be a republic unfettered by a hereditary aristocracy.
"Ceaselessly occupied with Rome and Athens; living, so to speak, with
their great men, myself born Citizen of a Republic, and son of a father
whose patriotism was his strongest passion, I took fire from his example;
I thought myself Greek or Roman; I became the personage whose life I
was reading." As passages in the *Social Contract* testify, he was enough
of a relativist—the disciple of Montesquieu in this matter as in others—
to see the possibility of freedom in moderate aristocracies or elective monarchies. But his ultimate preference was for a Geneva purified, the Geneva
in his fertile mind.

And "Geneva" also implied a powerful incentive toward a certain religious style. Rousseau's native city was, of course, a Calvinist stronghold
—the very home of Calvinism. And while secular doctrines of the Enlightenment had invaded cultivated circles in Geneva, the Calvinist atmosphere remained a palpable legacy even among Voltaire's sophisticated
Genevan friends. And this is the atmosphere that pervades Rousseau's
thinking. He was never an orthodox believer; never a good Calvinist,
never a good Catholic. As a mature thinker, he adopted the deism current
among the *philosophes* of his time: the doctrine that a beneficent god had
created the world with its laws and then withdrawn from it to leave virtuous men to discover its moral rules and live according to its dictates. It
is not an accident that Voltaire, the arch-deist who had little use for Rousseau, should applaud Rousseau's deistic "Profession of Faith of the Savoyard Vicar," that long set-piece he placed into his *Emile*. Rousseau therefore responded not to the Christian theology associated with Calvin's
name, but to what I would call its moral energy, its gospel of usefulness
and simplicity, its call for self-discipline and virtue, and its austerity. That
classical philosophical doctrines—especially Stoicism, which had some
significant affinities with this Calvinist posture—also appealed to Rousseau, only wove Calvinist earnestness all the more inextricably into the
texture of his thought. This—shall I call it Stoical Calvinism—probably
emerges most aggressively in Rousseau's *Lettre à d'Alembert sur les spectacles* of 1758, in which he vehemently rejected d'Alembert's playful proposal that the Genevan republic admit a theatre within its borders. The
suggestion, as his heated prose shows, hit Rousseau at a sensitive spot: it

struck him as a perilous invitation to immorality, an offensive defiance of prized Genevan virtue. In the diatribe he addressed to d'Alembert, Rousseau's virtuous austerity descends into plain philistinism: in the *Social Contract*, it serves the ideal of education: and that is why the *Social Contract* and *Emile* belong together. Yet a third work of this period, the epistolary novel *La nouvelle Héloïse*, published in 1761, is intimately related to his political masterpiece, and helps to clarify his political theory further.

The relevance of *La nouvelle Héloïse* to the *Social Contract* is not immediately apparent. Its hero, Saint-Preux, a striving, intelligent bourgeois, finds that the beautiful aristocratic Julie, whose tutor he is, has fallen in love with him; this bold though eminently virtuous girl first seduces and then dismisses him, and eventually chooses to marry an elderly, unemotional but highly eligible atheist, Wolmar. Even though her marriage is happy, blessed with children, money, local good works, and endless opportunities for self-examination and self-expression, Julie never forgets her first lover. But, though Saint-Preux returns and reawakens old temptations, she does not succumb to his charm but dies, in her accustomed self-sacrificing way, after saving one of her children from drowning. This allows her survivors to worship her as a secular saint. In portraying the idyllic little community that Julie and Wolmar govern with a light hand, superintending honest toil and decent festivals, and in permitting Julie to probe her moral and erotic condition in interminable exchanges with an understanding correspondent, Rousseau celebrates the virtues of candor, maturity, simplicity, self-restraint, good health, reason warmed by love and love ennobled by reason. The ethical religion which the leading characters explore with considerable gusto in *La nouvelle Héloïse* reads like the application of the "Profession of Faith of the Savoyard Vicar," while the social, cultural, economic, and implicitly political Utopia as well as the pedagogic practice in the novel, foreshadow the rest of *Emile*. The implicit, sometimes explicit message of *La nouvelle Héloïse* is that men and women must make themselves over if they are to be worthy of true self-government.

Emile gives this ideal its theoretical underpinning. It is only fitting that contemporaries should have thought the book a novel; its time of publication just a year after *La nouvelle Héloïse*, its free use of dialogue and interpolated stories, and the artificial environment in which Emile grows up, made *Emile* seem a work of the imagination. So it is, but its severely chronological structure, its coherent argument, and its polemical drive, make it the most radical educational treatise possible—radical in the original sense of the term: a treatise reaching down to the roots of man. Modern society, as Rousseau had already insisted at length in his discourses, is so corrupt and so unnatural that only a fundamental upheaval in the formation of human beings can make man truly human.

While *Emile* is substantial, its governing idea is simple. It is not just kindness to the young: that was not an invention of Rousseau's but can be found in earlier pedagogic treatises including John Locke's *Some*

Thoughts Concerning Education, of which Rousseau thought highly. It
is kindness with a purpose. Rousseau, the amateur of ancient philosophy,
wanted children educated in obedience to the Stoical doctrine that man
must live in accord with nature. The consequences of applying this maxim
to the training of the young are far-reaching: the child may be father to
the man, but he is a child first. Others, to be sure, had claimed to know
this; Locke had said as much in his book on education. But nobody had
seriously pursued the implications of this saying. Rousseau now spelled
out in detail precisely what it meant in practice. The educator must closely
consult the child's capacities and use them to help him grow. Rote learning and forced reading are nonsensical: they make the child into a parrot,
not a man. Even reasoning with the young, though superficially kind, is at
best futile and in effect cruel. For reason is the last capacity of the human
animal to awaken; it should therefore be the last to be brought into action.
It is absurd to make the child learn geography from books or maps; make
him ramble across rivers and meadows, teach him to keep his eyes open
as he walks; set him adrift on purpose to teach him how to find his way:
that is the only road to geography. And other disciplines must be acquired
in the same practical and memorable way. Young Emile, Rousseau says
emphatically, needs not "words, more words, still more words," but
"things, things!" Rousseau was the Bacon of education. Only the educator
who enters empathetically into the nature of the growing child's development and the range of his experience can lastingly enrich him.

While young Emile comes to reading late, this is not anti-intellectualism
on Rousseau's part, though in the hands of Rousseau's belated followers,
modern Progressive educators, it was often to become just that. It is,
rather, a perfectly logical inference from his developmental scheme. Emile
will begin to read when he is ready for it, at fifteen, and his first book will
be the bible of the self-reliant, *Robinson Crusoe.* But practicality is not
all there is to learning, even for Emile; in adolescence, Emile will discover,
and love, history and biography and, by the time he is twenty, the Latin
classics. A surprising agenda, but not a reading list for philistines.

This timetable is more than a pedagogic procedure designed to have
Emile remember what he has learned. It embodies a cultural criticism
and a cultural ideal. Since Emile's tutor discountenances pretty ways,
conventional lies, impressive displays of erudition, his charge will grow
up not with a false "civilized" facade, but with all the marks of authen-
ticity. He will be confident but not conceited, discriminating but not snob-
bish, rational but not cold, self-reliant but not self-centered; he will be
sound in mind and body alike, honest, affectionate, and disinterested. And
to be disinterested means to be public-spirited. Emile will be the one kind
of adult, in short, who can make the good community of Rousseau's
Social Contract work. The immoral society of his day was making immoral
men, incapable of reforming a culture in whose corruption they could not
help but connive. Hence they were compelled to perpetuate that which
they should destroy. The one way to break this impasse was to create a
new man who could, in turn, create a new society. It is an essential pre-

condition for this work that the young must be rapidly removed from corrupting influences: that is why Rousseau has his tutor live in isolation with his little charge.

The link between Rousseau's *Emile* and *Social Contract* should be obvious. Each requires the other. The makers and beneficiaries of the general will, which, Rousseau insists, is always right, are a gathering of Emiles. If man is born free yet is everywhere in chains, who but an Emile can do the work of liberation?

Once the community of Emiles has been formed, it will govern itself calmly, wisely, and generously. The key element in the citizen's activity is his participation in decision-making, and as a sound citizen he will cast his vote by listening not to his own selfish interests, but to his perception of the public weal. Of course, with the best of intentions, he may confound the two. But then the decision of the majority—not just any majority, but the intelligent, sensible, uncorrupted majority that Rousseau envisions— will recall the straying minority to its duty, to its true, larger interest. The closer private wills, as Rousseau puts it, approximate the general will, the more likely can that will realize itself in action. In a word, Rousseau seeks the virtuous citizen, who will, as he puts it in the *Social Contract,* "make virtue reign."

III

Rousseau's *Social Contract,* then, is a complex personal document drawing on all his experience and obliquely addressing his deepest problems, but it also forms a link in the great chain of treatises in political theory that began with Plato's *Republic.* Such treatises are about many things—the best form of government, the origins of the state, the place of religion in the polity, the relation of morals to laws, the interaction between legislature and executive. And Rousseau's *Social Contract* is about all these matters. But above all it is about the fundamental question agitating all political thinkers: that of authority. The question for the individual has always been: Why, and whom, should I obey? It is not simply a political question or, rather, the political question is a familial question writ large. It is a question the child may never consciously ask, but it is lodged somewhere in his mind. It is a question that the slave, or the subject wholly habituated to unconditional obedience, may never seriously canvass, but it will occur to him in rebellious moments. Rousseau raises the question again, and answers it in a wholly original way.

The liberals of Rousseau's time, and those both before and after him, had sought to delimit the respective boundaries of freedom and constraint, giving freedom as much scope as seemed reasonable. And Rousseau, like them, attempts to establish the respective rights of the sovereign and the citizen. But he goes further. He sees this tension not as a relation to be mapped, but as a paradox to be resolved. In Rousseau's version of the *Social Contract,* man surrenders all his rights without becoming a slave.

This is how he formulates the problem: "To find a form of association which defends and protects with the whole common power the person and property of each associate, and in which each, uniting himself to all, yet obeys himself alone, and remains as free as before." As one reflects on Rousseau's earlier writings, notably the discourses, one recognizes that the "one principle" which he professed had always guided him, is at work once again, on a larger stage. Man is good. And he can afford to exchange his natural for his civic freedom, to translate his original goodness into social action. Rousseau, we must remember, was not a primitivist; he did not condemn all organized society, and he believed that there was one society, one yet to be constructed, that was infinitely preferable to pre-political conditions. Man can surrender his natural freedom because, while he becomes a subject, he remains a master. In the good community he essentially obeys himself.

This position, which Rousseau works out in considerable detail in the *Social Contract,* is certainly not without its difficulties. But one difficulty, imported by critics into Rousseau's text, is not there, and we may therefore dismiss it quickly: the state, in Rousseau's system, is never the master, always the servant. For the body to which the individual yields his natural rights is not the government but society—a community of beings like himself. Just as Rousseau insisted that force does not create rights, so he insists that government, though it holds the monopoly of force, is always an agent of the citizens it protects.

Another difficulty, though, that surrounding Rousseau's civil religion, is a real stumbling block for the modern reader. Rousseau was, as a true *philosophe,* anticlerical. And he had particular reasons, implicit in his political philosophy, for inveighing against clerical establishments: he vehemently opposed any associations, lay or clerical, that might impose obligations on individuals and thus divide their loyalties. Rousseau's good society needed all of the citizen. At the same time, Rousseau, again with the *philosophes* on this point, thought that men require the prod and the curb of religion to assure their moral conduct. This notion was a commonplace among the men of the Enlightenment, though just what kind of frightening superstitions enlightened rulers should inculcate in their subjects to keep them docile was a matter of earnest debate and real uncertainty. Voltaire, for one, believed that thoughtful men did not need any superstition whatever; even if they should fall into the error of atheism they would not surrender to a life of self-indulgence or crime. It was different with illiterate laborers or peasants: freed from the spectre of eternal divine punishment, they might well take to stealing and murdering. Yet some *philosophes,* at least, were so implacably hostile to the superstitions which, in their view, all organized religions professed, that they were willing to take their chances with the truth, and leave the securing of society to the police.

Rousseau took part in this debate, and, as his chapter on the civil religion, added to the *Social Contract* late, reveals, was torn by it. On the one hand, he wanted no part of intolerance, of persecutions, of lying. On the other hand, he was convinced, as I have said, that men—all men— must have some religious beliefs that would make, and keep, them moral beings. This meant that the sovereign of the good society must devise "a purely civil profession of faith, the articles of which it belongs to the sovereign to establish, not exactly as dogmas of religion, but as sentiments of sociability, without which it is impossible to be a good citizen or a faithful subject." The dogmas should be simple and few in number, in- cluding belief in the existence of a powerful, intelligent, beneficent deity, a life to come, the good fortune of the just and the punishment of the wicked, the sacredness of the social contract and of the laws. Whoever does not believe these dogmas can be banished from the state, and who- ever has officially subscribed to them and then acts as if he does not believe in them should be put to death.

This harsh set of propositions is not a casual or accidental addition to Rousseau's political thinking; it lies squarely at the heart of his earnest Calvinist commitment to virtue. And as the reader of his *Social Contract,* with all its imaginativeness, all its rich panoply of ideas, must recognize, the dictatorship of virtue is a strenuous and in many ways a dangerous ideal.

PETER GAY

ROUSSEAU BIBLIOGRAPHY

1. COLLECTED WORKS

Bernard Gagnebin and Marcel Raymond, general editors, *Oeuvres Complètes de Jean-Jacques Rousseau*. Paris: Pléiade, 1959 ff.

C.E. Vaughn, *The Political Writings of Jean-Jacques Rousseau*, 2 vols. Cambridge: Cambridge University Press, 1915; reprinted Oxford: Basil Blackwell, 1962.

2. BIBLIOGRAPHIES

Bibliographies of recent work on Rousseau are published annually in the *Annales de la Société Jean-Jacques Rousseau*.

3. STUDIES

Pierre Burgelin, *La Philosophie de l'existence de J.J. Rousseau*. Paris: PUF, 1952.

David R. Cameron, *The Social Thought of Rousseau and Burke: A Comparative Study*. Toronto: University of Toronto Press, 1973.

Ernst Cassirer, *The Question of Jean-Jacques Rousseau*. Translated and edited by Peter Gay. Bloomington: Indiana University Press, 1963.

Alfred Cobban, *Rousseau and the Modern State*. 2nd revised edition, London: Allen and Unwin, 1964.

Maurice Cranston and Richard S. Peters, eds., *Hobbes and Rousseau: A Collection of Critical Essays*. New York: Doubleday, 1972.

Lester G. Crocker, *Rousseau's Social Contract: An Interpretative Essay*. Cleveland: Case Western Reserve Press, 1968.

Robert Derathé, *Le rationalisme de Jean-Jacques Rousseau*. Paris: PUF, 1948.

Robert Derathé, *Jean-Jacques Rousseau et la science politique de son temps*. Paris: PUF, 1950.

Stephen Ellenburg, *Rousseau's Political Philosophy: An Interpretation From Within*. Ithaca: Cornell University Press, 1976.

Etudes sur le Contrat social de Jean-Jacques Rousseau. Journées d'étude sur le contrat social, Dijon, 3-6 mai 1962. Paris: Société les Belles Lettres, 1964.

Peter Gay, "Reading About Rousseau," in *The Party of Humanity: Essays in the French Enlightenment*. New York: W.W. Norton, 1971.

Hilail Gildin, *Rousseau's Social Contract: The Design of the Argument.* Chicago: University of Chicago Press, 1983.

Victor Goldschmidt, *Anthropologie et politique: les principes du système de Rousseau.* Paris: Vrin, 1974.

Henri Gouhier, *Les Méditations métaphysiqus de Jean-Jacques Rousseau.* Paris: Vrin, 1970.

Henri Gouhier, *Rousseau et Voltaire: portraits dans deux miroirs.* Paris: Vrin, 1983.

F.C. Green, *Jean-Jacques Rousseau: A Critical Study of His Life and Writings.* Cambridge: Cambridge University Press, 1955.

Ronald Grimsley, *Jean-Jacques Rousseau: A Study of Self-Awareness.* Cardiff: University of Wales Press, 1961.

Ronald Grimsley, *The Philosophy of Rousseau.* New York: Oxford University Press, 1973.

Jean Guéhenno, *Jean-Jacques Rousseau,* 2 vols. Translated by John and Doreen Weightman. New York: Columbia University Press, 1966.

Charles W. Hendel, *Jean-Jacques Rousseau: Moralist,* 2 vols. London: Oxford University Press, 1934; reprinted Indianapolis: Library of Liberal Arts, 1962.

_____ , *Jean-Jacques Rousseau et son oeuvre: problèmes et recherches.* Commémoration et colloque de Paris, 16–20 Oct. 1962 organisès par la Comitè national pour la commæmoration de Jean-Jacques Rousseau. Paris: Klincksieck, 1964.

R. A. Leigh, *Rousseau after Two Hundred Years: Proceedings of the Cambridge Bicentennial Colloquium.* Cambridge: Cambridge University Press, 1982.

Ramon Lemos, *Rousseau's Political Philosophy: An Exposition and Interpretation.* Athens: University of Georgia Press, 1977.

Andrew Levine, *The Politics of Autonomy: A Kantian Reading of Rousseau's Social Contract.* Amherst: University of Massachusetts Press, 1976.

Alasdair C. MacIntyre, *A Short History of Ethics.* New York: Macmillan, 1966.

Roger D. Masters, *The Political Philosophy of Rousseau.* Princeton University Press, 1968.

James Miller, *Rousseau, Dreamer of Democracy.* New Haven: Yale University Press, 1984.

ROUSSEAU Bibliography

John B. Noone, *Rousseau's Social Contract: A Conceptual Analysis*. Athens: University of Georgia Press, 1980.

Marc. F. Plattner, *Rousseau's State of Nature: An Interpretation of the Discourse on Inequality*. Dekalb: Northern Illinois University Press, 1979.

Judith N. Shklar, *Men and Citizens: A Study of Rousseau's Social Theory*. Cambridge: Cambridge University Press, 1969.

Jean Starobinski, *Jean-Jacques Rousseau: La transparence et l'obstacle*. Paris: Plon, 1957.

Jacob Leib Talmon, *The Origins of Totalitarian Democracy*. New York: Praeger, 1960.

DISCOURSE WHICH WON THE PRIZE ON THE ACADEMY OF DIJON[1] IN THE YEAR 1750

On this Question Proposed by that Academy:
Whether the Restoration of the Sciences and the Arts
Contributed to the Purification of Mores[2]

by a Citizen of Geneva

"Here I am the barbarian
because they do not
understand me." — Ovid[3]

1. [Editor's Note: The Académie des sciences et belles lettres de Dijon was founded by Hector Bernard Pouffier, Dean of the Parliament of Bourgogne. In the October 1749 issue of *Mercure de France*, the Académie announced the topic of its 1750 essay competition: whether the restoration of the sciences and the arts contributed to the purification of morals. The prize consisted of a gold medallion.]

2. [Editor's Note: See Translator's Note, p. vi.]

3. [Editor's Note: *Tristia*, Book V, x. 37. Rousseau here quotes the Latin.]

FOREWORD[4]

What is celebrity? Here is the unhappy work to which I owe mine. Certainly this piece, which earned me a prize and made a name for me, is at best mediocre, and I dare to add that it is one of the least of this collection.[5] What an abyss of miseries the author would have avoided, had his first work been received as it deserved to be! But it was inevitable that a favor, unjust from the beginning, visited upon me by degrees a stiff penalty that is even more unjust.

4. [Editor's Note: This Foreword did not appear in print until 1781.]

5. [Editor's Note: The reference is to an edition of Rousseau's collected works which the author himself was preparing for publication.]

DISCOURSE ON THE SCIENCES AND THE ARTS

His prize-winning first Discourse (1750) made Rousseau famous — or, rather, notorious — overnight. As we know, he later described his first reading of the contest question from the Academy of Dijon that started it all — "Has the reestablishment of the sciences and the arts served to purify or to corrupt manners and morals?" — as a searing emotional upheaval. Whether this episode took place precisely as he recalled it, whether he embroidered or imagined it in retrospect, it was a decisive moment in his career as philosopher and philosophe. *Other cultural critics before him had taken the negative of the question, and denounced times of abundance and luxury as times of corruption. But Rousseau was living in an age and a society in which this stern point of view represented a distinct minority opinion. What is more, Rousseau already showed, in this first important publication, his fatal gift for eloquent, memorable epigrams. He pleaded more vigorously than he knew. The very nature of the question from the Academy of Dijon, inviting extreme statement, only exacerbated his natural disposition in that direction. In later years, Rousseau himself confessed that his first* Discourse *was hardly a masterpiece of logic. But he did not coin, and never used, that evocative phrase, "the noble savage;" his discourse on the sciences and the arts foisted that facile notion on him. A careful reading of this work reveals that it was far more than a naive plea for primitivism, far more than an exhortation to his contemporaries to abandon culture and return to some happy precivilized condition.*

P.G.

PREFACE

Here is one of the great and finest questions ever debated. This discourse is not concerned with those metaphysical subtleties that have found their way into every branch of learning and from which academy-sponsored competitions are not always exempt. Rather, it is concerned with one of those truths which are bound up with the happiness of mankind.

I foresee that I will not easily be forgiven for the side I have dared to choose. Running head on into everything that men admire today, I can expect only universal blame; and the fact of having been honored by the approval of a few wise men does not lead me to count on the approval of the public. Thus I have taken my stand. I do not care about pleasing either the witty or the fashionable. There will always be men destined to be subjugated by the opinions of their century, their country, their society.

1

A man who plays the freethinker and the philosopher today would, for the same reason, have merely been a fanatic at the time of the League.[6] One should not write for such readers when one wants to live beyond one's century.

One more word and I am finished. Counting little on the honor that I have received, I had, since sending it, recast and enlarged this discourse to the point of, in a sense, making another work of it. Today I believe I am obliged to restore it to the state in which it was awarded the prize. I have merely inserted some notes and allowed two easily recognized additions to remain, of which the Academy might perhaps not have approved. I thought that fair-mindedness, respect, and gratitude demanded this notice of me.

DISCOURSE

"We are deceived by the
appearance of right."[7]

Has the restoration of the sciences and the arts contributed to the purification of mores, or to their corruption? That is what is to be examined. Which side should I take in this question? The one, gentlemen, that is appropriate to an honest man who knows nothing and who thinks no less of himself for it.

It will be difficult, I feel, to adapt what I have to say to the tribunal before which I appear. How can I dare to blame the sciences before one of Europe's most learned societies, praise ignorance in a famous Academy, and reconcile contempt for study with respect for the truly learned? I have seen these points of conflict, and they have not daunted me. I am not abusing science, I told myself; I am defending virtue before virtuous men. Integrity is even dearer to good men than erudition is to the studious. What then have I to fear? The enlightenment of the assembly that listens to me? I admit it; but this is owing to the composition of the discourse and not to the sentiment of the speaker. Fair-minded sovereigns have never hesitated to pass judgments against themselves in disputes whose outcomes are uncertain; and the position most advantageous for a just cause is to have to defend oneself against an upright and enlightened opponent who is judge in his own case.

To this motive which heartens me is joined another which determines me, namely that, having upheld, according to my natural light, the side of truth, whatever my success, there is a prize which I cannot fail to receive; I will find it within the depths of my heart.

6. [Editor's Note: Founded in 1576 by Henri, third Duc de Guise, the Holy League was an organization of Catholics dedicated to the suppression of French Protestantism.]

7. [Editor's Note: Horace, *On the Art of Poetry*, v. 25. Rousseau here quotes the Latin.]

PART ONE

It is a grand and beautiful sight to see man emerge somehow from
nothing by his own efforts; dissipate, by the light of his reason, the
shadows in which nature had enveloped him; rise above himself; soar by
means of his mind into the heavenly regions; traverse, like the sun, the
vast expanse of the universe with giant steps; and, what is even grander
and more difficult, return to himself in order to study man and know his
nature, his duties, and his end. All of these marvels have been revived in
the past few generations.

Europe had relapsed into the barbarism of the first ages. A few
centuries ago the peoples of that part of the world, who today live such
enlightened lives, lived in a state worse than ignorance. Some nondes-
cript scientific jargon, even more contemptible than ignorance, had
usurped the name of knowledge, and posed a nearly invincible obstacle
to its return. A revolution was needed to bring men back to common
sense; it finally came from the least expected quarter. It was the stupid
Moslem, the eternal scourge of letters, who caused them to be reborn
among us. The fall of the throne of Constantinople[8] brought into Italy
the debris of ancient Greece. France in turn was enriched by these
precious spoils. Soon the sciences followed letters. To the art of writing
was joined the art of thinking — a sequence of events that may seem
strange, but which perhaps is only too natural. And the chief advantage
of commerce with the Muses began to be felt, namely, that of making
men more sociable by inspiring in them the desire to please one another
with works worthy of their mutual approval.

The mind has its needs, as does the body. The needs of the latter are
the foundations of society; the needs of the former make it pleasant.
While the government and the laws see to the safety and well-being of
assembled men, the sciences, letters and the arts, less despotic and
perhaps more powerful, spread garlands of flowers over the iron chains
with which they are burdened, stifle in them the sense of that original
liberty for which they seem to have been born, make them love their
slavery, and turn them into what is called civilized peoples. Need raised
up thrones; the sciences and the arts have strengthened them. Earthly
powers, love talents and protect those who cultivate them![9] Civilized

8. [Editor's Note: Constantinople (present day Istanbul) was the former capital of the
Byzantine Empire. It was captured by Sultan Mohammed II and the Turks in 1453.]

9. Princes always view with pleasure the spread, among their subjects, of the taste for
pleasant arts and luxuries not resulting in the exporting of money. For, in addition to
nurturing in them that pettiness of soul so appropriate to servitude, they know very well
that all the needs the populace imposes on itself are so many chains which burden it.
Alexander, wishing to keep the Ichthyophagi in a state of dependency, forced them to
renounce fishing and to eat foods common to other peoples. And the savages of America
who go totally naked and who live off the fruit of their hunting have never been tamed.
Indeed, what yoke could be imposed upon men who need nothing?

peoples, cultivate them! Happy slaves, you owe them that delicate and refined taste on which you pride yourselves; that sweetness of character and that urbanity in mores which make relationships among you so cordial and easy; in a word, the appearances of all the virtues without having any.

By this sort of civility, all the more agreeable as it puts on fewer airs, Athens and Rome once distinguished themselves in the much vaunted days of their magnificence and splendor. By it our century and our nation will doubtlessly surpass all times and all peoples. A philosophic tone without pedantry, manners natural yet engaging, equally removed from Teutonic rusticity as from Italian pantomime. These are the fruits of the taste acquired by good schooling and perfected in social interaction.

How sweet it would be to live among us, if outer appearances were always the likeness of the heart's dispositions, if decency were virtue, if our maxims served as our rules, if true philosophy were inseparable from the title of philosopher! But so many qualities are all too rarely found in combination, and virtue seldom goes forth in such great pomp. Expensive finery can betoken a wealthy man, and elegance a man of taste. The healthy and robust man is recognized by other signs. It is in the rustic clothing of the fieldworker and not underneath the gilding of the courtier that one will find bodily strength and vigor. Finery is no less alien to virtue, which is the strength and vigor of the soul. The good man is an athlete who enjoys competing in the nude. He is contemptuous of all those vile ornaments which would impair the use of his strength, most of which were invented merely to conceal some deformity.

Before art had fashioned our manners and taught our passions to speak an affected language, our mores were rustic but natural, and differences in behavior heralded, at first glance, differences of character. At base, human nature was no better, but men found their safety in the ease with which they saw through each other, and that advantage, which we no longer value, spared them many vices.

Today, when more subtle inquiries and a more refined taste have reduced the art of pleasing to established rules, a vile and deceitful uniformity reigns in our mores, and all minds seem to have been cast in the same mold. Without ceasing, politeness makes demands, propriety gives orders; without ceasing, common customs are followed, never one's own lights. One no longer dares to seem what one really is; and in this perpetual constraint, the men who make up this herd we call society will, if placed in the same circumstances, do all the same things unless stronger motives deter them. Thus no one will ever really know those with whom he is dealing. Hence in order to know one's friend, it would be necessary to wait for critical occasions, that is, to wait until it is too late, since it is for these very occasions that it would have been essential to know him.

What a retinue of vices must attend this incertitude! No more sincere friendships, no more real esteem, no more well-founded confidence. Suspicions, offenses, fears, coldness, reserve, hatred, betrayal will unceasingly hide under that uniform and deceitful veil of politeness, under that much vaunted urbanity that we owe to the enlightenment of our century. The name of the master of the universe will no longer be profaned with oaths; rather it will be insulted with blasphemies without our scrupulous ears being offended by them. No one will boast of his own merit, but will disparage that of others. No one will crudely wrong his enemy, but will skillfully slander him. National hatreds will die out, but so will love of country. Scorned ignorance will be replaced by a dangerous Pyrrhonism. Some excesses will be forbidden, some vices held in dishonor, but others will be adorned with the name of virtues. One must either have them or affect them. Let those who wish extoll the sobriety of the wise men of the present. For my part, I see in it merely a refinement of intemperance as unworthy of my praise as their artful simplicity.[10]

Such is the purity that our mores have acquired. Thus have we become decent men. It is for letters, the sciences, and the arts to claim their part in so wholesome an achievement. I will add but one thought: an inhabitant of some distant lands who sought to form an idea of European mores on the basis of the state of the sciences among us, the perfection of our arts, the seemliness of our theatrical performances, the civilized quality of our manners, the affability of our speech, our perpetual displays of goodwill, and that tumultuous competition of men of every age and circumstance who, from morning to night, seem intent on being obliging to one another; that foreigner, I say, would guess our mores to be exactly the opposite of what they are.

Where there is no effect, there is no cause to seek out. But here the effect is certain, the depravation real, and our souls have become corrupted in proportion as our sciences and our arts have advanced toward perfection. Will it be said that this is a misfortune peculiar to our age? No, gentlemen, the evils caused by our vain curiosity are as old as the world. The daily rise and fall of the ocean's waters have not been more unvaryingly subjected to the star which provides us with light during the night, than has the fate of mores and integrity been to the progress of the sciences and the arts. Virtue has been seen taking flight in proportion as their light rose on our horizon, and the same phenomenon has been observed in all times and in all places.

Consider Egypt, that first school of the universe, that climate so fertile beneath a brazen sky, that famous country from which Sesostris[11] departed long ago to conquer the world. She became the mother of philosophy and the fine arts, and soon thereafter was conquered by Cambyses,[12] then by Greeks, Romans, Arabs, and finally Turks.

10. "I love," says Montaigne, "to debate and discuss, but only with a few men and for my own sake. For I find it an especially unworthy profession for a man of honor to serve as a spectacle to the great and shamelessly parade one's mind and one's prattling." It is the profession of all our wits, save one. [Editor's Note: This citation is from Montaigne's "On the Art of Discussion," *Essays*, Book III, chapter 8.]

11. [Editor's Note: A fairly common name among the Egyptian pharaohs. The Sesostris in question here seems to be legendary.]

12. [Editor's Note: Cambyses, King of Persia, conquered Egypt in 525 B.C.]

Consider Greece, formerly populated by heroes who twice conquered Asia, once at Troy and once on their own home ground. The nascent letters had not yet brought corruption into the hearts of her inhabitants; but the progress of the arts, the dissolution of mores and the Macedonian's yoke followed closely upon one another; and Greece, ever learned, ever voluptuous, and ever the slave, experienced nothing in her revolutions but changes of masters. All the eloquence of Demosthenes could never revive a body which luxury and the arts had enervated.

It is at the time of the likes of Ennius and Terence[13] that Rome, founded by a shepherd and made famous by fieldworkers, began to degenerate. But after the likes of Ovid, Catullus, Martial,[14] and that crowd of obscene writers whose names alone offend modesty, Rome, formerly the temple of virtue, became the theater of crime, the disgrace of nations, and the plaything of barbarians. Finally, that capital of the world falls under the yoke which she had imposed on so many peoples, and the day of her fall was the eve of the day when one of her citizens was given the title of Arbiter of Good Taste.[15]

What shall I say about that capital of the Eastern Empire, which, by virtue of its location, seemed destined to be the capital of the entire world, that refuge of the sciences and the arts banished from the rest of Europe — more perhaps out of wisdom than barbarism. All that is most shameful about debauchery and corruption; blackest in betrayals, assassinations, and poisons; most atrocious in the coexistence of every sort of crime: that is what constitutes the fabric of the history of Constantinople. That is the pure source whence radiates to us the enlightenment on which our century prides itself.

But why seek in remote times proofs of a truth for which we have existing evidence before our eyes? In Asia there is an immense country where acknowledgement in the field of letters leads to the highest offices of the state. If the sciences purified mores, if they taught men to shed their blood for their country, if they enlivened their courage, the peoples of China should be wise, free and invincible. But if there is not a single vice that does not have mastery over them; not a single crime that is unfamiliar to them; if neither the enlightenment of the ministers, nor the

---

13. [Editor's Note: Quintus Ennius (239-c.170 B.C.) was an early Latin poet, revered as the father of Roman poetry. Publius Terentius Afer (c.190-c.159 B.C.) was a famous Roman playwright.]

14.   [Editor's Note: Publius Ovidius Naso (43 B.C.-18 A.D.) was a Roman writer, among whose works were *Metamorphoses* and *Ars Amatoris*. Caius Valerius Catullus (c.84-c.54 B.C.) is generally considered one of the greatest of the lyric poets of ancient Rome. Marcus Valerius Martialis (c.40-c.104 A.D.) was a Roman satyrist and epigrammatist. All three writers are perhaps best known for their graphically erotic poetry.]

15. [Editor's Note: Tacitus, in his *Annals*, XVI, 18, states that this title was given to Petronius (d. 66 A.D.), a satyrist and courtier to the Emperor Nero. An indolent and profligate lover of comfort and luxury, Petronius enjoyed a reputation as a man of elegant and refined taste. In recognition of these traits, Petronius was made the "Arbiter of Good Taste," responsible for orchestrating the Emperor's entertainment.]

alleged wisdom of the laws, nor the multitude of the inhabitants of that vast empire have been able to shield her from the yoke of the ignorant and coarse Tartar, what purpose has all her learned men served? What benefit has been derived from the honors bestowed upon them? Could it be to be peopled by slaves and wicked men?

Contrast these scenes with that of the mores of the small number of peoples who, protected against this contagion of vain knowledge, have by their virtues brought about their own happiness and the model for other nations. Such were the first Persians, a singular nation in which virtue was learned just as science is among us, which subjugated Asia so easily, and which alone has enjoyed the distinction of having the history of its institutions taken for a philosophical novel.[16] Such were the Scythians, about whom we have been left such magnificent praises. Such were the Germans, whose simplicity, innocence, and virtues a pen — weary of tracing the crimes and atrocities of an educated, opulent and voluptuous people — found relief in depicting. Such had been Rome herself in the times of her poverty and ignorance. Such, finally, has that rustic nation shown herself to this day — so vaunted for her courage which adversity could not overthrow, and for her faithfulness which example could not corrupt.[17]

It is not out of stupidity that these people have preferred other forms of exercise to those of the mind. They were not unaware of the fact that in other lands idle men spent their lives debating about the sovereign good, about vice and about virtue; and that arrogant reasoners, bestowing on themselves the highest praises, grouped other peoples under the contemptuous name of barbarians. However, they considered their mores and learned to disdain their teaching.[18]

Could I forget that it was in the very bosom of Greece that there was seen to arise that city as famous for her happy ignorance as for the wisdom of her laws, that republic of demi-gods rather than men, so superior to humanity did their virtues seem? O Sparta! Eternal shame to

---

16. [Editor's Note: An apparent reference to Xenophon's (430-354 B.C.) *Education of Cyrus.*]

17. I dare not speak of those happy nations which do not know even by name the vices that we have so much trouble repressing, those savages in America whose simple and natural polity Montaigne unhesitatingly prefers not only to Plato's *Laws* but even to everything philosophy could ever imagine as most perfect for the government of peoples. He cites a number of examples that are striking for someone who would know how to admire them. "What!" he says, "why they don't wear pants!"[Editor's note: This citation is from Montaigne's "Of Cannibals," *Essays,* Book I, chapter 31.]

18. Will someone honestly tell me what opinion the Athenians themselves must have held regarding eloquence, when they were so fastidious about banning it from that upright tribunal whose judgments the gods themselves did not appeal? What did the Romans think of medicine, when they banished it from their republic? And when a remnant of humanity led the Spanish to forbid their lawyers to enter America, what idea must they have had of jurisprudence? Could it not be said that they believed that by this single act they had made reparation for all the evils they had brought upon those unfortunate Indians?

a vain doctrine! While the vices, led by the fine arts, intruded themselves together into Athens, while a tyrant there gathered so carefully the works of the prince of poets,[19] you drove out from your walls the arts and artists, the sciences and scientists.

The event confirmed this difference. Athens became the abode of civility and good taste, the country of orators and philosophy. The elegance of her buildings paralleled that of the language. Marble and canvas, animated by the hands of the most capable masters, were to be seen everywhere. From Athens came those astonishing works that will serve as models in every corrupt age. The picture of Lacedaemon is less brilliant. "There," said the other peoples, "men are born virtuous, and the very air of the country seems to inspire virtue." Nothing of her inhabitants is left to us except the memory of their heroic actions. Are such monuments worth less to us than the curious marbles that Athens has left us?

Some wise men, it is true, had resisted the general torrent and protected themselves from vice in the abode of the Muses. But listen to the judgment that the first and unhappiest of them made of the learned men and artists of his time.

"I have," he says, "examined the poets, and I view them as people whose talent makes an impression on them and on others who claim to be wise, who are taken to be such, and who are nothing of the sort.

"From poets," continues Socrates, "I moved on to artists. No one knew less about the arts than I; no one was more convinced that artists possessed some especially fine secrets. Still, I perceived that their condition is no better than that of the poets, and that they are both laboring under the same prejudice. Because the most skillful among them excel in their specialty, they view themselves as the wisest of men. To my way of thinking, this presumption has completely tarnished their knowledge. From this it follows that, as I put myself in the place of the oracle and ask myself whether I would prefer to be what I am or what they are, to know what they have learned or to know that I know nothing, I answered myself and God: I want to remain what I am.

"We do not know — neither the sophists, nor the poets, nor the orators, nor the artists, nor I — what is the true, the good, and the beautiful. But there is this difference between us: that although these people know nothing, they all believe they know something. I, however, if I know nothing, at least am not in doubt about it. Thus all that superiority in wisdom accorded me by the oracle, reduces to being convinced that I am ignorant of what I do not know."

Here then is the wisest of men in the judgment of the gods, and the most learned of Athenians in the opinion of all Greece, Socrates, speaking in praise of ignorance! Does anyone believe that, were he to be reborn among us, our learned men and our artists would make him change his mind? No, gentlemen, this just man would continue to hold

19. [Editor's Note: Pisistratus (c.605-527 B.C.) was said to have directed the collection, transcription, and organization of the works of Homer.]

our vain sciences in contempt. He would not aid in the enlargement of that mass of books which inundate us from every quarter; and the only precept he would leave is the one left to his disciples and to our descendants: the example and the memory of his virtue. Thus is it noble to teach men!

Socrates had begun in Athens, Cato[20] the Elder continued in Rome to rail against those artful and subtle Greeks who seduced the virtue and enervated the courage of his fellow citizens. But the sciences, the arts, and dialectic prevailed once again. Rome was filled with philosophers and orators; military discipline was neglected, agriculture scorned, sects embraced, and the homeland forgotten. The sacred names of liberty, disinterestedness, obedience to the laws were replaced by the names of Epicurus, Zeno, Arcesilaus.[21] "Ever since learned men have begun to appear in our midst," their own philosophers said, "good men have vanished." Until then the Romans had been content to practice virtue; all was lost when they began to study it.

O Fabricius![22] What would your great soul have thought, if, had it been your misfortune to be returned to life, you had seen the pompous countenance of that Rome saved by your arm and honored more by your good name than by all her conquests? "Gods!" you would have said, "what has become of those thatched roofs and those rustic hearths where moderation and virtue once dwelt? What fatal splendor has followed upon Roman simplicity? What is this strange speech? What are these effeminate mores? What is the meaning of these statues, these paintings, these buildings? Fools, what have you done? You, the masters of nations, have you made yourselves the slaves of the frivolous men you conquered? Do rhetoricians govern you? Was it to enrich architects, painters, sculptors, and actors that you soaked Greece and Asia with your blood? Are the spoils of Carthage the prey of a flute player? Romans make haste to tear down these amphitheaters; shatter these marbles; burn these paintings; drive out these slaves who subjugate you and whose fatal arts corrupt you. Let others achieve notoriety by vain talents; the only talent worthy of Rome is that of conquering the world and making virtue reign in it. When Cineas[23] took our Senate for an assembly of kings, he

20. [Editor's Note: Marcus Porcius Cato (Cato the Elder) (234-149 B.C.) was a Roman general and statesman, renowned for his devotion to the old Roman ideals of simplicity, honesty, courage, loyalty, and steadfastness.]

21. [Editor's Note: Epicurus (c.341-270 B.C.) was the founder of the Epicurean school of philosophy. Zeno of Citium (c.336-264 B.C.) was the founder of the Stoic school of philosophy. Arcesilaus (c.316-241 B.C.) was a figure in the Middle Academy who played a pivotal role in the transmission and development of philosophical scepticism.]

22. [Editor's Note: Caius Fabricius Luscinus (d. 250 B.C.) was a Roman general and statesman, renowned for his uncomplicated integrity and dignity.]

23. [Editor's Note: Cineas, a Thessalian, was an ambassador of King Pyrrhus. Reputed to be possessed of good sense, he was also the student of Demosthenes who most reminded people of his teacher.]

was dazzled neither by vain pomp nor by studied elegance. There he did not hear that frivolous eloquence, the focus of study and delight of futile men. What then did Cineas see that was so majestic? O citizens! He saw a sight which neither your riches nor all your arts could ever display; the most beautiful sight ever to have appeared under the heavens, the assembly of two hundred virtuous men, worthy of commanding in Rome and of governing the earth."

But let us leap over the distance of place and time and see what has happened in our countries and before our eyes; or rather, let us set aside odious pictures that offend our delicate sensibilities, and spare ourselves the trouble of repeating the same things under different names. It was not in vain that I summoned the shade of Fabricius; and what did I make that great man say that I could not have placed in the mouth of Louis XII or Henry IV? Among us, it is true, Socrates would not have drunk the hemlock; but he would have drunk from a cup more bitter still: the insulting ridicule and scorn that are a hundred times worse than death.

That is how luxury, dissolution and slavery have at all times been the punishment for the arrogant efforts that we have made to leave the happy ignorance where eternal wisdom had placed us. The heavy veil with which she had covered all her operations seemed to give us sufficient warning that she had not destined us for vain inquiries. But is there even one of her lessons from which we have learned to profit, or which we have neglected with impunity? Peoples, know then once and for all that nature wanted to protect you from science just as a mother wrests a dangerous weapon from the hands of her child; that all the secrets she hides from you are so many evils from which she is protecting you, and that the difficulty you find in teaching yourselves is not the least of her kindnesses. Men are perverse; they would be even worse if they had had the misfortune of being born learned.

How humiliating are these reflections for humanity! How mortified our pride must be! What! Could probity be the daughter of ignorance? Science and virtue incompatible? What consequences might not be drawn from these prejudices? But to reconcile these apparent points of conflict, one need merely examine at close range the vanity and the emptiness of those proud titles which overpower us and which we so gratuitously bestow upon human knowledge. Let us then consider the sciences and the arts in themselves. Let us see what must result from their progress; and let us no longer hesitate to be in agreement on all the points where our reasoning will be found to be in accord with historical inductions.

PART TWO

It was an ancient tradition, passed from Egypt to Greece, that a god who was antagonistic toward the tranquility of men was the inventor of the sciences.[24] What opinion then must have been held about them by the Egyptians themselves, among whom the sciences were born? They saw at close quarters the sources that had produced them. Indeed, whether one leafs through the annals of the world, or supplements uncertain chronicles with philosophical inquiries, one will not find an origin for human knowledge corresponding to the idea that one wants to form of it. Astronomy was born of superstition, eloquence of ambition, hatred, flattery, lying; geometry of avarice; physics of vain curiosity; all of them, even moral philosophy, of human pride. Thus the sciences and the arts owe their birth to our vices; we would be less in doubt about their advantages, if they owed it to our virtues.

The defect of their origin is only too clearly called to mind for us in their objects. What would we do with the arts without the luxury that feeds them? What purposes would jurisprudence serve without the injustices of men? What would history become, if there were no tyrants, no wars, no conspirators? In a word, who would want to spend his life in fruitless speculations if each person, consulting only the duties of man and the needs of nature, had time for nothing but the homeland, the unfortunate, and his friends? Are we destined then to die fastened to the edge of the pit where truth has retreated? This reflection alone should block from the start any man who would seriously seek to teach himself through the study of philosophy.

What dangers! What false pathways in the investigation of the sciences! How many errors, a thousand times more dangerous than the truth is useful, must be endured in order to reach it? The disadvantage is apparent, for falsity is susceptible to an infinity of combinations; but truth has but one mode of being. Besides, who seeks it sincerely? Even with the best will, by what marks is one sure of recognizing it? In this crowd of different sentiments, what will be our criterion for judging it properly?[25] And, what is most difficult, if perchance we finally find it, who among us will know how to make good use of it?

If our sciences are vain in the objects they have in view, they are even more dangerous in the effects they produce. Born in idleness, they

---

24. The allegory of the fable of Prometheus is easy to see; and it does not appear that the Greeks who nailed him to the Caucasus thought any more favorably of him than the Egyptians did of their god Theuth. "The satyr," says an ancient fable, "wanted to kiss and embrace fire the first time he saw it. But Prometheus cried out to him, 'Satyr, you will mourn the loss of the beard on your chin, for it burns when touched.'" It is the subject of the frontispiece.

25. The less one knows, the more one believes one knows. Did the Peripatetics doubt anything? Did Descartes not construct the universe with cubes and vortices? And is there in Europe even today a physicist, however humble, who does not boldly explain the profound mystery of electricity, which will perhaps forever be the despair of true philosophers? [Editor's Note: Peripatetics were followers of the philosophy of Aristotle. René Descartes (1596-1650), French mathematician and philosopher, is often cited as "the father of modern philosophy." He is the author of the *Discourse on Method*, the *Meditations on First Philosophy*, and the *Principles of Philosophy*.]

nourish it in turn; and the irreparable loss of time is the first injury they necessarily cause society. In politics, as in moral philosophy, it is a great evil not to do good, and every useless citizen may be viewed as a pernicious man. Answer me, then, illustrious philosophers, you thanks to whom we know the ratios in which bodies attract one another in a vacuum; the relationships of areas covered in equal periods of time in the revolutions of the planets; what curves have conjugate points, which have points of inflection, and which have cusps; how man sees everything in God; how the soul and the body are in harmony with one another, like two clocks, without communicating; what stars can be inhabited; what insects reproduce in some extraordinary manner? Answer me, I say, you from whom we have received so much sublime knowledge; if you had never taught us any of these things, would we therefore have been any less numerous, less well governed, less formidable, less flourishing or more perverse? Reconsider, then, the importance of your productions; and if the labors of the most enlightened of our learned men and our best citizens obtain for us so little that is useful, tell us what we should think about that crowd of obscure writers and idle men of letters who to no purpose devour the substance of the state.

What did I say? Idle? Would to God they really were! Mores would then be healthier and society would be more peaceful. But these vain and futile declaimers go off in every direction, armed with their deadly paradoxes, undermining the foundations of faith and annihilating virtue. They smile contemptuously at such old-fashioned words as homeland and religion, and dedicate their talents and their philosophy to destroying and degrading all that is sacred among men. Not that at bottom they hate either virtue or our dogmas; they are enemies of public opinion, and to bring them back to the feet of the altars it would be enough to consign them among the atheists. O fury to gain distinction, of what are you not capable?

The misuse of time is great evil. Other evils that are even worse follow after letters and the arts. Luxury, born like them of idleness and men's vanity, is one such. Luxury seldom thrives without the sciences and the arts, and they never thrive without it. I know that our philosophy, ever fecund with singular maxims, claims, contrary to the experience of all centuries, that luxury causes the splendor of states. But after having forgotten the need for sumptuary laws, will it still dare deny that good mores are essential to the continuance of empires, and that luxury is diametrically opposed to good mores? Granted luxury is a sure sign of wealth; that it even serves, if you will, to increase wealth. What conclusion must we draw from this paradox so worthy of being born in our times; and what will become of virtue when one must become wealthy at any cost? Ancient politicians spoke incessantly about mores and virtue; ours speak only of commerce and money. One will tell you that in a given country a man is worth the price he would sell for in Algiers; another, following this calculation, will find some countries where a man is worth nothing and others where he is worth less than nothing. They value men the way they would herds of cattle. According to them, a man is worth no more to the state than what he consumes. Thus one Sybarite would have been worth at least thirty Lacedaemonians. So guess which of these two republics, Sparta and Sybaris,[26] was subjugated by a handful of peasants, and which caused Asia to tremble.

The monarchy of Cyrus[27] was conquered with thirty thousand men by a prince who was poorer than the humblest of Persian satraps; and the Scythians, the most miserable of all peoples, resisted the most powerful monarchs in the universe. Two famous republics competed for world domination. One was very rich and the other had nothing, and it was the latter which destroyed the former. The Roman Empire, in turn, after having swallowed up all the wealth of the universe, fell prey to men who did not even know what wealth was. The Franks conquered the Gauls, the Saxons conquered England — with no other treasures than their bravery and their poverty. A band of poor mountaineers, all of whose greed was limited to a few sheepskins, after having tamed Austrian arrogance, crushed that opulent and formidable House of Burgundy which caused the potentates of Europe to tremble. Finally, all the power and wisdom of Charles V's heir, supported by all the treasures of the Indies, were beaten by a handful of herring fishers. Let our politicians deign to suspend their calculations in order to reflect on these examples, and let them learn for once that with money one has everything but mores and citizens.

Precisely what, then, is at issue in this question of luxury? To know whether it is more important for empires to be brilliant and fleeting, or virtuous and long-lasting. I say brilliant, but by what luster? The taste for ostentation is hardly ever combined in the same souls with the taste for honesty. No, it is not possible for minds degraded by a multitude of futile needs ever to rise to anything great; and even if they had the strength, they would lack the courage.

Every artist wants to be applauded. The praises of his contemporaries are the most precious part of his reward. What then will he do to obtain praise, if he has the misfortune to be born among a people and at a time when learned men, having become fashionable, have placed a frivolous youth in a position to set the tone; when men have sacrificed their taste to the tyrants of their liberty;[28] when, because one of the sexes dares

26. [Editor's Note: Sparta was an ancient Greek city known for its emphasis on military discipline and training. In decline for many years, it was finally abandoned during the period of Roman domination. Sybaris was a city in Magna Graecia (now southern Italy), founded in 770. B.C. It was a wealthy city whose citizens were reputed to have pursued lives of pleasure and luxury — "Sybaritic" pastimes. The city was destroyed in 510 B.C.]

27. [Editor's Note: Cyrus the Great (d. 529 B.C.), King of Persia and founder of the Achaemenian dynasty and the Persian Empire. The military defeat mentioned here did not involve Cyrus himself but one of his successors.]

28. I am very far from thinking that this ascendancy of women is in itself an evil. It is a gift bestowed on them by nature for the happiness of mankind. Better directed, it could produce as much good as it today does harm. We are not sufficiently aware of the

approve only what is a match for the other's pusillanimity, masterpieces of dramatic poetry are dropped and harmonic prodigies rejected? What will he do, gentlemen? He will lower his genius to the level of his century, and will prefer to compose popular works which are admired during his lifetime instead of marvels which would not be admired until long after his death. Tell us, famed Aroüet,[29] how many manly and strong beauties you have sacrificed to our false delicacy, and how many great things has the spirit of gallantry, so fertile in small things, cost you?

In this way the dissolution of mores, a necessary consequence of luxury, leads in turn to the corruption of taste. If perchance there is, among men of extraordinary talents, someone who has firmness of soul and who refuses to yield to the genius of his century and to degrade himself by childish productions, woe to him! He will die in poverty and oblivion. Would that I were making a prediction and not reporting an experience! Carle, Pierre;[30] the moment has come when that brush destined to enhance the majesty of our temples with sublime and saintly images will either fall from your hands or be prostituted to embellish carriage panels with lascivious pictures. And you, rival of the likes of Praxiteles and Phidias,[31] you whose chisel the ancients would have employed to make them gods capable of excusing their idolatry in our eyes; inimitable Pigalle,[32] either your hand will be determined to rough out the belly of a grotesque or it will have to remain idle.

One cannot reflect on mores without taking delight in recalling the image of the simplicity of the earliest times. It is a beautiful shore, adorned by the hands of nature alone, toward which one continually turns one's eyes, and from which one regretfully feels oneself moving away. When innocent and virtuous men wanted to have the gods as witnesses of their actions, they lived together in the same huts. But having soon become wicked, they wearied of these inconvenient spectators and banished them to magnificent temples. Finally, they chased them from the temples in order to take up residence in them themselves,

---

advantages that would come to pass in society if a better education were given to that half of mankind which governs the other. Men will always be what is pleasing to women. Thus if you want men to become great and virtuous, teach women what greatness of soul and virtue are. The reflections afforded by this subject and made long ago by Plato richly deserve a better development by a pen worthy of writing in the tradition of such a teacher and to defend so great a cause.

29. [Editor's Note: Francois Marie Aroüet de Voltaire (1694-1778), better known simply as Voltaire, was a French poet, dramatist, essayist, historian, philosopher and scientist.]

30. [Editor's Note: Charles-André (Carle) Vanloo (1705-1765) and Jean-Baptiste-Marie Pierre (1713-1789) enjoyed international reputations as painters.]

31. [Editor's Note: Praxiteles (fl. c.370-330 B.C.) and Phidias (c.500-c.432 B.C.) are among the most famous of ancient Greek sculptors.]

32. [Editor's Note: Jean-Baptiste Pigalle (1714-1785) was a French sculptor who achieved fame through a life of hardship and sacrifice.]

or at least the temples of the gods were no longer distinguishable from the homes of the citizens. That period was the height of depravity, and vices were never impelled further than when they were, so to speak, seen propped up on columns of marble and carved on Corinthian capitals at the entrance to the palaces of the great.

While the conveniences of life increase, the arts are perfected and luxury spreads, true courage is enervated, military virtues disappear, and this too is the work of the sciences and of all those arts which are practiced in the darkness of the study. When the Goths ravaged Greece, all of the libraries were saved from fire only because of the opinion, spread by one of them, that the enemy should be left the furnishings so well suited to distracting them from military exercise and to amusing them with idle and sedentary occupations. Charles VIII found himself master of Tuscany and the Kingdom of Naples practically without having drawn his sword, and his entire court attributed this unexpected ease to the fact that the princes and the nobility of Italy had a good time becoming ingenious and learned more than they exerted themselves trying to become vigorous and warlike. In fact, says the sensible man who reports these two cases, all examples teach us that in this martial polity and in all those that resemble it, the study of the sciences is much more apt to soften and enervate courage than to strengthen and enliven it.

The Romans admitted that military virtue died out among them in proportion as they had begun to become connoisseurs of paintings, engravings, goldsmiths' vessels, and to cultivate the fine arts. And, as if that famous country were destined to serve unceasingly as an example to other peoples, the rise of the Medicis and the revival of letters brought down once again and perhaps forever that warlike reputation which Italy seemed to have recovered a few centuries ago.

The ancient republics of Greece, with that wisdom that radiated through most of their institutions, had forbidden their citizens to engage in all those tranquil and sedentary professions which, by weighing down and corrupting the body, soon enervate the vigor of the soul. Indeed, with what eye does one think that men who are crushed by the smallest need and stopped cold by the least pain could face hunger, thirst, periods of fatigue, dangers and death? With what courage will soldiers stand up under excessive labors to which they are unaccustomed? With what fervor will they go on forced marches under officers who lack even the strength to travel on horseback? Let no one raise as an objection against me the renowned valor of all those modern warriors who are so scientifically disciplined. People brag to me of their bravery on a day of battle, but they do not tell me how they handle overwork, how they withstand the harshness of the seasons and the inclemency of the weather. All that is needed is a bit of sunshine or snow, a lack of a few superfluities, to melt and destroy the best of our armies in a few days. Intrepid warriors, suffer for once the truth you so rarely hear: you are brave, I know; you would have triumphed with Hannibal at Cannae and at Trasimene; with you Caesar would have crossed the Rubicon and enslaved his country; but it was not with you that the former would have crossed the Alps, and the latter would have vanquished your ancestors.

Battles do not always make for success in war, and for generals there is an art superior to that of winning battles. A man who runs intrepidly into the line of fire is still a very bad officer. Even in a soldier, a little more strength and vigor would perhaps be more necessary than that sort of bravery, which does not protect him from death; and what difference does it make to the state whether its troops die from fever and cold or by the enemy's sword?

If the cultivation of the sciences is harmful to warlike qualities, it is even more so to moral qualities. From our earliest years a foolish education adorns our mind and corrupts our judgment. Everywhere I see immense establishments where youths are brought up at great expense to learn everything but their duties. Your children will not know their own language, but will speak others which are nowhere in use. They will know how to compose verses they will scarcely be capable of comprehending. Without knowing how to separate error from truth, they will possess the art of making them unrecognizable to others by means of specious arguments. But they will not know the meaning of the words magnanimity, fair-mindedness, temperance, humanity, courage. That sweet name homeland will never strike their ear; and if they hear God spoken of at all, it will be less to be in awe of him than to be in fear of him.[33] I would just as soon, said a wise man, my pupil had passed time on the tennis court; at least his body would have been more fit because of it. I know that children need to be kept occupied and that, for them, idleness is the greatest danger to fear. What then should they learn? That is certainly a fine question! Let them learn what they ought to do when they are men,[34] and not what they ought to forget.

---

33. *Pens. Philosoph.* [Editor's Note: the reference is to Diderot, *Pensées philosophiques*, VIII.]

34. Such was the education of the Spartans according to the greatest of their kings. It is, says Montaigne, well worth considering that in that excellent administration of Lycurgus (in truth monstrously perfect), although it was conscientious about the nurture of children, as if this were its chief responsibility; and although it was in the very home of the Muses, so little mention was made of the doctrine, as if those great-souled youths, disdaining every other yoke, required only the teachers of valor, prudence, and justice, instead of our teachers of science.

Let us now see how the same author speaks of the ancient Persians. Plato, he says, relates that the eldest son of their royal line was brought up as follows. After his birth he was given over not to women but to eunuchs, who, because of their virtue, had the greatest influence with the king. They took charge of making his body fair and healthy, and after seven years they taught him to ride and hunt. When he turned fourteen, they placed him in the hands of four people: the most wise, the most just, the most temperate, the most valiant in the nation. The first taught him religion; the second always to be truthful; the third to conquer his appetites; the fourth to fear nothing. All, I would add, to make him good, none to make him learned.

Astyages, in Xenophon, asks Cyrus for an account of his last lesson. It is, he says, that in our school a large boy who had a small tunic gave it to one of his companions who was smaller and took from him his tunic which was larger. When our tutor made me the judge of this dispute, I judged that things should be allowed to stand as they are, and that they both seemed to be better taken care of in this matter. Whereupon he chastised me for having done wrong, for I had stopped to consider seemliness, and one ought first to have

Our gardens are decorated with statues and our galleries with pictures. What would you think these masterpieces of art, exhibited for public admiration, represent? The defenders of the homeland? or those even greater men who have enriched it with their virtues? No. They are images of all the aberrations of the heart and reason, carefully drawn from ancient mythology, and presented at an early age to the curiosity of our children, doubtless so that they may have models of bad actions before their eyes even before they know how to read.

Where do all these abuses come from, if not from the fatal inequality introduced among men by the distinction of talents and the degradation of virtues? That is the most evident effect of all our studies, and the most dangerous of all their consequences. One no longer asks whether a man has integrity, but whether he has talents; not whether a book is useful, but whether it is well written. Rewards are showered upon the wit, and virtue is left without honors. There are a thousand prizes for fine discourses, none for fine actions. Meanwhile, would someone tell me whether the glory attached to the best of discourses that will be crowned in this Academy is comparable to the merit of having established the prize?

The wise man does not chase after fortune, but he is not insensitive to glory; and he sees it so ill distributed, that his virtue, which a little emulation would have enlivened and made advantageous to society, languishes and dies out in misery and oblivion. This is what, in the long run, the preference for congenial talents over useful ones must everywhere produce, and what experience since the revival of the sciences and the arts has only too well confirmed. We have physicists, geometers, chemists, astronomers, poets, musicians, painters; we no longer have citizens. Or if there still are some left to us, dispersed in our abandoned countryside, they perish there indigent and despised. Such is the state to which those who give us bread and our children milk are reduced; such are the sentiments they get from us.

Nevertheless, I confess that the evil is not as great as it could have become. By placing health-restoring herbs next to various harmful plants, and by placing the remedy for their wounds in several injurious animals, eternal foresight has taught sovereigns, who are its ministers, to imitate its wisdom. By following this example, that great monarch, whose glory will only acquire a new luster from one age to another, drew from the very bosom of the sciences and the arts, sources of a thousand disorders, those famed societies which are charged simultaneously with the dangerous trust of human knowledge and the sacred trust of mores, by the attention they pay to maintaining them in all their purity, and to requiring it in the members they admit.

---

taken justice into account, which requires that no one be subjected to force in matters pertaining to what belongs to him. And he said that he was punished, just as we are punished in our villages for having forgotten the first aorist of $\tau\acute{\upsilon}\pi\tau\omega$. My schoolmaster would have to give me a fine harangue *in genere demonstrativo*, before he persuaded me that his school is as good as that one.

These wise institutions, strengthened by his august successor and imitated by all the kings of Europe, will at least serve as a restraint on men of letters, who, since they all aspire to the honor of being admitted to the academies, will keep watch over themselves and try to make themselves worthy by means of useful works and irreproachable mores. Those among these organizations that will select, for the prize competitions honoring literary merit, subjects suitable for reviving the love of virtue in the hearts of citizens, will show that such love reigns among them, and will give the people that very rare and sweet pleasure of seeing learned societies devote themselves to spreading throughout mankind not only congenial enlightenment but also salutary teachings.

Do not therefore raise an objection against me which for me is merely a new proof. So many precautions show all too well the necessity for taking them, and no one seeks remedies for non-existent evils. Why should these, by their inadequacy, also have the character of ordinary remedies? So many establishments brought into being for the benefit of the learned are thus all the more capable of causing deception in regard to the objects of the sciences and of turning minds toward their cultivation. To judge from the precautions taken, it seems that there are too many laborers and a shortage of philosophers is feared. I have no desire to venture here a comparison between agriculture and philosophy; it would not be tolerated. I will ask merely, what is philosophy? What do the writings of the best known philosophers contain? What are the lessons of these friends of wisdom? To listen to them, would one not take them for a troop of charlatans, each crying from his own place on a public square, "Come to me; I alone do not deceive?" One claims there are no bodies and that everything is appearance; another that there is no substance but matter, nor any God but the world. This one proposes that there are neither virtues nor vices, and that moral good and evil are chimeras; that one that men are wolves and can devour one another with a clear conscience. O great philosophers! Why do you not save these useful lessons for your friends and for your children? You would soon reap the reward for them, and we would have no fear of finding one of your followers among our own.

These then are the wonderful men on whom the esteem of their contemporaries was squandered during their lifetimes, and for whom immortality was set aside after their deaths! These are the wise maxims we have received from them and which we will transmit from generation to generation to our descendants. Since it has been given over to all the aberrations of human reason, has paganism left to posterity anything comparable to the shameful monuments prepared for it by the printing press under the reign of the Gospel? The impious writings of the likes of Leucippus and Diagoras[35] perished with them. The art of immortalizing

35. [Editor's Note: Leucippus (fl. 5th century B.C.) was an ancient Greek philosopher reputed by Aristotle to have been the inspiration for the atomistic theory associated with Democritus. Diagoras of Melos (fl. 5th century B.C.), Greek poet and philosopher. When Spartan forces overran Melos, he fled to Athens, where he gained a reputation for

the extravagances of the human mind had not yet been invented. But thanks to typography[36] and the use we make of it, the dangerous reveries of the likes of Hobbes and Spinoza[37] will remain forever. Go, famed writings of which the ignorance and rusticity of our forefathers would have been incapable. Go among our descendants in company with those even more dangerous works which reek of the corruption of the mores of our century; and together send on to future centuries a faithful history of the progress and advantages of our sciences and our arts. If they read you, you will not leave them in any doubt about the question we are dealing with today; and unless they are more foolish than we, they will raise their hands to heaven and will say with bitterness of heart: "Almighty God, you who hold minds in your hands, deliver us from the enlightenment and the deadly arts of our fathers, and give back to us ignorance, innocence, and poverty — the only goods that can bring about our happiness and that are precious in your sight."

But if the progress of the sciences and the arts has added nothing to our genuine felicity, if it has corrupted our mores, and if the corruption of mores has damaged the purity of taste, what are we to think of that crowd of elementary-level writers who have removed from the Temple of the Muses the difficulties which protected its approach and which nature had spread out before it as a test of strength for those who might be

---

his outspoken scepticism and atheism. He was an ardent follower of the atomistic philosophy of Democritus.]

36. Considering the frightful disorders that the printing press has already caused in Europe, and judging the future by the progress that the evil makes from one day to the next, it is easy to foresee that sovereigns will not delay in taking as many pains to banish this terrible art from their states as they took to establish it in them. The Sultan Achmed, yielding to the importunities of some alleged men of taste, had consented to establish a printing press in Constantinople. But the press had hardly begun operations when it had to be destroyed and the equipment thrown into a pit. It is said that the Caliph Omar, when asked what ought to be done with the library of Alexandria, answered in these terms: "If the books in this library contain things opposed to the Koran, they are bad and should be burned. If they contain nothing but the doctrine of the Koran, burn them anyway; they are superfluous." Our learned men have cited this reasoning as the height of absurdity. Nevertheless, imagine Gregory the Great in place of Omar and the Gospel in place of the Koran. The library would still have been burned, and this perhaps would be the finest deed in the life of that illustrious pontiff. [Editor's Note: Achmed III (1673-1736), Ottoman sultan who ruled from 1703 until 1730, when he was overthrown and later died in prison. Omar (c.581-644) became caliph in 634 and was assassinated ten years later. He is largely responsible for the early spread of Mohammedanism in the Near East. Pope Gregory I, also known as Gregory the Great, (c.540-604) ruled as pope from 590 to 604. He is best known for his establishment of the supremacy and temporal power of the papacy.]

37. [Editor's Note: Thomas Hobbes (1588-1679) was an English philosopher who espoused the doctrine of mechanistic materialism. He was the author of *De Cive*, the *Leviathan*, and *De Homine*. Baruch (or Benedict) de Spinoza (1632-1677) was a member of the community of Sephardic Jews living in Holland who had fled persecution in Spain and Portugal. His chief writings were the *Ethics, On the Improvement of the Understanding*, and the *Theological-Political Treatise*.]

tempted to know? While it would be desirable for all those who could not go far in a career in letters to be deterred from the outset and become involved with arts useful to society, what are we to think of those compilers of works who have indiscreetly broken down the door of the sciences and ushered into their sanctuary a populace unworthy of approaching it? Someone who will be a bad versifier or an inferior geometer all his life, might perhaps have become a great cloth maker. Those whom nature destined to be her disciples had no need of teachers. The likes of Verulam, Descartes, Newton,[38] these tutors of mankind had none themselves. Indeed, what guides would have led them as far as their own vast genius has carried them? Ordinary teachers could only have constricted their understanding by confining it to the narrow capacity of their own. The first obstacles taught them to work hard and to exert themselves in order to cover the immense area they traversed. If a few men must be permitted to devote themselves to the study of the sciences and the arts, it should only be those who feel the strength to venture forth alone in their footsteps and to overtake them. It is for this small number to raise monuments to the glory of the human mind. But if we want nothing to be beyond their genius, nothing must be beyond their hopes. That is the only encouragement they need. The soul imperceptibly proportions itself to the objects that occupy it, and it is great events that make great men. The prince of eloquence was consul of Rome, and perhaps the greatest of philosophers, chancellor of England. Does anyone believe that if the one had merely occupied a chair at some university and the other had obtained only a modest pension from an academy; does anyone, I say, believe that their works would not have felt the effects of their condition? Therefore let kings not disdain to admit into their councils the men most capable of counseling them well. Let them renounce the old prejudice invented by the pride of the great, that the art of leading peoples is more difficult than that of enlightening them, as if it were easier to induce men to act well of their own accord than to compel them to do it by force. May learned men of the first rank find honorable asylum in their courts. May they obtain the only recompense worth of them: that of contributing by their influence to the happiness of the peoples to whom they have taught wisdom. Only then will we see what can be done by virtue, science, and authority, enlivened by a noble emulation and working in concert for the felicity of mankind. But so long as power is alone on one side, with enlightenment and wisdom alone on the other, learned men will rarely think about great things, princes will more rarely perform noble deeds, and peoples will continue to be vile, corrupt, and unhappy.

---

38. [Editor's Note: Francis Bacon (1561-1626), English statesman and philosopher, was created Baron Verulam in 1618 and Viscount of St. Albans in 1621. He is the author of *The Advancement of Learning* and the *Novum Organum*. René Descartes is described in Note 25. Isaac Newton (1642-1727), English physicist and philosopher, inventor of the reflecting telescope and best known for his formulation of the laws of motion and the laws of gravitation. His principal works were *Philosophiae naturalis principia mathematica* and the *Opticks*.]

For us — ordinary men to whom heaven has not distributed such great talents and whom it does not destine for so much glory — let us remain in our obscurity. Let us not chase after a reputation that would escape us and which, in the present state of things, would never return to us what it would have cost us, even if we had all the qualifications to obtain it. What good is it to seek our happiness in the opinion of another if we can find it in ourselves? Let us leave to others the care of instructing peoples in their duties, and confine ourselves to fulfilling our own duties well. We have no need to know more than this.

O virtue! Sublime science of simple souls, are there so many difficulties and so much preparation necessary in order to know you? Are your principles not engraved in all hearts, and is it not enough, in order to learn your laws, to commune with oneself and, in the silence of the passions, to listen to the voice of one's conscience? That is the true philosophy; let us know how to be satisfied with it. And without envying the glory of those famous men who are immortalized in the republic of letters, let us try to place between them and ourselves that glorious distinction observed long ago between two great peoples: that the one knew how to speak well, the other how to act well.

DISCOURSE ON THE ORIGIN AND

FOUNDATIONS OF

INEQUALITY AMONG MEN

BY

JEAN-JACQUES ROUSSEAU,

Citizen of Geneva

"Not in depraved things but in those well oriented according to nature, are we to consider what is natural."
— Aristotle, *Politics*, II.

DISCOURSE ON THE ORIGIN OF INEQUALITY

In 1754 Jean-Jacques Rousseau wrote his second Discourse, on the Origin of Inequality, in response to the same prize competition—that of the Dijon Academy—that had awarded him first prize in 1749 for his first, on the Sciences and Arts. He published his work the following year, in 1755, but without the blessing of the Academy's recognition. Whatever the jury may have thought, the second discourse is of transcendent importance for the student of Rousseau's work as well as for the history of political theory. It was as controversial an essay as the first, and as rhetorical. Less ridden by paradox and more complex than the first essay, it was also, in its own way, even more radical, for Rousseau had read and thought much in the years separating the two. The entire French moralizing tradition, with Montaigne and Montesquieu at its head, had now become his possession. Thus he could buttress his arguments with quotations from philosophers and travelers, and with an eloquence matured by intense reflection and active literary practice. He could differentiate speculatively between an original state of nature, one of primitive isolation, a kind of prepolitical community, one of simplicity and happiness—and the vice-ridden societies which, according to Rousseau, dominated the civilized world of his time.

As more than one commentator has noted, the present discourse is not a reformist tract, but an assault on all organized society. For Rousseau, it was the emergence of private property, of which this discourse is a vehement critique, that also marked the emergence of this latest and fateful stage in human evolution. "The first man who enclosed a plot of ground and thought of saying, 'This is mine,' and found others stupid enough to believe him, was the true founder of civil society." It is this famous sentence, and the arguments that sustain it, that fed the fervor of revolutionaries and socialists for a century.

P. G.

To

The Republic

of Geneva

Magnificent, Most Honored and Sovereign Lords:

Convinced that only a virtuous man may bestow on his homeland those honors which it can acknowledge, I have labored for thirty years to earn the right to offer you public homage. And since this happy occasion supplements to some extent what my efforts have been unable to accomplish, I believed I might be allowed here to give heed to the zeal that urges me on, instead of the right that ought to have given me authorization. Having had the good fortune to be born among you, how could I meditate on the equality which nature has established among men and upon the inequality they have instituted without thinking of the profound wisdom with which both, felicitously combined in this state, cooperate in the manner that most closely approximates the natural law and that is most favorable to society, to the maintenance of public order and to the happiness of private individuals? In searching for the best maxims that good sense could dictate concerning the constitution of a government, I have been so struck on seeing them all in operation in your own, that even if I had not been born within your walls, I would have believed myself incapable of dispensing with offering this picture of human society to that people which, of all peoples, seems to me to be in possession of the greatest advantages, and to have best prevented its abuses.

If I had had to choose my birthplace, I would have chosen a society of a size limited by the extent of human faculties, that is to say, limited by the possibility of being well governed, and where, with each being sufficient to his task, no one would have been forced to relegate to others the functions with which he was charged; a state where, with all private individuals being known to one another, neither the obscure maneuvers of vice nor the modesty of virtue could be hidden from the notice and the judgment of the public, and where that pleasant habit of seeing and knowing one another turned love of homeland into love of the citizens rather than into love of the land.

I would have wanted to be born in a country where the sovereign and the people could have but one and the same interest, so that all the movements of the machine always tended only to the common happiness. Since this could not have taken place unless the people and the sovereign were one and the same person, it follows that I would have wished to be born under a democratic government, wisely tempered.

I would have wanted to live and die free, that is to say, subject to the laws in such wise that neither I nor anyone else could shake off their honorable yoke: that pleasant and salutary yoke, which the most arrogant heads bear with all the greater docility, since they are made to bear no other.

I would therefore have wanted it to be impossible for anyone in the state to say that he was above the law and for anyone outside to demand that the state was obliged to give him recognition. For whatever the constitution of a government may be, if a single man is found who is not subject to the law, all the others are necessarily at his discretion.[1] And if there is a national leader and a foreign leader as well, whatever the division of authority they may make, it is impossible for both of them to be strictly obeyed and for the state to be well governed.

I would not have wanted to dwell in a newly constituted republic, however good its laws may be, out of fear that, with the government perhaps constituted otherwise than would be required for the moment and being unsuited to the new citizens or the citizens to the new government, the state would be subject to being overthrown and destroyed almost from its inception. For liberty is like those solid and tasty foods or those full-bodied wines which are appropriate for nourishing and strengthening robust constitutions that are used to them, but which overpower, ruin and intoxicate the weak and delicate who are not suited for them. Once peoples are accustomed to masters, they are no longer in a position to get along without them. If they try to shake off the yoke, they put all the more distance between themselves and liberty, because, in mistaking for liberty an unbridled license which is its opposite, their revolutions nearly always deliver them over to seducers who simply make their chains heavier. The Roman people itself—that model of all free peoples—was in no position to govern itself when it emerged from the oppression of the Tarquins. Debased by slavery and the ignominious labors the Tarquins had imposed on it, at first it was but a stupid rabble that needed to be managed and governed with the greatest wisdom, so that, as it gradually became accustomed to breathe the salutary air of liberty, these souls, enervated or rather brutalized under tyranny, acquired by degrees that severity of mores and that high-spirited courage which eventually made them, of all the peoples, most worthy of respect. I would therefore have sought for my homeland a happy and tranquil republic, whose antiquity was somehow lost in the dark recesses of time, which had experienced only such attacks as served to manifest and strengthen in its inhabitants courage and love of homeland, and where the citizens, long accustomed to a wise independence, were not only free but worthy of being so.

I would have wanted to choose for myself a homeland diverted by a fortunate impotence from the fierce love of conquest, and protected by an even more fortunate position from the fear of becoming itself the conquest of another state; a free city, situated among several peoples none of whom had any interest in invading it, while each had an interest in preventing the others from invading it themselves; in a word, a republic that did not tempt the ambition of its neighbors and that could reasonably count on their assistance in time of need. It follows that in so fortunate a position, it would have had nothing to fear except from itself; and that, if its citizens were trained in the use of arms, it would have been more to maintain in them that martial fervor and that high-spirited courage that suit liberty so well and whet the appetite for it, than out of the necessity to provide for their defense.

I would have searched for a country where the right of legislation was common to all citizens, for who can know better than they the conditions under which it suits them to live together in a single society? But I would not have approved of plebiscites like those of the Romans where the state's leaders and those most interested in its preservation were excluded from the deliberations on which its safety often depended, and where, by an absurd inconsistency, the magistrates were deprived of the rights enjoyed by ordinary citizens.

On the contrary, I would have desired that, in order to stop the self-centered and ill-conceived projects and the dangerous innovations that finally ruined Athens, no one would have the power to propose new laws according to his fancy; that this right belonged exclusively to the magistrates; that even they used it with such caution that the populace, for its part, was so hesitant about giving its consent to these laws, and that their promulgation could only be done with such solemnity that before the constitution was overturned one had time to be convinced that it is above all the great antiquity of the laws that makes them holy and venerable; that the populace soon holds in contempt those laws that it sees change daily; and that in becoming accustomed to neglect old usages on the pretext of making improvements, great evils are often introduced in order to correct the lesser ones.

Above all, I would have fled, as necessarily ill-governed, a republic where the people, believing it could get along without its magistrates or permit them but a precarious authority, would imprudently have held on to the administration of civil affairs and the execution of its own laws. Such must have been the rude constitution of the first governments immediately emerging from the state of nature, and such too was one of the vices which ruined the republic of Athens.

But I would have chosen that republic where private individuals, being content to give sanction to the laws and to decide as a body and upon the recommendation of their leaders the most important public affairs, would establish respected tribunals, distinguish with care their various departments, annually elect the most capable and most upright of their fellow citizens to administer justice and to govern the state; and where, with the virtue of the magistrates thus bearing witness to the wisdom of the people, they would mutually honor one another. Thus if some fatal misunderstandings were ever to disturb public concord, even those periods of blindness and errors were marked by indications of moderation, reciprocal esteem, and a common respect for the laws: presages and guarantees of a sincere and perpetual reconciliation.

Such, MAGNIFICENT, MOST HONORED, AND SOVEREIGN LORDS, are the advantages that I would have sought in the homeland that I would have chosen for myself. And if in addition providence had joined to it a charming location, a temperate climate, a fertile country and the most delightful appearance there is under the heavens, to complete my happiness I would have desired only to enjoy all these goods in the bosom of that happy homeland, living peacefully in sweet society with my fellow citizens, and practicing toward them (following their own example), humanity, friendship, and all the virtues; and leaving behind me the honorable memory of a good man and a decent and virtuous patriot.

If, less happy or too late grown wise, I had seen myself reduced to end an infirm and languishing career in other climates, pointlessly regretting the repose and peace of which an imprudent youth deprived me, I would at least have nourished in my soul those same sentiments I could not have used in my native country; and penetrated by a tender and disinterested affection for my distant fellow citizens, I would have addressed them from the bottom of my heart more or less along the following lines:

My dear fellow citizens, or rather my brothers, since the bonds of blood as well as the laws unite almost all of us, it gives me pleasure to be incapable of thinking of you without at the same time thinking of all the good things you enjoy, and of which perhaps none of you appreciates the value more deeply than I who have lost them. The more I reflect upon your political and civil situation, the less I am capable of imagining that the nature of human affairs could admit of a better one. In all other governments, when it is a question of assuring the greatest good of the state, everything is always limited to imaginary projects, and at most to simple possibilities. As for you, your happiness is complete; it remains merely to enjoy it. And to become perfectly happy you are in need of nothing more than to know how to be satisfied with being so. Your sovereignty, acquired or recovered at the point of a sword, and preserved for two centuries by dint of valor and wisdom, is at last fully and universally recognized. Honorable treaties fix your boundaries, secure your rights and strengthen your repose. Your constitution is excellent, since it is dictated by the most sublime reason and is guaranteed by friendly powers deserving of respect. Your state is tranquil; you have neither wars nor conquerors to fear. You have no other masters but the wise laws you have made, administered by upright magistrates of your own choosing. You are neither rich enough to enervate yourself with softness and to lose in vain delights the taste for true happiness and solid virtues, nor poor enough to need more foreign assistance than your industry procures for you. And this precious liberty, which in large nations is maintained only by exorbitant taxes, costs you almost nothing to pursue.

For the happiness of its citizens and the examples of the peoples, may a republic so wisely and so happily constituted last forever! This is the only wish left for you to make, and the only precaution left for you to take. From here on, it is for you alone, not to bring about your own happiness, your ancestors having saved you the trouble, but to render it lasting by the wisdom of using it well. It is upon your perpetual union, your obedience to the laws, your respect for their ministers that your preservation depends. If there remains among you the slightest germ of bitterness or distrust, hasten to destroy it as a ruinous leaven that sooner or later results in your misfortunes and the ruin of the state. I beg you all to look deep inside your hearts and to heed the secret voice of your conscience. Is there anyone among you who knows of a body that is more upright, more enlightened, more worthy of respect than that of your magistracy? Do not all its members give you the example of moderation, of simplicity of mores, of respect for the laws, and of the most sincere reconciliation? Then freely give such wise chiefs that salutary confidence that reason owes to virtue. Bear in mind that they are of your choice, that they justify it, and that the honors due to those whom you have established in dignity necessarily reflect back upon yourselves. None of you is so unenlightened as to be ignorant of the fact that where the vigor of laws and the authority of their defenders cease, there can be neither security nor freedom for anyone. What then is the point at issue among you except to do wholeheartedly and with just confidence what you should always be obliged to do by a true self-interest, by duty and for the sake of reason? May a sinful and ruinous indifference to the maintenance of the constitution never make you neglect in time of need the wise teachings of the most enlightened and most zealous among you. But may equity, moderation, and the most respectful firmness continue to regulate all your activities and display in you, to the entire universe, the example of a proud and modest people, as jealous of its glory as of its liberty. Above all, beware (and this will be my last counsel) of ever listening to sinister interpretations and venomous speeches, whose secret motives are often more dangerous than the actions that are their object. An entire household awakens and takes warning at the first cries of a good and faithful watchdog who never barks except at the approach of burglars. But people hate the nuisance caused by those noisy animals that continually disturb the public repose and whose continual and ill-timed warnings are not heeded even at the moment when they are necessary.

And you, MAGNIFICENT AND MOST HONORED LORDS, you upright and worthy magistrates of a free people, permit me to offer you in particular my compliments and my respects. If there is a rank in the world suited to conferring honor on those who hold it, it is without doubt the one that is given by talents and virtue, that of which you have made yourselves worthy, and to which your fellow citizens have raised you. Their own merit adds still a new luster to yours. And I that find you, who were chosen by men capable of governing others in order that they themselves may be governed, are as much above other magistrates as a free people; and above all that the one which you have the honor of leading, is, by its enlightenment and reason, above the populace of the other states.

May I be permitted to cite an example of which better records ought to remain, and which will always be near to my heart. I never call to mind without the sweetest emotion the memory of the virtuous citizen to whom I owe my being, and who often spoke to me in my childhood of the respect that was owed you. I still see him living from the work of his hands, and nourishing his soul on the most sublime truths. I see Tacitus, Plutarch and Grotius mingled with the instruments of his craft before him. I see at his side a beloved son receiving with too little profit the tender instruction of the best of fathers. But if the aberrations of foolish youth made me forget such wise lessons for a time, I have the happiness to sense at last that whatever the inclination one may have toward vice, it is difficult for an education in which the heart is involved to remain forever lost.

Such, MAGNIFICENT AND MOST HONORED LORDS, are the citizens and even the simple inhabitants born in the state you govern. Such are those educated and sensible men concerning whom, under the name of workers and people, such base and false ideas are entertained in other nations. My father, I gladly acknowledge, was in no way distinguished among his fellow citizens; he was only what they all are; and such as he was, there was no country where his company would not have been sought after, cultivated, and profitably too, by the most upright men. It does not behoove me, nor, thank heaven, is it necessary to speak to you of the regard which men of that stamp can expect from you: your equals by education as well as by the rights of nature and of birth; your inferiors by their will and by the preference they owe your merit, which they have granted to it, and for which you in turn owe them some sort of gratitude. It is with intense satisfaction that I learn how much, in your dealings with them, you temper with gentleness and cooperativeness the gravity suited to the ministers of the law; how much you repay them in esteem and attention for the obedience and respect they owe you; conduct full of justice and wisdom, suited to putting at a greater and greater distance the memory of unhappy events which must be forgotten so as never to see them again; conduct all the more judicious because this equitable and generous people makes a pleasure out of its duty, because it naturally loves to honor you, and because those who are most zealous in upholding their rights are the ones who are most inclined to respect yours.

It should not be surprising that the leaders of a civil society love its glory and happiness; but, unfortunately for the tranquility of men, that those who consider themselves as the magistrates, or rather as the masters, of a more holy and more sublime homeland manifest some love for the earthly homeland which nourishes them. How sweet it is for me to be able to make such a rare exception in our favor, and to place in the rank of our best citizens those zealous trustees of the sacred dogmas authorized by the laws, those venerable pastors of souls, whose lively and sweet eloquence the better instills the maxims of the Gospel into people's hearts as they themselves always begin by practicing them. Everyone knows the success with which the great art of preaching is cultivated in Geneva. But since people are too accustomed to seeing things said in one way and done in another, few of them know the extent to which the spirit of Christianity, the saintliness of mores, severity to oneself and gentleness to others reign in the body of our ministers. Perhaps it behooves only the city of Geneva to provide the edifying example of such a perfect union between a society of theologians and of men of letters. It is in large part upon their wisdom and their acknowledged moderation and upon their zeal for the prosperity of the state that I base my hopes for its eternal tranquility. And I note, with a pleasure mixed with amazement and respect, how much they abhor the atrocious maxims of those sacred and barbarous men of whom history provides more than one example, and who, in order to uphold the alleged rights of God—that is to say, their own interests—were all the less sparing of human blood because they hoped their own would always be respected.

Could I forget that precious half of the republic which produces the happiness of the other and whose gentleness and wisdom maintain peace and good mores? Amiable and virtuous women citizens, it will always be the fate of your sex to govern ours. Happy it is when your chaste power, exercised only within the conjugal union, makes itself felt only for the glory of the state and the public happiness! Thus it was that in Sparta women were in command, and thus it is that you deserve to be in command in Geneva. What barbarous man could resist the voice of honor and reason in the mouth of an affectionate wife? And who would not despise vain luxury on seeing your simple and modest attire, which, from the luster it derives from you, seems the most favorable to beauty? It is for you to maintain always, by your amiable and innocent dominion and by your insinuating wit, the love of laws in the state and concord among the citizens; to reunite, by happy marriages, divided families; and above all, to correct, by the persuasive sweetness of your lessons and by the modest graces of your conversation, those extravagances which our young people come to acquire in other countries, whence, instead of the many useful things they could profit from, they bring back, with a childish manner and ridiculous airs adopted among fallen women, nothing more than an admiration for who knows what pretended grandeurs, frivolous compensations for servitude, which will never be worth as much as august liberty. Therefore always be what you are, the chaste guardians of mores and the gentle bonds of peace; and continue to assert on every occasion the rights of the heart and of nature for the benefit of duty and virtue.

I flatter myself that events will not prove me wrong in basing upon such guarantees hope for the general happiness of the citizens and for the glory of the republic. I admit that with all these advantages it will not shine with that brilliance which dazzles most eyes; and the childish and fatal taste for this is the deadliest enemy of happiness and liberty. Let a dissolute youth go elsewhere in search of easy pleasures and lengthy repentances. Let the alleged men of taste admire someplace else the grandeur of palaces, the beauty of carriages, the sumptuous furnishings, the pomp of spectacles, and all the refinements of softness and luxury. In Geneva we will find only men; but such a sight has a value of its own, and those who seek it are well worth the admirers of the rest.

May you all, MAGNIFICENT, MOST HONORED AND SOVEREIGN LORDS, deign to receive with the same goodness the respectful testimonies of the interest I take in your common prosperity. If I were unfortunate enough to be guilty of some indiscreet rapture in this lively effusion of my heart, I beg you to pardon it as the tender affection of a true patriot, and to the ardent and legitimate zeal of a man who envisages no greater happiness for himself than that of seeing all of you happy.

With the most profound respect, I am, MAGNIFICENT, MOST HONORED AND SOVEREIGN LORDS, your most humble and most obedient servant and fellow citizen.

Jean-Jacques Rousseau

Chambéry
12 June 1754

PREFACE

Of all the branches of human knowledge, the most useful and the least advanced seems to me to be that of man;[2] and I dare say that the inscription on the temple at Delphi alone contained a precept more important and more difficult than all the huge tomes of the moralists. Thus I regard the subject of this discourse as one of the most interesting questions that philosophy is capable of proposing, and unhappily for us, one of the thorniest that philosophers can attempt to resolve. For how can the source of the inequality among men be known unless one begins by knowing men themselves? And how will man be successful in seeing himself as nature formed him, through all the changes that the succession of time and things must have produced in his original constitution, and in separating what he derives from his own wherewithal from what circumstances and his progress have added to or changed in his primitive state? Like the statue of Glaucus, which time, sea and storms had disfigured to such an extent that it looked less like a god than a wild beast, the human soul, altered in the midst of society by a thousand constantly recurring causes, by the acquisition of a multitude of bits of knowledge and of errors, by changes that took place in the constitution of bodies, by the constant impact of the passions, has, as it were, changed its appearance to the point of being nearly unrecognizable. And instead of a being active always by certain and invariable principles, instead of that heavenly and majestic simplicity whose mark its author had left on it, one no longer finds anything but the grotesque contrast of passion which thinks it reasons and an understanding in a state of delirium.

What is even more cruel is that, since all the progress of the human species continually moves away from its primitive state, the more we accumulate new knowledge, the more we deprive ourselves of the means of acquiring the most important knowledge of all. Thus, in a sense, it is by dint of studying man that we have rendered ourselves incapable of knowing him.

It is easy to see that it is in these successive changes of the human constitution that we must seek the first origin of the differences that distinguish men, who, by common consensus, are naturally as equal among themselves as were the animals of each species before various physical causes had introduced into certain species the varieties we now observe among some of them. In effect, it is inconceivable that these first changes, by whatever means they took place, should have altered all at once and in the same manner all the individuals of the species. But while some improved or declined and acquired various good or bad qualities which were not inherent in their nature, the others remained longer in their original state. And such was the first source of inequality among men, which it is easier to demonstrate thus in general than to assign with precision its true causes.

Let my readers not imagine, then, that I dare flatter myself with having seen what appears to me so difficult to see. I have begun some lines of reasoning; I have hazarded some guesses, less in the hope of resolving the question than with the intention of clarifying it and of reducing it to its true state. Others will easily be able to go farther on this same route, though it will not be easy for anyone to reach the end of it. For it is no light undertaking to separate what is original from what is artificial in the present nature of man, and to have a proper understanding of a state which no longer exists, which perhaps never existed, which probably never will exist, and yet about which it is necessary to have accurate notions in order to judge properly our own present state. He who would attempt to determine precisely which precautions to take in order to make solid observations on this subject would need even more philosophy than is generally supposed; and a good solution of the following problem would not seem to me unworthy of the Aristotles and Plinys of our century: *What experiments would be necessary to achieve knowledge of natural man? And what are the means of carrying out these experiments in the midst of society?* Far from undertaking to resolve this problem, I believe I have meditated sufficiently on the subject to dare respond in advance that the greatest philosophers will not be too good to direct these experiments, nor the most powerful sovereigns to carry them out. It is hardly reasonable to expect such a combination, especially with the perseverance or rather the succession of understanding and good will needed on both sides in order to achieve success.

These investigations, so difficult to carry out and so little thought about until now, are nevertheless the only means we have left of removing a multitude of difficulties that conceal from us the knowledge of the real foundations of human society. It is this ignorance of the nature of man which throws so much uncertainty and obscurity on the true definition of natural right. For the idea of right, says M. Burlamaqui, and even more that of natural right, are manifestly ideas relative to the nature of man. Therefore, he continues, the principles of this science must be deduced from this very nature of man from man's constitution and state.

It is not without surprise and a sense of outrage that one observes the paucity of agreement that prevails among the various authors who have treated it. Among the most serious writers one can hardly find two who are of the same opinion on this point. The Roman jurists—not to mention the ancient philosophers who seem to have done their best to contradict each other on the most fundamental principles—subject man and all other animals indifferently to the same natural law, because they take this expression to refer to the law that nature imposes on itself rather than the law she prescribes, or rather because of the particular sense in which those jurists understood the word "law," which on this occasion they seem to have taken only for the expression of the general relations established by nature among all animate beings for their common preservation. The moderns, in acknowledging under the word "law" merely a rule prescribed to a moral being, that is to say, intelligent, free and considered in his relations with other beings, consequently limit the competence of the natural law to the only animal endowed with reason, that is, to man. But with each one defining this law in his own fashion, they all establish it on such metaphysical principles that even among us there are very few people in a position to grasp these principles, far from being able to find them by themselves. So that all the definitions of these wise men, otherwise in perpetual contradiction with one another, agree on this alone, that it is impossible to understand the law of nature and consequently to obey it without being a great reasoner and a profound metaphysician, which means precisely that for the establishment of society, men must have used enlightenment which develops only with great difficulty and by a very small number of people within the society itself.

Knowing nature so little and agreeing so poorly on the meaning of the word "law," it would be quite difficult to come to some common understanding regarding a good definition of natural law. Thus all those definitions that are found in books have, over and above a lack of uniformity, the added fault of being drawn from several branches of knowledge which men do not naturally have, and from advantages the idea of which they cannot conceive until after having left the state of nature. Writers begin by seeking the rules on which, for the common utility, it would be appropriate for men to agree among themselves; and then they give the name *natural law* to the collection of these rules, with no other proof than the good which presumably would result from their universal observance. Surely this is a very convenient way to compose definitions and to explain the nature of things by virtually arbitrary views of what is seemly.

But as long as we are ignorant of natural man, it is futile for us to attempt to determine the law he has received or which is best suited to his constitution. All that we can see very clearly regarding this law is that, for it to be law, not only must the will of him who is obliged by it be capable of knowing submission to it, but also, for it to be natural, it must speak directly by the voice of nature.

Leaving aside therefore all the scientific books which teach us only to see men as they have made themselves, and meditating on the first and most simple operations of the human soul, I believe I perceive in it two principles that are prior to reason, of which one makes us ardently interested in our well-being and our self-preservation, and the other inspires in us a natural repugnance to seeing any sentient being, especially our fellow man, perish or suffer. It is from the conjunction and combination that our mind is in a position to make regarding these two principles, without the need for introducing that of sociability, that all the rules of natural right appear to me to flow; rules which reason is later forced to reestablish on other foundations, when, by its successive developments, it has succeeded in smothering nature.

In this way one is not obliged to make a man a philosopher before making him a man. His duties toward others are not uniquely dictated to him by the belated lessons of wisdom; and as long as he does not resist the inner impulse of compassion, he will never harm another man or even another sentient being, except in the legitimate instance where, if his preservation were involved, he is obliged to give preference to himself. By this means, an end can also be made to the ancient disputes regarding the participation of animals in the natural law. For it is clear that, lacking intelligence and liberty, they cannot recognize this law; but since they share to some extent in our nature by virtue of the sentient quality with which they are endowed, one will judge that they should also participate in natural right, and that man is subject to some sort of duties toward them. It seems, in effect, that if I am obliged not to do any harm to my fellow man, it is less because he is a rational being than because he is a sentient being: a quality that, since it is common to both animals and men, should at least give the former the right not to be needlessly mistreated by the latter.

This same study of original man, of his true needs and the fundamental principles of his duties, is also the only good means that can be used to remove those multitudes of difficulties which present themselves regarding the origin of moral inequality, the true foundations of the body politic, the reciprocal rights of its members, and a thousand other similar questions that are as important as they are poorly explained.

In considering human society from a tranquil and disinterested point of view it seems at first to manifest merely the violence of powerful men and the oppression of the weak. The mind revolts against the harshness of the former; one is inclined to deplore the blindness of the latter. And since nothing is less stable among men than those external relationships which chance brings about more often than wisdom, and which are called weakness or power, wealth or poverty, human establishments appear at first glance to be based on piles of shifting sand. It is only in examining them closely, only after having cleared away the dust and sand that surround the edifice, that one perceives the unshakeable base on which it is raised and one learns to respect its foundations. Now without a serious study of man, of his natural faculties and their successive developments, one will never succeed in making these distinctions and in separating, in the present constitution of things, what the divine will has done from what human art has pretended to do. The political and moral investigations occasioned by the important question I am examining are therefore useful in every way; and the hypothetical history of governments is an instructive lesson for man in every respect. In considering what we would have become, left to ourselves, we ought to learn to bless him whose beneficent hand, in correcting our institutions and giving them an unshakeable foundation, has prevented the disorders that must otherwise result from them, and has brought about our happiness from the means that seemed likely to add to our misery.

Learn whom God has ordered you to be, and in what part of human affairs you have been placed.

Notice on the Notes

I have added some notes to this work, following my indolent custom of working in fits and starts. Occasionally these notes wander so far from the subject that they are not good to read with the text. I therefore have consigned them to the end of the Discourse, in which I have tried my best to follow the straightest path. Those who have the courage to begin again will be able to amuse themselves the second time as they beat the bushes and try to run through the notes. There will be little harm done if others do not read them at all.

[Translator's note: These notes are presented on p. 83. Additions to the text, made by Rousseau in the 1782 edition, are translated here and enclosed by brackets.]

QUESTION

Proposed by the Academy of Dijon

What is the Origin of Inequality

Among Men, and is it Authorized

by the Natural Law?

DISCOURSE ON THE ORIGIN AND

FOUNDATIONS OF INEQUALITY

AMONG MEN

It is of man that I have to speak, and the question I am examining indicates to me that I am going to be speaking to men, for such questions are not proposed by those who are afraid to honor the truth. I will therefore confidently defend the cause of humanity before the wise men who invite me to do so, and I will not be displeased with myself if I make myself worthy of my subject and my judges.

I conceive of two kinds of inequality in the human species: one which I call natural or physical, because it is established by nature and consists in the difference of age, health, bodily strength, and qualities of mind or soul. The other may be called moral or political inequality, because it depends on a kind of convention and is established, or at least authorized, by the consent of men. This latter type of inequality consists in the different privileges enjoyed by some at the expense of others, such as being richer, more honored, more powerful than they, or even causing themselves to be obeyed by them.

There is no point in asking what the source of natural inequality is, because the answer would be found enunciated in the simple definition of the word. There is still less of a point in asking whether there would not be some essential connection between the two inequalities, for that would amount to asking whether those who command are necessarily better than those who obey, and whether strength of body or mind, wisdom or virtue are always found in the same individuals in proportion to power or wealth. Perhaps this is a good question for slaves to discuss within earshot of their masters, but it is not suitable for reasonable and free men who seek the truth.

Precisely what, then, is the subject of this discourse? To mark, in the progress of things, the moment when, right taking the place of violence, nature was subjected to the law. To explain the sequence of wonders by which the strong could resolve to serve the weak, and the people to buy imaginary repose at the price of real felicity.

The philosophers who have examined the foundations of society have all felt the necessity of returning to the state of nature, but none of them has reached it. Some have not hesitated to ascribe to man in that state the notion of just and unjust, without bothering to show that he had to have that notion, or even that it was useful to him. Others have spoken of the natural right that everyone has to preserve what belongs to him, without explaining what they mean by "belonging." Others started out by giving authority to the stronger over the weaker, and immediately brought about government, without giving any thought to the time that had to pass before the meaning of the words "authority" and "government" could exist among men. Finally, all of them, speaking continually of need, avarice, oppression, desires, and pride, have transferred to the state of nature the ideas they acquired in society. They spoke about savage man, and it was civil man they depicted. It did not even occur to most of our philosophers to doubt that the state of nature had existed, even though it is evident from reading the Holy Scriptures that the first man, having received enlightenment and precepts immediately from God, was not himself in that state; and if we give the writings of Moses the credence that every Christian owes them, we must deny that, even before the flood, men were ever in the pure state of nature, unless they had fallen back into it because of some extraordinary event: a paradox that is quite awkward to defend and utterly impossible to prove.

Let us therefore begin by putting aside all the facts, for they have no bearing on the question. The investigations that may be undertaken concerning this subject should not be taken for historical truths, but only for hypothetical and conditional reasonings, better suited to shedding light on the nature of things than on pointing out their true origin, like those our physicists make everyday with regard to the formation of the world. Religion commands us to believe that since God himself drew men out of the state of nature, they are unequal because he wanted them to be so; but it does not forbid us to form conjectures, drawn solely from the nature of man and the beings that surround him, concerning what the human race could have become, if it had been left to itself. That is what I am asked, and what I propose to examine in this discourse. Since my subject concerns man in general, I will attempt to speak in terms that suit all nations, or rather, forgetting times and places in order to think only of the men to whom I am speaking, I will imagine I am in the Lyceum in Athens, reciting the lessons of my masters, having men like Plato and Xenocrates for my judges, and the human race for my audience.

O man, whatever country you may be from, whatever your opinions may be, listen: here is your history, as I have thought to read it, not in the books of your fellowmen, who are liars, but in nature, who never lies. Everything that comes from nature will be true; there will be nothing false except what I have unintentionally added. The times about which I am going to speak are quite remote: how much you have changed from what you were! It is, as it were, the life of your species that I am about to describe to you according to the qualities you have received, which your education and your habits have been able to corrupt but have been unable to destroy. There is, I feel, an age at which an individual man would want to stop. You will seek the age at which you would want your species to have stopped. Dissatisfied with your present state for reasons that portend even greater grounds for dissatisfaction for your unhappy posterity, perhaps you would like to be able to go backwards in time. This feeling should be a hymn in praise of your first ancestors, the criticism of your contemporaries, and the dread of those who have the unhappiness of living after you.

PART ONE

However important it may be, in order to render sound judgments regarding the natural state of man, to consider him from his origin and to examine him, so to speak, in the first embryo of the species, I will not follow his nature through its successive developments. I will not stop to investigate in the animal kingdom what he might have been at the beginning so as eventually to become what he is. I will not examine whether, as Aristotle thinks, man's elongated nails were not at first hooked claws, whether man was not furry like a bear, and whether, if man walked on all fours,[3] his gaze, directed toward the ground and limited to a horizon of a few steps—did not provide an indication of both the character and the limits of his ideas. On this subject I could form only vague and almost imaginary conjectures. Comparative anatomy has as yet made too little progress; the observations of naturalists are as yet too uncertain for one to be able to establish the basis of solid reasoning on such foundations. Thus, without having recourse to the supernatural knowledge we have on this point, and without taking note of the changes that must have occurred in the internal as well as the external conformation of man, as he applied his limbs to new purposes and nourished himself on new foods, I will suppose him to have been formed from all time as I see him today: walking on two feet, using his hands as we use ours, directing his gaze over all of nature, and measuring with his eyes the vast expanse of the heavens.

When I strip that being, thus constituted, of all the supernatural gifts he could have received and of all the artificial faculties he could have acquired only through long progress; when I consider him, in a word, as he must have left the hands of nature, I see an animal less strong than some, less agile than others, but all in all, the most advantageously organized of all. I see him satisfying his hunger under an oak tree, quenching his thirst at the first stream, finding his bed at the foot of the same tree that supplied his meal; and thus all his needs are satisfied.

When the earth is left to its natural fertility[4] and covered with immense forests that were never mutilated by the axe, it offers storehouses and shelters at every step to animals of every species. Men, dispersed among the animals, observe and imitate their industry, and thereby raise themselves to the level of animal instinct, with the advantage that, whereas each species has only its own instincts, man, who may perhaps have none that belongs to him, appropriates all of them to himself, feeds himself equally well on most of the various foods[5] which the other animals divide among themselves, and consequently finds his sustenance more easily than any of the rest can.

Accustomed from childhood to inclement weather and the rigors of the seasons, acclimated to fatigue, and forced, naked and without arms, to defend their lives and their prey against other ferocious beasts, or to escape them by taking flight, men develop a robust and nearly unalterable temperament. Children enter the world with the excellent constitution of their parents and strengthen it with the same exercises that produced it, thus acquiring all the vigor that the human race is capable of having. Nature treats them precisely the way the law of Sparta treated the children of its citizens: it renders strong and robust those who are well constituted and makes all the rest perish, thereby differing from our present-day societies, where the state, by making children burdensome to their parents, kills them indiscriminately before their birth.

Since the savage man's body is the only instrument he knows, he employs it for a variety of purposes that, for lack of practice, ours are incapable of serving. And our industry deprives us of the force and agility that necessity obliges him to acquire. If he had had an axe, would his wrists break such strong branches? If he had had a sling, would he throw a stone with so much force? If he had had a ladder, would he climb a tree so nimbly? If he had had a horse, would he run so fast? Give a civilized man time to gather all his machines around him, and undoubtedly he will easily overcome a savage man. But if you want to see an even more unequal fight, pit them against each other naked and disarmed, and you will soon realize the advantage of constantly having all of one's forces at one's disposal, of always being ready for any event, and of always carrying one's entire self, as it were, with one.[6]

Hobbes maintains that man is naturally intrepid and seeks only to attack and to fight. On the other hand, an illustrious philosopher thinks, and Cumberland and Pufendorf also affirm, that nothing is as timid as man in the state of nature, and that he is always trembling and ready to take flight at the slightest sound he hears or at the slightest movement he perceives. That may be the case with regard to objects with which he is not acquainted. And I do not doubt that he is frightened by all the new sights that present themselves to him every time he can neither discern the physical good and evil he may expect from them nor compare his forces with the dangers he must run: rare circumstances in the state of nature, where everything takes place in such a uniform manner and where the face of the earth is not subject to those sudden and continual changes caused by the passions and inconstancy of peoples living together. But since a savage man lives dispersed among the animals and, finding himself early on in a position to measure himself against them, he soon makes the comparison; and, aware that he surpasses them in skillfulness more than they surpass him in strength, he learns not to fear them any more. Pit a bear or a wolf against a savage who is robust, agile, and courageous, as they all are, armed with stones and a hefty cudgel, and you will see that the danger will be at least equal on both sides, and that after several such experiences, ferocious beasts, which do not like to attack one another, will be quite reluctant to attack a man, having found him to be as ferocious as themselves. With regard to animals that actually have more strength than man has skillfulness, he is in the same position as other weaker species, which nevertheless subsist. Man has the advantage that, since he is no less adept than they at running and at finding almost certain refuge in trees, he always has the alternative of accepting or leaving the encounter and the choice of taking flight or entering into combat. Moreover, it appears that no animal naturally attacks man, except in the case of self-defense or extreme hunger, or shows evidence of those violent antipathies toward him that seem to indicate that one species is destined by nature to serve as food for another.

[No doubt these are the reasons why negroes and savages bother themselves so little about the ferocious beasts they may encounter in the woods. In this respect, the Caribs of Venezuela, among others, live in the most profound security and without the slightest inconvenience. Although they are practically naked, says Francisco Coreal, they boldly expose themselves in the forest, armed only with bow and arrow, but no one has ever heard of one of them being devoured by animals.]

There are other, more formidable enemies, against which man does not have the same means of self-defense: natural infirmities, childhood, old age, and illnesses of all kinds—sad signs of our weakness, of which the first two are common to all animals, with the last belonging principally to man living in society. On the subject of childhood, I even observe that a mother, by carrying her child everywhere with her, can feed it much more easily than females of several animal species, which are forced to be continually coming and going, with great fatigue, to seek their food and to suckle or feed their young. It is true that if a woman were to perish, the child runs a considerable risk of perishing with her. But this danger is common to a hundred other species, whose young are for quite some time incapable of going off to seek their nourishment for themselves. And although childhood is longer among us, our lifespan is also longer; thus things are more or less equal in this respect,[7] although there are other rules, not relevant to my subject, which are concerned with the duration of infancy and the number of young.[8] Among the elderly, who are less active and perspire little, the need for food diminishes with the faculty of providing for it. And since savage life shields them from gout and rheumatism, and since old age is, of all ills, the one that human assistance can least alleviate, they eventually die without anyone being aware that they are ceasing to exist, and almost without being aware of it themselves.

With regard to illnesses, I will not repeat the vain and false pronouncements made against medicine by the majority of people in good health. Rather, I will ask whether there is any solid observation on the basis of which one can conclude that the average lifespan is shorter in those countries where the art of medicine is most neglected than in those where it is cultivated most assiduously. And how could that be the case, if we give ourselves more ills than medicine can furnish us remedies? The extreme inequality in our lifestyle: excessive idleness among some, excessive labor among others; the ease with which we arouse and satisfy our appetites and our sensuality; the overly refined foods of the wealthy, which nourish them with irritating juices and overwhelm them with indigestion; the bad food of the poor, who most of the time do not have even that, and who, for want of food, are inclined to stuff their stomachs greedily whenever possible; staying up until all hours, excesses of all kinds, immoderate outbursts of every passion, bouts of fatigue and mental exhaustion; countless sorrows and afflictions which are felt in all levels of society and which perpetually gnaw away at souls: these are the fatal proofs that most of our ills are of our own making, and that we could have avoided nearly all of them by preserving the simple, regular and solitary lifestyle prescribed to us by nature. If nature has destined us to be healthy, I almost dare to affirm that the state of reflection is a state contrary to nature and that the man who meditates is a depraved animal. When one thinks about the stout constitutions of the savages, at least of those whom we have not ruined with our strong liquors; when one becomes aware of the fact that they know almost no illnesses but wounds and old age, one is strongly inclined to believe that someone could easily write the history of human maladies by following the history of civil societies. This at least was the opinion of Plato, who believed that, from certain remedies used or approved by

Podalirius and Machaon at the siege of Troy, various illnesses which these remedies should exacerbate were as yet unknown among men. [And Celsus reports that diet, so necessary today, was only an invention of Hippocrates.]

With so few sources of ills, man in the state of nature hardly has any need therefore of remedies, much less of physicians. The human race is in no worse condition than all the others in this respect; and it is easy to learn from hunters whether in their chases they find many sick animals. They find quite a few that have received serious wounds that healed quite nicely, that have had bones or even limbs broken and reset with no other surgeon than time, no other regimen than their everyday life, and that are no less perfectly cured for not having been tormented with incisions, poisoned with drugs, or exhausted with fasting. Finally, however correctly administered medicine may be among us, it is still certain that although a sick savage, abandoned to himself, has nothing to hope for except from nature, on the other hand, he has nothing to fear except his illness. This frequently makes his situation preferable to ours.

Therefore we must take care not to confuse savage man with the men we have before our eyes. Nature treats all animals left to their own devices with a predilection that seems to show how jealous she is of that right. The horse, the cat, the bull, even the ass, are usually taller, and all of them have a more robust constitution, more vigor, more strength, and more courage in the forests than in our homes. They lose half of these advantages in becoming domesticated; it might be said that all our efforts at feeding them and treating them well only end in their degeneration. It is the same for man himself. In becoming habituated to the ways of society and a slave, he becomes weak, fearful, and servile; his soft and effeminate lifestyle completes the enervation of both his strength and his courage. Let us add that the difference between the savage man and the domesticated man should be still greater than that between the savage animal and the domesticated animal; for while animal and man have been treated equally by nature, man gives more comforts to himself than to the animals he tames, and all of these comforts are so many specific causes that make him degenerate more noticeably.

It is therefore no great misfortune for those first men, nor, above all, such a great obstacle to their preservation, that they are naked, that they have no dwelling, and that they lack all those useful things we take to be so necessary. If they do not have furry skin, they have no need for it in warm countries, and in cold countries they soon learn to help themselves to the skins of animals they have vanquished. If they have but two feet to run with, they have two arms to provide for their defense and for their needs. Perhaps their children learn to walk late and with difficulty, but mothers carry them easily: an advantage that is lacking in other species, where the mother, on being pursued, finds herself forced to abandon her young or to conform her pace to theirs. [It is possible there are some exceptions to this. For example, the animal from the province of Nicaragua which resembles a fox and which has feet like a man's hands, and, according to Coreal, has a pouch under its belly in which the mother places her young when she is forced to take flight. No doubt this is the same animal that is called *tlaquatzin* in Mexico; the female of the species Laët describes as having a similar pouch for the same purpose.] Finally, unless we suppose those singular and fortuitous combinations of circumstances of which I will speak later, and which might very well have never taken place, at any rate it is clear that the first man who made clothing or a dwelling for himself was giving himself things that were hardly necessary, since he had done without them until then and since it is not clear why, as a grown man, he could not endure the kind of life he had endured ever since he was a child.

Alone, idle, and always near danger, savage man must like to sleep and be a light sleeper like animals which do little thinking and, as it were, sleep the entire time they are not thinking. Since his self-preservation was practically his sole concern, his best trained faculties ought to be those that have attack and defense as their principal object, either to subjugate his prey or to prevent his becoming the prey of another animal. On the other hand, the organs that are perfected only by softness and sensuality must remain in a state of crudeness that excludes any kind of refinement in him. And with his senses being divided in this respect, he will have extremely crude senses of touch and taste; those of sight, hearing and smell will have the greatest subtlety. Such is the state of animals in general, and, according to the reports of travellers, such also is that of the majority of savage peoples. Thus we should not be surprised that the Hottentots of the Cape of Good Hope can sight ships with the naked eye as far out at sea as the Dutch can with telescopes; or that the savages of America were as capable of trailing Spaniards by smell as the best dogs could have done; or that all these barbarous nations endure their nakedness with no discomfort, whet their appetites with hot peppers, and drink European liquors like water.

So far I have considered only physical man. Let us now try to look at him from a metaphysical and moral point of view.

In any animal I see nothing but an ingenious machine to which nature has given senses in order for it to renew its strength and to protect itself, to a certain point, from all that tends to destroy or disturb it. I am aware of precisely the same things in the human machine, with the difference that nature alone does everything in the operations of an animal, whereas man contributes, as a free agent, to his own operations. The former chooses or rejects by instinct and the later by an act of freedom. Hence an animal cannot deviate from the rule that is prescribed to it, even when it would be advantageous to do so, while man deviates from it, often to his own detriment. Thus a pigeon would die of hunger near a bowl filled with choice meats, and so would a cat perched atop a pile of fruit or grain, even though both could nourish themselves quite well with the food they disdain, if they were of a mind to try some. And thus dissolute men abandon themselves to excesses which cause them fever and death, because the mind perverts the senses and because the will still speaks when nature is silent.

Every animal has ideas, since it has senses; up to a certain point it even combines its ideas, and in this regard man differs from an animal only in degree. Some philosophers have even suggested that there is a greater difference between two given men than between a given man and an animal. Therefore it is not so much understanding which causes the specific distinction of man from all other animals as it is his being a free agent. Nature commands every animal, and beasts obey. Man feels the same impetus, but he knows he is free to go along or to resist; and it is above all in the awareness of this freedom that the spirituality of his soul is made manifest. For physics explains in some way the mechanism of the senses and the formation of ideas; but in the power of willing, or rather of choosing, and in the feeling of this power, we find only purely spiritual acts, about which the laws of mechanics explain nothing.

But if the difficulties surrounding all these questions should leave some room for dispute on this difference between man and animal, there is another very specific quality which distinguishes them and about which there can be no argument: the faculty of self-perfection, a faculty which, with the aid of circumstances, successively develops all the others, and resides among us as much in the species as in the individual. On the other hand, an animal, at the end of a few months, is what it will be all its life; and its species, at the end of a thousand years, is what it was in the first of those thousand years. Why is man alone subject to becoming an imbecile? Is it not that he thereby returns to his primitive state, and that, while the animal which has acquired nothing and which also has nothing to lose, always retains its instinct, man, in losing through old age or other accidents all that his *perfectibility* has enabled him to acquire, thus falls even lower than the animal itself? It would be sad for us to be forced to agree that this distinctive and almost unlimited faculty is the source of all man's misfortunes; that this is what, by dint of time, draws him out of that original condition in which he would pass tranquil and innocent days; that this is what, through centuries of giving rise to his enlightenment and his errors, his vices and his virtues, eventually makes him a tyrant over himself and nature.[9] It would be dreadful to be obliged to praise as a beneficent being the one who first suggested to the inhabitant on the banks of the Orinoco the use of boards which he binds to his children's temples, and which assure them of at least part of their imbecility and their original happiness.

Savage man, left by nature to instinct alone, or rather compensated for the instinct he is perhaps lacking by faculties capable of first replacing them and then of raising him to the level of instinct, will therefore begin with purely animal functions.[10] Perceiving and feeling will be his first state, which he will have in common with all animals. Willing and not willing, desiring, and fearing will be the first and nearly the only operations of his soul until new circumstances bring about new developments in it.

Whatever the moralists may say about it, human understanding owes much to the passions, which, by common consensus, also owe a great deal to it. It is by their activity that our reason is perfected. We seek to know only because we desire to find enjoyment; and it is impossible to conceive why someone who had neither desires nor fears would go to the bother of reasoning. The passions in turn take their origin from our needs, and their progress from our knowledge. For one can desire or fear things only by virtue of the ideas one can have of them, or from the simple impulse of nature; and savage man, deprived of every sort of enlightenment, feels only the passion of this latter sort. His desires do not go beyond his physical needs.[11] The only goods he knows in the universe are nourishment, a woman and rest; the only evils he fears are pain and hunger. I say pain and not death because an animal will never know what it is to die; and knowledge of death and its terrors is one of the first acquisitions that man has made in withdrawing from the animal condition.

Were it necessary, it would be easy for me to support this view with facts and to demonstrate that, among all the nations of the world, the progress of the mind has been precisely proportionate to the needs received by peoples from nature or to those needs to which circumstances have subjected them, and consequently to the passions which inclined them to provide for those needs. I would show the arts coming into being in Egypt and spreading with the flooding of the Nile. I would follow their progress among the Greeks, where they were seen to germinate, grow and rise to the heavens among the sands and rocks of Attica, though never being able to take root on the fertile banks of the Eurotas. I would point out that in general the peoples of the north are more industrious than those of the south, because they cannot get along as well without being so, as if nature thereby wanted to equalize things by giving to their minds the fertility it refuses their soil.

But without having recourse to the uncertain testimony of history, does anyone fail to see that everything seems to remove savage man from the temptation and the means of ceasing to be savage? His imagination depicts nothing to him; his heart asks nothing of him. His modest needs are so easily found at hand, and he is so far from the degree of knowledge necessary to make him desire to acquire greater knowledge, that he can have neither foresight nor curiosity. The spectacle of nature becomes a matter of indifference to him by dint of its becoming familiar to him. It is always the same order, always the same succession of changes. He does not have a mind for marveling at the greatest wonders; and we must not seek in him the philosophy that a man needs in order to know how to observe once what he has seen everyday. His soul, agitated by nothing, is given over to the single feeling of his own present existence, without any idea of the future, however, near it may be, and his projects, as limited as his views, hardly extend to the end of the day. Such is, even today, the extent of the Carib's foresight. In the morning he sells his bed of cotton and in the evening he returns in tears to buy it back, for want of having foreseen that he would need it that night.

The more one meditates on this subject, the more the distance from pure sensations to the simplest knowledge increases before our eyes; and it is impossible to conceive how a man could have crossed such a wide gap by his forces alone, without the aid of communication and without the provocation of necessity. How many centuries have perhaps gone by before men were in a position to see any fire other than that from the heavens? How many different risks did they have to run before they learned the most common uses of that element? How many times did they let it go out before they had acquired the art of reproducing it? And how many times perhaps did each of these secrets die with the one who had discovered it? What will we say about agriculture, an art that requires so much labor and foresight, that depends on so many other arts, that quite obviously is practicable only in a society which is at least in its beginning stages, and that serves us not so much to derive from the earth food it would readily provide without agriculture, as to force from it those preferences that are most to our taste? But let us suppose that men multiplied to the point where the natural productions were no longer sufficient to nourish them: a supposition which, it may be said in passing, would show a great advantage for the human species in that way of life. Let us suppose that, without forges or workshops, farm implements had fallen from the heavens into the hands of the savages; that these men had conquered the mortal hatred they all have for continuous work; that they had learned to foresee their needs far enough in advance; that they had guessed how the soil is to be cultivated, grains sown, and trees planted; that they had discovered the arts of grinding wheat and fermenting grapes: all things they would need to have been taught by the gods, for it is inconceivable how they could have picked these things up on their own. Yet, after all this, what man would be so foolish as to tire himself out cultivating a field that will be plundered by the first comer, be it man or beast, who takes a fancy to the crop? And how could each man resolve to spend his life in hard labor, when, the more necessary to him the fruits of his labor may be, the surer he is of not realizing them? In a word, how could this situation lead men to cultivate the soil as long as it is not divided among them, that is to say, as long as the state of nature is not wiped out?

Were we to want to suppose a savage man as skilled in the art of thinking as our philosophers make him out to be; were we, following their example, to make him a full-fledged philosopher, discovering by himself the most sublime truths, and, by chains of terribly abstract reasoning, forming for himself maxims of justice and reason drawn from the love of order in general or from the known will of his creator; in a word, were we to suppose there was as much intelligence and enlightenment in his mind as he needs, and is in fact found to have been possessed of dullness and stupidity, what use would the species have for all that metaphysics, which could not be communicated and which would perish with the individual who would have invented it? What progress could the human race make, scattered in the woods among the animals? And to what extent could men mutually perfect and enlighten one another, when, with neither a fixed dwelling nor any need for one another, they would hardly encounter one another twice in their lives, without knowing or talking to one another.

Let us consider how many ideas we owe to the use of speech; how much grammar trains and facilitates the operations of the mind. And let us think of the inconceivable difficulties and the infinite amount of time that the first invention of languages must have cost. Let us join their reflections to the preceding ones, and we will be in a position to judge how many thousands of centuries would have been necessary to develop successively in the human mind the operations of which it was capable.

May I be permitted to consider for a moment the obstacles to the origin of languages. I could be content here to cite or repeat the investigations that the Abbé de Condillac has made on this matter, all of which completely confirm my view, and may perhaps have given me the idea in the first place. But since the way in which this philosopher resolves the difficulties he himself raises concerning the origin of conventional signs shows that he assumed what I question (namely, a kind of society already established among the inventors of language), I believe that, in referring to his reflections, I must add to them my own, in order to present the same difficulties from a standpoint that is pertinent to my subject. The first that presents itself is to imagine how languages could have become necessary; for since men had no communication among themselves nor any need for it, I fail to see either the necessity of this invention or its possibility, if it were not indispensable. I might well say, as do many others, that languages were born in the domestic intercourse among fathers, mothers, and children. But aside from the fact that this would not resolve the difficulties, it would make the mistake of those who, reasoning about the state of nature, intrude into it ideas taken from society. They always see the family gathered in one and the same dwelling, with its members maintaining among themselves a union as intimate and permanent as exists among us, where so many common interests unite them. But the fact of the matter is that in that primitive state, since nobody had houses or huts or property of any kind, each one bedded down in some random spot and often for only one night. Males and females came together fortuitously as a result of chance encounters, occasion, and desire, without there being any great need for words to express what they had to say to one another. They left one another with the same nonchalance.[12] The mother at first nursed her children for her own need; then, with habit having endeared them to her, she later nourished them for their own need. Once they had the strength to look for their food, they did not hesitate to leave the mother herself. And since there was practically no other way of finding one another than not to lose sight of one another, they were soon at the point of not even recognizing one another. It should also be noted that, since the child had all his needs to explain and consequently more things to say to the mother than the mother to the child, it is the child who must make the greatest effort toward inventing a language, and that the language he uses should in large part be of his own making, which multiplies languages as many times as there are individuals to speak them. This tendency was abetted by a nomadic and vagabond life, which does not give any idiom time to gain a foothold. For claiming that the mother teaches her child the words he ought to use in asking her for this or that is a good way of showing how already formed languages are taught, but it does not tell us how languages are formed.

Let us suppose this first difficulty has been overcome. Let us disregard for a moment the immense space that there must have been between the pure state of nature and the need for languages. And, on the supposition that they are necessary,[13] let us inquire how they might have begun to be established. Here we come to a new difficulty, worse still than the preceding one. For if men needed speech in order to learn to think, they had a still greater need for knowing how to think in order to discover the art of speaking. And even if it were understood how vocal sounds had been taken for the conventional expressions of our ideas, it would still remain for us to determine what could have been the conventional expressions for ideas that, not having a sensible object, could not be indicated either by gesture or by voice. Thus we are scarcely able to form tenable conjectures regarding the birth of this art of communicating thoughts and establishing intercourse between minds, a sublime art which is already quite far from its origin, but which the philosopher still sees at so prodigious a distance from its perfection that there is no man so foolhardy as to claim that it will ever achieve it, even if the sequences of change that time necessarily brings were suspended in its favor, even if prejudices were to be barred from the academies or be silent before them, and even if they were able to occupy themselves with that thorny problem for whole centuries without interruption.

Man's first language, the most universal, the most energetic and the only language he needed before it was necessary to persuade men assembled together, is the cry of nature. Since this cry was elicited only by a kind of instinct in pressing circumstances, to beg for help in great dangers, or for relief of violent ills, it was not used very much in the ordinary course of life, where more moderate feelings prevail. When the ideas of men begin to spread and multiply, and closer communication was established among them, they sought more numerous signs and a more extensive language. They multiplied vocal inflections and combined them with gestures, which, by their nature, are more expressive, and whose meaning is less dependent on a prior determination. They therefore signified visible and mobile objects by means of gestures, and audible ones by imitative sounds. But since a gesture indicates hardly anything more than present or easily described objects and visible actions; since its use is not universal, because darkness or the interposition of a body renders it useless; and since it requires rather than stimulates attention, men finally thought of replacing them with vocal articulations, which, while not having the same relationship to certain ideas, were better suited to represent all ideas as conventional signs. Such a substitution could only be made by a common consent and in a way rather difficult to practice for men whose crude organs had as yet no exercise, and still more difficult to conceive in itself, since that unanimous agreement had to have had a motive, and speech appears to have been necessary in order to establish the use of speech.

We must infer that the first words men used had a much broader meaning in their mind than do those used in languages that are already formed; and that, being ignorant of the division of discourse into its constitutive parts, at first they gave each word the meaning of a whole sentence. When they began to distinguish subject from attribute and verb from noun, which was no mean effort of genius, substantives were at first only so many proper nouns; the [present] infinitive was the only verb tense; and the notion of adjectives must have developed only with considerable difficulty, since every adjective is an abstract word, and abstractions are difficult and not particularly natural operations.

At first each object was given a particular name, without regard to genus and species which those first founders were not in a position to distinguish; and all individual things presented themselves to their minds in isolation, as they are in the spectacle of nature. If one oak tree was called A, another was called B. [For the first idea one draws from two things is that they are not the same; and it often requires quite some time to observe what they have in common.] Thus the more limited the knowledge, the more extensive becomes the dictionary. The difficulty inherent in all this nomenclature could not easily be alleviated, for in order to group beings under various common and generic denominations, it was necessary to know their properties and their differences. Observations and definitions were necessary, that is to say, natural history and metaphysics, and far more than men of those times could have had.

Moreover, general ideas can be introduced into the mind only with the aid of words, and the understanding grasps them only through sentences. That is one reason why animals cannot form such ideas or even acquire the perfectibility that depends on them. When a monkey moves unhesitatingly from one nut to another, does anyone think the monkey has the general idea of that type of fruit and that he compares its archetype with these two individuals? Undoubtedly not; but the sight of one of these nuts recalls to his memory the sensations he received of the other; and his eyes, modified in a certain way, announce to his sense of taste the modification it is about to receive. Every general idea is purely intellectual. The least involvement of the imagination thereupon makes the idea particular. Try to draw for yourself the image of a tree in general; you will never succeed in doing it. In spite of yourself, it must be seen as small or large, barren or leafy, light or dark; and if you were in a position to see in it nothing but what you see in every tree, this image would no longer resemble a tree. Purely abstract beings are perceived in the same way, or are conceived only through discourse. The definition of a triangle alone gives you the true idea of it. As soon as you behold one in your mind, it is a particular triangle and not some other one, and you cannot avoid making its lines to be perceptible or its plane to have color. It is therefore necessary to utter sentences, and thus to speak, in order to have general ideas. For as soon as the imagination stops, the mind proceeds no further without the aid of discourse. If, then, the first inventors of language could give names only to ideas they already had, it follows that the first substantives could not have been anything but proper nouns.

But when, by means I am unable to conceive, our new grammarians began to extend their ideas and to generalize their words, the ignorance of the inventors must have subjected this method to very strict limitations. And just as they had at first unduly multiplied the names of individual things, owing to their failure to know the genera and species, they later made too few species and genera, owing to their failure to have considered beings in all their differences. Pushing these divisions far enough would have required more experience and enlightenment than they could have had, and more investigations and work than they were willing to put into it. Now if even today new species are discovered everyday that until now had escaped all our observations, just imagine how many species must have escaped the attention of men who judged things only on first appearance! As for primary classes and the most general notions, it is superfluous to add that they too must have escaped them. How, for example, would they have imagined or understood the words "matter," "mind," "substance," "mode," "figure," and "movement," when our philosophers, who for so long have been making use of them, have a great deal of difficulty understanding them themselves; and when, since the ideas attached to these words are purely metaphysical, they found no model of them in nature?

I stop with these first steps, and I implore my judges to suspend their reading here to consider, concerning the invention of physical substantives alone, that is to say, concerning the easiest part of the language to discover, how far language still had to go in order to express all the thoughts of men, assume a durable form, be capable of being spoken in public, and influence society. I implore them to reflect upon how much time and knowledge were needed to discover numbers,[14] abstract words, aorists, and all the tenses of verbs, particles, syntax, the connecting of sentences, reasoning, and the forming of all the logic of discourse. As for myself, being shocked by the unending difficulties and convinced of the almost demonstrable impossibility that languages could have arisen and been established by merely human means, I leave to anyone who would undertake it the discussion of the following difficult problem: which was the more necessary: an already formed society for the invention of languages, or an already invented language for the establishment of society?

Whatever these origins may be, it is clear, from the little care taken by nature to bring men together through mutual needs and to facilitate their use of speech, how little she prepared them for becoming habituated to the ways of society, and how little she contributed to all that men have done to establish the bonds of society. In fact, it is impossible to imagine why, in that primitive state, one man would have a greater need for another man than a monkey or a wolf has for another of its respective species; or, assuming this need, what motive could induce the other man to satisfy it; or even, in this latter instance, how could they be in mutual agreement regarding the conditions. I know that we are repeatedly told that nothing would have been so miserable as man in that state; and if it is true, as I believe I have proved, that it is only after many centuries that men could have had the desire and the opportunity to leave that state, that would be a charge to bring against nature, not against him whom nature has thus constituted. But if we understand the word *miserable* properly, it is a word which is without meaning or which signifies merely a painful privation and suffering of the body or the soul. Now I would very much like someone to explain to me what kind of misery can there be for a free being whose heart is at peace and whose body is in good health? I ask which of the two, civil or natural life, is more likely to become insufferable to those who live it? We see about us practically no people who do not complain about their existence; many even deprive themselves of it to the extent they are able, and the combination of divine and human laws is hardly enough to stop this disorder. I ask if anyone has ever heard tell of a savage who was living in liberty ever dreaming of complaining about his life and of killing himself. Let the judgment therefore be made with less pride on which side real misery lies. On the other hand, nothing would have been so miserable as savage man, dazzled by enlightenment, tormented by passions, and reasoning about a state different from his own. It was by a very wise providence that the latent faculties he possessed should develop only as the occasion to exercise them presents itself, so that they would be neither superfluous nor troublesome to him beforehand, nor underdeveloped and useless in time of need. In instinct alone, man had everything he needed in order to live in the state of nature; in a cultivated reason, he has only what he needs to live in society.

At first it would seem that men in that state, having among themselves no type of moral relations or acknowledged duties, could be neither good nor evil, and had neither vices nor virtues, unless, if we take these words in a physical sense, we call those qualities that can harm an individual's preservation "vices" in him, and those that can contribute to it "virtues." In that case it would be necessary to call the one who least resists the simple impulses of nature the most virtuous. But without departing from the standard meaning of these words, it is appropriate to suspend the judgment we could make regarding such a situation and to be on our guard against our prejudices, until we have examined with scale in hand whether there are more virtues than vices among civilized men; or whether their virtues are more advantageous than their vices are lethal; or whether the progress of their knowledge is sufficient compensation for ills they inflict on one another as they learn of the good they ought to do; or whether, all things considered, they would not be in a happier set of circumstances if they had neither evil to fear nor good to hope for from anyone, rather than subjecting themselves to a universal dependence and obliging themselves to receive everything from those who do not oblige themselves to give them anything.

Above all, let us not conclude with Hobbes that because man has no idea of goodness he is naturally evil; that he is vicious because he does not know virtue; that he always refuses to perform services for his fellow men he does not believe he owes them; or that, by virtue of the right, which he reasonably attributes to himself, to those things he needs, he foolishly imagines himself to be the sole proprietor of the entire universe. Hobbes has very clearly seen the defect of all modern definitions of natural right, but the consequences he draws from his own definition show that he takes it in a sense that is no less false. Were he to have reasoned on the basis of the principles he establishes, this author should have said that since the state of nature is the state in which the concern for our self-preservation is the least prejudicial to that of others, that state was consequently the most appropriate for peace and the best suited for the human race. He says precisely the opposite, because he had wrongly injected into the savage man's concern for self-preservation the need to satisfy a multitude of passions which are the product of society and which have made laws necessary. The evil man, he says, is a robust child. It remains to be seen whether savage man is a robust child. Were we to grant him this, what would we conclude from it? That if this man were as dependent on others when he is robust as he is when he is weak, there is no type of excess to which he would not tend: he would beat his mother if she were too slow in offering him her breast; he would strangle one of his younger brothers, should he find him annoying; he would bite someone's leg, should he be assaulted or aggravated by him. But being robust and being dependent are two contradictory suppositions in the state of nature. Man is weak when he is dependent, and he is emancipated from that dependence before he is robust. Hobbes did not see that the same cause preventing savages from using their reason, as our jurists claim, is what prevents them at the same time from abusing their faculties, as he himself maintains. Hence we could say that savages are not evil precisely because they do not know what it is to be good; for it is neither the development of enlightenment nor the restraint imposed by the law, but the calm of the passions and the ignorance of vice which prevents them from doing evil. *So much more profitable to these is the ignorance of vice than the knowledge of virtue is to those.* Moreover, there is another principle that Hobbes failed to notice, and which, having been given to man in order to mitigate, in certain circumstances, the ferocity of his egocentrism or the desire for self-preservation before this egocentrism of his came into being,[15] tempers the ardor he has for his own well-being by an innate repugnance to seeing his fellow men suffer. I do not believe I have any contradiction to fear in granting the only natural virtue that the most excessive detractor of human virtues was forced to recognize. I am referring to pity, a disposition that is fitting for beings that are as weak and as subject to ills as we are; a virtue all the more universal and all the more useful to man in that it precedes in him any kind of reflection, and so natural that even animals sometimes show noticeable signs of it. Without speaking of the tenderness of mothers for their young and of the perils they have to brave in order to protect them, one daily observes the repugnance that horses have for trampling a living body with their hooves. An animal does not go undisturbed past a dead animal of its own species. There are even some animals that give them a kind of sepulchre; and the mournful lowing of cattle entering a slaughterhouse voices the impression they receive of the horrible spectacle that strikes them. One notes with pleasure the author of *The Fable of the Bees,* having been forced to acknowledge man as a compassionate and sensitive being, departing from his cold and subtle style in the example he gives, to offer us the pathetic image of an imprisoned man who sees outside his cell a ferocious animal tearing a child from its mother's breast, mashing its frail limbs with its murderous teeth, and ripping with its claws the child's quivering entrails. What horrible agitation must be felt by this witness of an event in which he has no personal interest! What anguish must he suffer at this sight, being unable to be of any help to the fainting mother or to the dying child?

Such is the pure movement of nature prior to all reflection. Such is the force of natural pity, which the most depraved mores still have difficulty destroying, since everyday one sees in our theaters someone affected and weeping at the ills of some unfortunate person, and who, were he in the tyrant's place, would intensify the torments of his enemy still more; [like the bloodthirsty Sulla, so sensitive to ills he had not caused, or like Alexander of Pherae, who did not dare attend the performance of any tragedy, for fear of being seen weeping with Andromache and Priam, and yet who listened impassively to the cries of so many citizens who were killed every day on his orders. *Nature, in giving men tears, bears witness that she gave the human race the softest hearts.*] Mandeville has a clear awareness that, with all their mores, men would never have been anything but monsters, if nature had not given them pity to aid their reason; but he has not seen that from this quality alone flow all the social virtues that he wants to deny in men. In fact, what are generosity, mercy, and humanity, if not pity applied to the weak, to the guilty, or to the human species in general. Benevolence and even friendship are, properly understood, the products of a constant pity fixed on a particular object; for is desiring that someone not suffer anything but desiring that he be happy? Were it true that commiseration were merely a sentiment that puts us in the position of the one who suffers, a sentiment that is obscure and powerful in savage man, developed but weak in man dwelling in civil society, what importance would this idea have to the truth of what I say, except to give it more force? In fact, commiseration will be all the more energetic as the witnessing animal identifies itself more intimately with the suffering animal. Now it is evident that this identification must have been infinitely closer in the state of nature than in the state of reasoning. Reason is what engenders egocentrism, and reflection strengthens it. Reason is what turns man in upon himself. Reason is what separates him from all that troubles him and afflicts him. Philosophy is what isolates him and what moves him to say in secret, at the sight of a suffering man, "Perish if you will; I am safe and sound." No longer can anything but danger to the entire society trouble the tranquil slumber of the philosopher and yank him from his bed. His fellow man can be killed with impunity underneath his window. He has merely to place his hands over his ears and argue with himself a little in order to prevent nature, which rebels within him, from identifying him with the man being assassinated. Savage man does not have this admirable talent, and for lack of wisdom and reason he is always seen thoughtlessly giving in to the first sentiment of humanity. When there is a riot or a street brawl, the populace gathers together; the prudent man withdraws from the scene. It is the rabble, the women of the marketplace, who separate the combatants and prevent decent people from killing one another.

It is therefore quite certain that pity is a natural sentiment, which, by moderating in each individual the activity of the love of oneself, contributes to the mutual preservation of the entire species. Pity is what carries us without reflection to the aid of those we see suffering. Pity is what, in the state of nature, takes the place of laws, mores, and virtue, with the advantage that no one is tempted to disobey its sweet voice. Pity is what will prevent every robust savage from robbing a weak child or an infirm old man of his hard-earned subsistence, if he himself expects to be able to find his own someplace else. Instead of the sublime maxim of reasoned justice, *Do unto others as you would have them do unto you,* pity inspires all men with another maxim of natural goodness, much less perfect but perhaps more useful than the preceding one: *Do what is good for you with as little harm as possible to others.* In a word, it is in this natural sentiment, rather than in subtle arguments that one must search for the cause of the repugnance at doing evil that every man would experience, even independently of the maxims of education. Although it might be appropriate for Socrates and minds of his stature to acquire virtue through reason, the human race would long ago have ceased to exist, if its preservation had depended solely on the reasonings of its members.

With passions so minimally active and such a salutary restraint, being more wild than evil, and more attentive to protecting themselves from the harm they could receive than tempted to do harm to others, men were not subject to very dangerous conflicts. Since they had no sort of intercourse among themselves; since, as a consequence, they knew neither vanity, nor deference, nor esteem, nor contempt; since they had not the slightest notion of mine and thine, nor any true idea of justice; since they regarded the acts of violence that could befall them as an easily redressed evil and not as an offense that must be punished; and since they did not even dream of vengeance except perhaps as a knee-jerk response right then and there, like the dog that bites the stone that is thrown at him, their disputes would rarely have had bloody consequences, if their subject had been no more sensitive than food. But I see a more dangerous matter that remains for me to discuss.

Among the passions that agitate the heart of man, there is an ardent, impetuous one that renders one sex necessary to the other; a terrible passion which braves all dangers, overcomes all obstacles, and which, in its fury, seems fitted to destroy the human race it is destined to preserve.

What would become of men, victimized by this unrestrained and brutal rage, without modesty and self-control, fighting everyday over the object of their passion at the price of their blood?

There must first be agreement that the more violent the passions are, the more necessary the laws are to contain them. But over and above the fact that the disorders and the crimes these passions cause daily in our midst show quite well the insufficiency of the laws in this regard, it would still be good to examine whether these disorders did not come into being with the laws themselves; for then, even if they were capable of repressing them, the least one should expect of them would be that they call a halt to an evil that would not exist without them.

Let us begin by distinguishing between the moral and the physical aspects of the sentiment of love. The physical aspect is that general desire which inclines one sex to unite with another. The moral aspect is what determines this desire and fixes it exclusively on one single object, or which at least gives it a greater degree of energy for this preferred object. Now it is easy to see that the moral aspect of love is an artificial sentiment born of social custom, and extolled by women with so much skill and care in order to establish their hegemony and make dominant the sex that ought to obey. Since this feeling is founded on certain notions of merit or beauty that a savage is not in a position to have, and on comparisons he is incapable of making, it must be almost non-existent for him. For since his mind could not form abstract ideas of regularity and proportion, his heart is not susceptible to sentiments of admiration and love, which, even without its being observed come into being from the application of these ideas. He pays exclusive attention to the temperament he has received from nature, and not the taste [aversion] he has been unable to acquire; any woman suits his purpose.

Limited merely to the physical aspect of love, and fortunate enough to be ignorant of those preferences which stir up the feeling and increase the difficulties in satisfying it, men must feel the ardors of their temperament less frequently and less vividly, and consequently have fewer and less cruel conflicts among themselves. Imagination, which wreaks so much havoc among us, does not speak to savage hearts; each man peacefully awaits the impetus of nature, gives himself over to it without choice, and with more pleasure than frenzy; and once the need is satisfied, all desire is snuffed out.

Hence it is incontestable that love itself, like all other passions, had acquired only in society that impetuous ardor which so often makes it lethal to men. And it is all the more ridiculous to represent savages as continually slaughtering each other in order to satisfy their brutality, since this opinion is directly contrary to experience; and since the Caribs, of all existing peoples, are the people that until now has wandered least from the state of nature, they are the people least subject to jealousy, even though they live in a hot climate which always seems to occasion greater activity in these passions.

As to any inferences that could be drawn, in the case of several species of animals, from the clashes between males that bloody our poultry yards throughout the year, and which make our forests resound in the spring with their cries as they quarrel over a female, it is necessary to begin by excluding all species in which nature has manifestly established, in the relative power of the sexes, relations other than those that exist among us. Hence cockfights do not form the basis for an inference regarding the human species. In species where the proportion is more closely observed, these fights can have for their cause only the scarcity of females in relation to the number of males, or the exclusive intervals during which the female continually rejects the advances of the male, which adds up to the cause just cited. For if each female receives the male for only two months a year, in this respect it is as if the number of females were reduced by five-sixths. Now neither of these two cases is applicable to the human species where the number of females generally surpasses the number of males, and where human females, unlike those of other species, have never been observed to have periods of heat and exclusion, even among savages. Moreover, among several of these animal species, where the entire species goes into heat simultaneously, there comes a terrible moment of common ardor, tumult, disorder and combat: a moment that does not happen in the human species where love is never periodic. Therefore one cannot conclude from the combats of certain animals for the possession of females that the same thing would happen to man in the state of nature. And even if one could draw that conclusion, given that these conflicts do not destroy the other species, one should conclude that they would not be any more lethal for ours. And it is quite apparent that they would wreak less havoc in the state of nature than in society, especially in countries where mores still count for something and where the jealousy of lovers and the vengeance of husbands every day give rise to duels, murders and still worse things; where the duty of eternal fidelity serves merely to create adulterers; and where even the laws of continence and honor necessarily spread debauchery and multiply the number of abortions.

Let us conclude that, wandering in the forests, without industry, without speech, without dwelling, without war, without relationships, with no need for his fellow men, and correspondingly with no desire to do them harm, perhaps never even recognizing any of them individually, savage man, subject to few passions and self-sufficient, had only the sentiments and enlightenment appropriate to that state; he felt only his true needs, took notice of only what he believed he had an interest in seeing; and that his intelligence made no more progress than his vanity. If by chance he made some discovery, he was all the less able to communicate it to others because he did not even know his own children. Art perished with its inventor. There was neither education nor progress; generations were multiplied to no purpose. Since each one always began from the same point, centuries went by with all the crudeness of the first ages; the species was already old, and man remained ever a child.

If I have gone on at such length about the supposition of that primitive condition, it is because, having ancient errors and inveterate prejudices to destroy, I felt I should dig down to the root and show, in the depiction of the true state of nature how far even natural inequality is from having as much reality and influence in that state as our writers claim.

In fact, it is easy to see that, among the differences that distinguish men, several of them pass for natural ones which are exclusively the work of habit and of the various sorts of life that men adopt in society. Thus a robust or delicate temperament, and the strength or weakness that depend on it, frequently derive more from the harsh or effeminate way in which one has been raised than from the primitive constitution of bodies. The same holds for mental powers; and not only does education make a difference between cultivated minds and those that are not, it also augments the difference among the former in proportion to their culture; for were a giant and a dwarf walking on the same road, each step they both take would give a fresh advantage to the giant. Now if one compares the prodigious diversity of educations and lifestyles in the different orders of the civil state with the simplicity and uniformity of animal and savage life, where all nourish themselves from the same foods live in the same manner, and do exactly the same things, it will be understood how much less the difference between one man and another must be in the state of nature than in that of society, and how much natural inequality must increase in the human species through inequality occasioned by social institutions.

But even if nature were to affect, in the distribution of her gifts, as many preferences as is claimed, what advantage would the most favored men derive from them, to the detriment of others, in a state of things that allowed practically no sort of relationships among them? Where there is no love, what use is beauty? What use is wit for people who do not speak, and ruse to those who have no dealing with others? I always hear it repeated that the stronger will oppress the weaker. But let me have an explanation of the meaning of the word "oppression." Some will dominate with violence; others will groan, enslaved to all their caprices. That is precisely what I observe among us; but I do not see how this could be said of savage men, to whom it would be difficult even to explain what servitude and domination are. A man could well lay hold of the fruit another has gathered, the game he has killed, the cave that served as his shelter. But how will he ever succeed in making himself be obeyed? And what can be the chains of dependence among men who possess nothing? If someone chases me from one tree, I am free to go to another; if someone torments me in one place, who will prevent me from going elsewhere? Is there a man with strength sufficiently superior to mine and who is, moreover, sufficiently depraved, sufficiently lazy and sufficiently ferocious to force me to provide for his subsistence while he remains idle? He must resolve not to take his eyes off me for a single instant, to keep me carefully tied down while he sleeps, for fear that I may escape or that I would kill him. In other words, he is obliged to expose himself voluntarily to a much greater hardship than the one he wants to avoid and gives me. After all that, were his vigilance to relax for an instant, were an unforeseen noise to make him turn his head, I take twenty steps into the forest; my chains are broken, and he never sees me again for the rest of his life.

Without needlessly prolonging these details, anyone should see that, since the bonds of servitude are formed merely from the mutual dependence of men and the reciprocal needs that unite them, it is impossible to enslave a man without having first put him in the position of being incapable of doing without another. This being a situation that did not exist in the state of nature, it leaves each person free of the yoke, and renders pointless the law of the strongest.

After having proved that inequality is hardly observable in the state of nature, and that its influence there is almost nonexistent, it remains for me to show its origin and progress in the successive developments of the human mind. After having shown that *perfectibility,* social virtues, and the other faculties that natural man had received in a state of potentiality could never develop by themselves, that to achieve this development they required the chance coming together of several unconnected causes that might never have come into being and without which he would have remained eternally in his primitive constitution, it remains for me to consider and to bring together the various chance happenings that were able to perfect human reason while deteriorating the species, make a being evil while rendering it habituated to the ways of society, and, from so distant a beginning, finally bring man and the world to the point where we see them now.

I admit that, since the events I have to describe could have taken place in several ways, I cannot make a determination among them except on the basis of conjecture. But over and above the fact that these conjectures become reasons when they are the most probable ones that a person can draw from the nature of things and the sole means that a person can have of discovering the truth, the consequences I wish to deduce from mine will not thereby be conjectural, since, on the basis of the principles I have just established, no other system is conceivable that would not furnish me with the same results, and from which I could not draw the same conclusions.

This will excuse me from expanding my reflections on the way in which the lapse of time compensates for the slight probability of events; concerning the surprising power that quite negligible causes may have when they act without interruption; concerning the impossibility, on the one hand, of a person's destroying certain hypotheses, even though, on the other hand, one is not in a position to accord them the level of factual certitude; concerning a situation in which two facts given as real are to be connected by a series of intermediate facts that are unknown or regarded as such, it belongs to history, when it exists, to provide the facts that connect them; it belongs to philosophy, when history is unavailable, to determine similar facts that can connect them; finally, concerning how, with respect to events, similarity reduces the facts to a much smaller number of different classes than one might imagine. It is enough for me to offer these objects to the consideration of my judges; it is enough for me to have seen to it that ordinary readers would have no need to consider them.

PART TWO

The first person who, having enclosed a plot of land, took it into his head to say *this is mine* and found people simple enough to believe him, was the true founder of civil society. What crimes, wars, murders, what miseries and horrors would the human race have been spared, had someone pulled up the stakes or filled in the ditch and cried out to his fellow men: "Do not listen to this impostor. You are lost if you forget that the fruits of the earth belong to all and the earth to no one!" But it is quite likely that by then things had already reached the point where they could no longer continue as they were. For this idea of property, depending on many prior ideas which could only have arisen successively, was not formed all at once in the human mind. It was necessary to make great progress, to acquire much industry and enlightenment, and to transmit and augment them from one age to another, before arriving at this final stage in the state of nature. Let us therefore take things farther back and try to piece together under a single viewpoint that slow succession of events and advances in knowledge in their most natural order.

Man's first sentiment was that of his own existence; his first concern was that of his preservation. The products of the earth provided him with all the help he needed; instinct led him to make use of them. With hunger and other appetites making him experience by turns various ways of existing, there was one appetite that invited him to perpetuate his species; and this blind inclination, devoid of any sentiment of the heart, produced a purely animal act. Once this need had been satisfied, the two sexes no longer took cognizance of one another, and even the child no longer meant anything to the mother once it could do without her.

Such was the condition of man in his nascent stage; such was the life of an animal limited at first to pure sensations, and scarcely profiting from the gifts nature offered him, far from dreaming of extracting anything from her. But difficulties soon presented themselves to him; it was necessary to learn to overcome them. The height of trees, which kept him from reaching their fruits, the competition of animals that sought to feed themselves on these same fruits, the ferocity of those animals that wanted to take his own life: everything obliged him to apply himself to bodily exercises. It was necessary to become agile, fleet-footed and vigorous in combat. Natural arms, which are tree branches and stones, were soon found ready at hand. He learned to surmount nature's obstacles, combat other animals when necessary, fight for his subsistence even with men, or compensate for what he had to yield to those stronger than himself.

In proportion as the human race spread, difficulties multiplied with the men. Differences in soils, climates and seasons could force them to inculcate these differences in their lifestyles. Barren years, long and hard winters, hot summers that consume everything required new resourcefulness from them. Along the seashore and the riverbanks they invented the fishing line and hook, and became fishermen and fish-eaters. In the forests they made bows and arrows, and became hunters and warriors. In cold countries they covered themselves with the skins of animals they had killed. Lightning, a volcano, or some fortuitous chance happening acquainted them with fire: a new resource against the rigors of winter. They learned to preserve this element, then to reproduce it, and finally to use it to prepare meats that previously they devoured raw.

This repeated appropriation of various beings to himself, and of some beings to others, must naturally have engendered in man's mind the perceptions of certain relations. These relationships which we express by the words "large," "small," "strong," "weak," "fast," "slow," "timorous," "bold," and other similar ideas, compared when needed and almost without thinking about it, finally produced in him a kind of reflection, or rather a mechanical prudence which pointed out to him the precautions that were most necessary for his safety.

The new enlightenment which resulted from this development increased his superiority over the other animals by making him aware of it. He trained himself to set traps for them; he tricked them in a thousand different ways. And although several surpassed him in fighting strength or in swiftness in running, of those that could serve him or hurt him, he became in time the master of the former and the scourge of the latter. Thus the first glance he directed upon himself produced within him the first stirring of pride; thus, as yet hardly knowing how to distinguish the ranks, and contemplating himself in the first rank by virtue of his species, he prepared himself from afar to lay claim to it in virtue of his individuality.

Although his fellowmen were not for him what they are for us, and although he had hardly anything more to do with them than with other animals, they were not forgotten in his observations. The conformities that time could make him perceive among them, his female, and himself, made him judge those he did not perceive. And seeing that they all acted as he would have done under similar circumstances, he concluded that their way of thinking and feeling was in complete conformity with his own. And this important truth, well established in his mind, made him follow, by a presentiment as sure as dialectic and more prompt, the best rules of conduct that it was appropriate to observe toward them for his advantage and safety.

Taught by experience that love of well-being is the sole motive of human actions, he found himself in a position to distinguish the rare occasions when common interest should make him count on the assistance of his fellowmen, and those even rarer occasions when competition ought to make him distrust them. In the first case, he united with them in a herd, or at most in some sort of free association, that obligated no one and that lasted only as long as the passing need that had formed it. In the second case, everyone sought to obtain his own advantage, either by overt force, if he believed he could, or by cleverness and cunning, if he felt himself to be the weaker.

This is how men could imperceptibly acquire some crude idea of mutual commitments and of the advantages to be had in fulfilling them, but only insofar as present and perceptible interests could require it, since foresight meant nothing to them, and far from concerning themselves about a distant future, they did not even give a thought to the next day. Were it a matter of catching a deer, everyone was quite aware that he must faithfully keep to his post in order to achieve this purpose; but if a hare happened to pass within reach of one of them, no doubt he would have pursued it without giving it a second thought, and that, having obtained his prey, he cared very little about causing his companions to miss theirs.

It is easy to understand that such intercourse did not require a language much more refined than that of crows or monkeys, which flock together in practically the same way. Inarticulate cries, many gestures, and some imitative noises must for a long time have made up the universal language. By joining to this in each country a few articulate and conventional sounds, whose institution, as I have already said, is not too easy to explain, there were individual languages, but crude and imperfect ones, quite similar to those still spoken by various savage nations today. Constrained by the passing of time, the abundance of things I have to say, and the practically imperceptible progress of the beginnings, I am flying like an arrow over the multitudes of centuries. For the slower events were in succeeding one another, the quicker they can be described.

These first advances enabled man to make more rapid ones. The more the mind was enlightened, the more industry was perfected. Soon they ceased to fall asleep under the first tree or to retreat into caves, and found various types of hatchets made of hard, sharp stones, which served to cut wood, dig up the soil, and make huts from branches they later found it useful to cover with clay and mud. This was the period of a first revolution which formed the establishment of the distinction among families and which introduced a kind of property, whence perhaps there already arose many quarrels and fights. However, since the strongest were probably the first to make themselves lodgings they felt capable of defending, presumably the weak found it quicker and safer to imitate them than to try to dislodge them; and as for those who already had huts, each of them must have rarely sought to appropriate that of his neighbor, less because it did not belong to him than because it was of no use to him, and because he could not seize it without exposing himself to a fierce battle with the family that occupied it.

The first developments of the heart were the effect of a new situation that united the husbands and wives, fathers and children in one common habitation. The habit of living together gave rise to the sweetest sentiments known to men: conjugal love and paternal love. Each family became a little society all the better united because mutual attachment and liberty were its only bonds; and it was then that the first difference was established in the lifestyle of the two sexes, which until then had had only one. Women became more sedentary and grew accustomed to watch over the hut and the children, while the man went to seek their common subsistence. With their slightly softer life the two sexes also began to lose something of their ferocity and vigor. But while each one separately became less suited to combat savage beasts, on the other hand it was easier to assemble in order jointly to resist them.

In this new state, with a simple and solitary life, very limited needs, and the tools they had invented to provide for them, since men enjoyed a great deal of leisure time, they used it to procure for themselves many types of conveniences unknown to their fathers; and that was the first yoke they imposed on themselves without realizing it, and the first source of evils they prepared for their descendants. For in addition to their continuing thus to soften body and mind (those conveniences having through habit lost almost all their pleasure, and being at the same time degenerated into true needs), being deprived of them became much more cruel than possessing them was sweet; and they were unhappy about losing them without being happy about possessing them.

At this point we can see a little better how the use of speech was established or imperceptibly perfected itself in the bosom of each family; and one can further conjecture how various particular causes could have extended the language and accelerated its progress by making it more necessary. Great floods or earthquakes surrounded the inhabited areas with water or precipices. Upheavals of the globe detached parts of the mainland and broke them up into islands. Clearly among men thus brought together and forced to live together, a common idiom must have been formed sooner than among those who wandered freely about the forests of the mainland. Thus it is quite possible that after their first attempts at navigation, the islanders brought the use of speech to us; and it is at least quite probable that society and languages came into being on islands and were perfected there before they were known on the mainland.

Everything begins to take on a new appearance. Having previously wandered about the forests and having assumed a more fixed situation, men slowly came together and united into different bands, eventually forming in each country a particular nation, united by mores and characteristic features, not by regulations and laws, but by the same kind of life and foods and by the common influence of the climate. Eventually a permanent proximity cannot fail to engender some intercourse among different families. Young people of different sexes live in neighboring huts; the passing intercourse demanded by nature soon leads to another, through frequent contact with one another, no less sweet and more permanent. People become accustomed to consider different objects and to make comparisons. Imperceptibly they acquire the ideas of merit and beauty which produce feelings of preference. By dint of seeing one another, they can no longer get along without seeing one another again. A sweet and tender feeling insinuates itself into the soul and at the least opposition becomes an impetuous fury. Jealousy awakens with love; discord triumphs, and the sweetest passion receives sacrifices of human blood.

In proportion as ideas and sentiments succeed one another and as the mind and heart are trained, the human race continues to be tamed, relationships spread and bonds are tightened. People grew accustomed to gather in front of their huts or around a large tree; song and dance, true children of love and leisure, became the amusement or rather the occupation of idle men and women who had flocked together. Each one began to look at the others and to want to be looked at himself, and public esteem had a value. The one who sang or danced the best, the handsomest, the strongest, the most adroit or the most eloquent became the most highly regarded. And this was the first step toward inequality and, at the same time, toward vice. From these first preferences were born vanity and contempt on the one hand, and shame and envy on the other. And the fermentation caused by these new leavens eventually produced compounds fatal to happiness and innocence.

As soon as men had begun mutually to value one another, and the idea of esteem was formed in their minds, each one claimed to have a right to it, and it was no longer possible for anyone to be lacking it with impunity. From this came the first duties of civility, even among savages; and from this every voluntary wrong became an outrage, because along with the harm that resulted from the injury, the offended party saw in it contempt for his person, which often was more insufferable than the harm itself. Hence each man punished the contempt shown him in a manner proportionate to the esteem in which he held himself; acts of revenge became terrible, and men became bloodthirsty and cruel. This is precisely the stage reached by most of the savage people known to us; and it is for want of having made adequate distinctions among their ideas or of having noticed how far these peoples already were from the original state of nature that many have hastened to conclude that man is naturally cruel, and that he needs civilization in order to soften him. On the contrary, nothing is so gentle as man in his primitive state, when, placed by nature at an equal distance from the stupidity of brutes and the fatal enlightenment of civil man, and limited equally by instinct and reason to protecting himself from the harm that threatens him, he is restrained by natural pity from needlessly harming anyone himself, even if he has been harmed. For according to the axiom of the wise Locke, *where there is no property, there is no injury.*

But it must be noted that society in its beginning stages and the relations already established among men required in them qualities different from those they derived from their primitive constitution; that, with morality beginning to be introduced into human actions, and everyone, prior to the existence of laws, being sole judge and avenger of the offenses he had received, the goodness appropriate to the pure state of nature was no longer what was appropriate to an emerging society; that it was necessary for punishments to become more severe in proportion as the occasions for giving offense became more frequent; and that it was for the fear of vengeance to take the place of the deterrent character of laws. Hence although men had become less forebearing, and although natural pity had already undergone some alteration, this period of the development of human faculties, maintaining a middle position between the indolence of our primitive state and the petulant activity of our egocentrism, must have been the happiest and most durable epoch. The more one reflects on it, the more one finds that this state was the least subject to upheavals and the best for man,[16] and that he must have left it only by virtue of some fatal chance happening that, for the common good, ought never have happened. The example of savages, almost all of whom have been found in this state, seems to confirm that the human race had been made to remain in it always; that this state is the veritable youth of the world; and that all the subsequent progress has been in appearance so many steps toward the perfection of the individual, and in fact toward the decay of the species.

As long as men were content with the rustic huts, as long as they were limited to making their clothing out of skins sewn together with thorns or fish bones, adorning themselves with feathers and shells, painting their bodies with various colors, perfecting or embellishing their bows and arrows, using sharp-edged stones to make some fishing canoes or some crude musical instruments; in a word, as long as they applied themselves exclusively to tasks that a single individual could do and to the arts that did not require the cooperation of several hands, they lived as free, healthy, good and happy as they could in accordance with their nature; and they continued to enjoy among themselves the sweet rewards of independent intercourse. But as soon as one man needed the help of another, as soon as one man realized that it was useful for a single individual to have provisions for two, equality disappeared, property came into existence, labor became necessary. Vast forests were transformed into smiling fields which had to be watered with men's sweat, and in which slavery and misery were soon seen to germinate and grow with the crops.

Metallurgy and agriculture were the two arts whose invention produced this great revolution. For the poet, it is gold and silver; but for the philosopher, it is iron and wheat that have civilized men and ruined the human race. Thus they were both unknown to the savages of America, who for that reason have always remained savages. Other peoples even appear to have remained barbarous, as long as they practiced one of those arts without the other. And perhaps one of the best reasons why Europe has been, if not sooner, at least more constantly and better governed than the other parts of the world, is that it is at the same time the most abundant in iron and the most fertile in wheat.

It is very difficult to guess how men came to know and use iron, for it is incredible that by themselves they thought of drawing the ore from the mine and performing the necessary preparations on it for smelting it before they knew what would result. From another point of view, it is even less plausible to attribute this discovery to some accidental fire, because mines are set up exclusively in arid places devoid of trees and plants, so that one would say that nature had taken precautions to conceal this deadly secret from us. Thus there remains only the extraordinary circumstance of some volcano that, in casting forth molten metal, would have given observers the idea of imitating this operation of nature. Even still we must suppose them to have had a great deal of courage and foresight to undertake such a difficult task and to have envisaged so far in advance the advantages they could derive from it. This is hardly suitable for minds already better trained than theirs must have been.

As for agriculture, its principle was known long before its practice was established, and it is hardly possible that men, constantly preoccupied with deriving their subsistence from trees and plants, did not rather quickly get the idea of the methods used by nature to grow plant life. But their industry probably did not turn in that direction until very late either because trees, which, along with hunting and fishing, provided their nourishment, had no need of their care; or for want of knowing how to use wheat; or for want of tools with which to cultivate it; or for want of foresight regarding future needs; or, finally, for want of the means of preventing others from appropriating the fruits of their labors. Having become more industrious, it is believable that, with sharp stones and pointed sticks, they began by cultivating some vegetables or roots around their huts long before they knew how to prepare wheat and had the tools necessary for large-scale cultivation. Moreover, to devote oneself to that occupation and to sow the lands, one must be resolved to lose something at first in order to gain a great deal later: a precaution quite far removed from the mind of the savage man, who, as I have said, finds it quite difficult to give thought in the morning to what he will need at night.

The invention of the other arts was therefore necessary to force the human race to apply itself to that of agriculture. Once men were needed in order to smelt and forge the iron, other men were needed in order to feed them. The more the number of workers increased, the fewer hands there were to obtain food for the common subsistence, without there being fewer mouths to consume it; and since some needed foodstuffs in exchange for their iron, the others finally found the secret of using iron to multiply foodstuffs. From this there arose farming and agriculture, on the one hand, and the art of working metals and multiplying their uses, on the other.

From the cultivation of land, there necessarily followed the division of land; and from property once recognized, the first rules of justice. For in order to render everyone what is his, it is necessary that everyone can have something. Moreover, as men began to look toward the future and as they saw that they all had goods to lose, there was not one of them who did not have to fear reprisals against himself for wrongs he might do to another. This origin is all the more natural as it is impossible to conceive of the idea of property arising from anything but manual labor, for it is not clear what man can add, beyond his own labor, in order to appropriate things he has not made. It is labor alone that, in giving the cultivator a right to the product of the soil he has tilled, consequently gives him a right, at least until the harvest, and thus from year to year. With this possession continuing uninterrupted, it is easily transformed into property. When the ancients, says Grotius, gave Ceres the epithet of legislatrix, gave the name Thesmophories to a festival celebrated in her honor, they thereby made it apparent that the division of lands has produced a new kind of right: namely, the right of property, different from that which results from the natural law.

Things in this state could have remained equal, if talents had been equal, and if the use of iron and the consumption of foodstuffs had always been in precise balance. But this proportion, which was not maintained by anything, was soon broken. The strongest did the most work; the most adroit turned theirs to better advantage: the most ingenious found ways to shorten their labor. The farmer had a greater need for iron, or the blacksmith had a greater need for wheat; and in laboring equally, the one earned a great deal while the other barely had enough to live. Thus it is that natural inequality imperceptibly manifests itself together with inequality occasioned by the socialization process. Thus it is that the differences among men, developed by those of circumstances, make themselves more noticeable, more permanent in their effects, and begin to influence the fate of private individuals in the same proportion.

With things having reached this point, it is easy to imagine the rest. I will not stop to describe the successive invention of the arts, the progress of languages, the testing and use of talents, the inequality of fortunes, the use or abuse of wealth, nor all the details that follow these and that everyone can easily supply. I will limit myself exclusively to taking a look at the human race placed in this new order of things.

Thus we find here all our faculties developed, memory and imagination in play, egocentrism looking out for its interests, reason rendered active, and the mind having nearly reached the limit of the perfection of which it is capable. We find here all the natural qualities put into action, the rank and fate of each man established not only on the basis of the quantity of goods and the power to serve or harm, but also on the basis of mind, beauty, strength or skill, on the basis of merit or talents. And since these qualities were the only ones that could attract consideration, he was soon forced to have them or affect them. It was necessary, for his advantage, to show himself to be something other than what he in fact was. Being something and appearing to be something became two completely different things; and from this distinction there arose grand ostentation, deceptive cunning, and all the vices that follow in their wake. On the other hand, although man had previously been free and independent, we find him, so to speak, subject, by virtue of a multitude of fresh needs, to all of nature and particularly to his fellowmen, whose slave in a sense he becomes even in becoming their master; rich, he needs their services; poor, he needs their help; and being midway between wealth and poverty does not put him in a position to get along without them. It is therefore necessary for him to seek incessantly to interest them in his fate and to make them find their own profit, in fact or in appearance, in working for his. This makes him two-faced and crooked with some, imperious and harsh with others, and puts him in the position of having to abuse everyone he needs when he cannot make them fear them and does not find it in his interests to be of useful service to them. Finally, consuming ambition, the zeal for raising the relative level of his fortune, less out of real need than in order to put himself above others, inspires in all men a wicked tendency to harm one another, a secret jealousy all the more dangerous because, in order to strike its blow in greater safety, it often wears the mask of benevolence; in short, competition and rivalry on the one hand, opposition of interest[s] on the other, and always the hidden desire to profit at the expense of someone else. All these ills are the first effect of property and the inseparable offshoot of incipient inequality.

Before representative signs of wealth had been invented, it could hardly have consisted of anything but lands and livestock, the only real goods men can possess. Now when inheritances had grown in number and size to the point of covering the entire landscape and of all bordering on one another, some could no longer be enlarged except at the expense of others; and the supernumeraries, whom weakness or indolence had prevented from acquiring an inheritance in their turn, became poor without having lost anything, because while everything changed around them, they alone had not changed at all. Thus they were forced to receive or steal their subsistence from the hands of the rich. And from that there began to arise, according to the diverse characters of the rich and the poor, domination and servitude, or violence and thefts. For their part, the wealthy had no sooner known the pleasure of domination, than before long they disdained all others, and using their old slaves to subdue new ones, they thought of nothing but the subjugation and enslavement of their neighbors, like those ravenous wolves which, on having once tasted human flesh, reject all other food and desire to devour only men.

Thus, when both the most powerful or the most miserable made of their strength or their needs a sort of right to another's goods, equivalent, according to them, to the right of property, the destruction of equality was followed by the most frightful disorder. Thus the usurpations of the rich, the acts of brigandage by the poor, the unbridled passions of all, stifling natural pity and the still weak voice of justice, made men greedy, ambitious and wicked. There arose between the right of the strongest and the right of the first occupant a perpetual conflict that ended only in fights and murders.[17] Emerging society gave way to the most horrible state of war; since the human race, vilified and desolated, was no longer able to retrace its steps or give up the unfortunate acquisitions it had made, and since it labored only toward its shame by abusing the faculties that honor it, it brought itself to the brink of its ruin. *Horrified by the newness of the ill, both the poor man and the rich man hope to flee from wealth, hating what they once had prayed for.*

It is not possible that men should not have eventually reflected upon so miserable a situation and upon the calamities that overwhelm them. The rich in particular must have soon felt how disadvantageous to them it was to have a perpetual war in which they alone paid all the costs, and in which the risk of losing one's life was common to all and the risk of losing one's goods was personal. Moreover, regardless of the light in which they tried to place their usurpations, they knew full well that they were established on nothing but a precarious and abusive right, and that having been acquired merely by force, force might take them away from them without their having any reason to complain. Even those enriched exclusively by industry could hardly base their property on better claims. They could very well say: "I am the one who built that wall; I have earned this land with my labor." In response to them it could be said: "Who gave you the boundary lines? By what right do you claim to exact payment at our expense for labor we did not impose upon you? Are you unaware that a multitude of your brothers perish or suffer from need of what you have in excess, and that you needed explicit and unanimous consent from the human race for you to help yourself to anything from the common subsistence that went beyond your own?" Bereft of valid reasons to justify himself and sufficient forces to defend himself; easily crushing a private individual, but himself crushed by troops of bandits; alone against all and unable on account of mutual jealousies to unite with his equals against enemies united by the common hope of plunder, the rich, pressed by necessity, finally conceived the most thought-out project that ever entered the human mind. It was to use in his favor the very strength of those who attacked him, to turn his adversaries into his defenders, to instill in them other maxims, and to give them other institutions which were as favorable to him as natural right was unfavorable to him.

With this end in mind, after having shown his neighbors the horror of a situation which armed them all against each other and made their possessions as burdensome as their needs, and in which no one could find safety in either poverty or wealth, he easily invented specious reasons to lead them to his goal. "Let us unite," he says to them, "in order to protect the weak from oppression, restrain the ambitious, and assure everyone of possessing what belongs to him. Let us institute rules of justice and peace to which all will be obliged to conform, which will make special exceptions for no one, and which will in some way compensate for the caprices of fortune by subjecting the strong and the weak to mutual obligations. In short, instead of turning our forces against ourselves, let us gather them into one supreme power that governs us according to wise laws, that protects and defends all the members of the association, repulses common enemies, and maintains us in an eternal concord."

Considerably less than the equivalent of this discourse was needed to convince crude, easily seduced men who also had too many disputes to settle among themselves to be able to get along without arbiters, and too much greed and ambition to be able to get along without masters for long. They all ran to chain themselves, in the belief that they secured their liberty, for although they had enough sense to realize the advantages of a political establishment, they did not have enough experience to foresee its dangers. Those most capable of anticipating the abuses were precisely those who counted on profiting from them; and even the wise saw the need to be resolved to sacrifice one part of their liberty to preserve the other, just as a wounded man has his arm amputated to save the rest of his body.

Such was, or should have been, the origin of society and laws, which gave new fetters to the weak and new forces to the rich,[18] irretrievably destroyed natural liberty, established forever the law of property and of inequality, changed adroit usurpation into an irrevocable right, and for the profit of a few ambitious men henceforth subjected the entire human race to labor, servitude and misery. It is readily apparent how the establishment of a single society rendered indispensable that of all the others, and how, to stand head to head against the united forces, it was necessary to unite in turn. Societies, multiplying or spreading rapidly, soon covered the entire surface of the earth; and it was no longer possible to find a single corner in the universe where someone could free himself from the yoke and withdraw his head from the often ill-guided sword which everyone saw perpetually hanging over his own head. With civil right thus having become the common rule of citizens, the law of nature no longer was operative except between the various societies, when, under the name of the law of nations, it was tempered by some tacit conventions in order to make intercourse possible and to serve as a substitute for natural compassion which, losing between one society and another nearly all the force it had between one man and another, no longer resides anywhere but in a few great cosmopolitan souls, who overcome the imaginary barriers that separate peoples, and who, following the example of the sovereign being who has created them, embrace the entire human race in their benevolence.

Remaining thus among themselves in the state of nature, the bodies politic soon experienced the inconveniences that had forced private individuals to leave it; and that state became even more deadly among these great bodies than that state had among the private individuals of whom they were composed. Whence came the national wars, battles, murders, and reprisals that make nature tremble and offend reason, and all those horrible prejudices that rank the honor of shedding human blood among the virtues. The most decent people learned to consider it one of their duties to kill their fellow men. Finally, men were seen massacring one another by the thousands without knowing why. More murders were committed in a single day of combat and more horrors in the capture of a single city than were committed in the state of nature during entire centuries over the entire face of the earth. Such are the first effects one glimpses of the division of mankind into different societies. Let us return to the founding of these societies.

I know that many have ascribed other origins to political societies, such as conquests by the most powerful, or the union of the weak; and the choice among these causes is indifferent to what I want to establish. Nevertheless, the one I have just described seems to me the most natural, for the following reasons. 1. In the first case, the right of conquest, since it is not a right, could not have founded any other, because the conqueror and conquered peoples always remain in a state of war with one another, unless the nation, returned to full liberty, were to choose voluntarily its conqueror as its leader. Until then, whatever the capitulations that may have been made, since they have been founded on violence alone and are consequently null by this very fact, on this hypothesis there can be neither true society nor body politic, nor any other law than that of the strongest. 2. These words *strong* and *weak* are equivocal in the second case, because in the interval between the establishment of the right of property or of the first occupant and that of political governments, the meaning of these terms is better rendered by the words *poor* and *rich,* because, before the laws, man did not in fact have any other means of placing his equals in subjection except by attacking their goods or by giving them part of his. 3. Since the poor had nothing to lose but their liberty, it would have been utter folly for them to have voluntarily surrendered the only good remaining to them, gaining nothing in return. On the contrary, since the rich men were, so to speak, sensitive in all parts of their goods, it was much easier to do them harm, and consequently they had to take greater precautions to protect themselves. And finally it is reasonable to believe that a thing was invented by those to whom it is useful rather than by those to whom it is harmful.

Incipient government did not have a constant and regular form. The lack of philosophy and experience permitted only present inconveniences to be perceived, and there was thought of remedying the others only as they presented themselves. Despite all the labors of the wisest legislators, the political state always remained imperfect, because it was practically the work of chance and, because it had been badly begun, time, in discovering faults and suggesting remedies, could never repair the vices of the constitution. People were continually patching it up, whereas they should have begun by clearing the air and putting aside all the old materials, as Lycurgus did in Sparta, in order to raise a good edifice later on. At first, society consisted merely of some general conventions that all private individuals promised to observe, and concerning which the community became the guarantor for each of them. Experience had to demonstrate how weak such a constitution was, and how easy it was for lawbreakers to escape conviction or punishment for faults of which the public alone was to be witness and judge. The law had to be evaded in a thousand ways; inconveniences and disorders had to multiply continually in order to make them finally give some thought to confiding to private individuals the dangerous trust of public authority, and to make them entrust to magistrates the care of enforcing the observance of the deliberations of the people. For to say that the leaders were chosen before the confederation was brought about and that the ministers of the laws existed before the laws themselves is a supposition that does not allow of serious debate.

It would be no more reasonable to believe that initially the peoples threw themselves unconditionally and for all time into the arms of an absolute master, and that the first means of providing for the common security dreamed up by proud and unruly men was to rush headlong into slavery. In fact, why did they give themselves over to superiors, if not to defend themselves against oppression and to protect their goods, their liberties and their lives, which are, as it were, the constitutive elements of their being? Now, since, in relations between men, the worst that can happen to someone is for him to see himself at the discretion of someone else, would it not have been contrary to good sense to begin by surrendering into the hands of a leader the only things for whose preservation they needed his help? What equivalent could he have offered them for the concession of so fine a right? And if he had dared to demand it on the pretext of defending them, would he not have immediately received the reply given in the fable: "what more will the enemy do to us?" It is therefore incontestable, and it is a fundamental maxim of all political right, that peoples have given themselves leaders in order to defend their liberty and not to enslave themselves. *If we have a prince,* Pliny said to Trajan, *it is so that he may preserve us from having a master.*

[Our] political theorists produce the same sophisms about the love of liberty that [our] philosophers have made about the state of nature. By the things they see they render judgments about very different things they have not seen; and they attribute to men a natural inclination to servitude owing to the patience with which those who are before their eyes endure their servitude, without giving a thought to the fact that it is the same for liberty as it is for innocence and virtue: their value is felt only as long as one has them oneself, and the taste for them is lost as soon as one has lost them. "I know the delights of your country," said Brasidas to a satrap who compared the life of Sparta to that of Persepolis, "but you cannot know the pleasures of mine."

As an unbroken steed bristles his mane, paws the ground with his hoof, and struggles violently at the mere approach of the bit, while a trained horse patiently endures the whip and the spur, barbarous man does not bow his head for the yoke that civilized man wears without a murmur, and he prefers the most stormy liberty to tranquil subjection. Thus it is not by the degradation of enslaved peoples that man's natural dispositions for or against servitude are to be judged, but by the wonders that all free peoples have accomplished to safeguard themselves from oppression. I know that enslaved peoples do nothing but boast of the peace and tranquillity they enjoy in their chains and that *they give the name 'peace' to the most miserable slavery.* But when I see free peoples sacrificing pleasures, tranquillity, wealth, power, and life itself for the preservation of this sole good which is regarded so disdainfully by those who have lost it; when I see animals born free and abhorring captivity break their heads against the bars of their prison; when I see multitudes of utterly naked savages scorn European pleasures and brave hunger, fire, sword and death, simply to preserve their independence, I sense that it is inappropriate for slaves to reason about liberty.

As for paternal authority, from which several have derived absolute government and all society, it is enough, without having recourse to the contrary proofs of Locke and Sidney, to note that nothing in the world is farther from the ferocious spirit of despotism than the gentleness of that authority which looks more to the advantage of the one who obeys than to the utility of the one who commands; that by the law of nature, the father is master of the child as long as his help is necessary for him; that beyond this point they become equals, and the son, completely independent of the father, then owes him merely respect and not obedience; for gratitude is clearly a duty that must be rendered, but not a right that can be demanded. Instead of saying that civil society derives from paternal power, on the contrary it must be said that it is from civil society that this power draws its principal force. An individual was not recognized as the father of several children until the children remained gathered about him. The goods of the father, of which he is truly the master, are the goods that keep his children in a state of dependence toward him, and he can cause their receiving a share in his estate to be consequent upon the extent to which they will have well merited it from him by continuous deference to his wishes. Now, far from having some similar favor to expect from their despot (since they belong to him as personal possessions—they and all they possess—or at least he claims this to be the case), subjects are reduced to receiving as a favor what he leaves them of their goods. He does what is just when he despoils them; he does them a favor when he allows them to live.

In continuing thus to examine facts from the viewpoint of right, no more solidity than truth would be found in the belief that the establishment of tyranny was voluntary; and it would be difficult to show the validity of a contract that would obligate only one of the parties, where all the commitments would be placed on one side with none on the other, and that it would turn exclusively to the disadvantage of the one making the commitments. This odious system is quite far removed from being, even today, that of wise and good monarchs, and especially of the kings of France, as may be seen in various places in their edicts, and particularly in the following passage of a famous writing published in 1667 in the name of and by order of Louis XIV: *Let it not be said therefore that the sovereign is not subject to the laws of his state, for the contrary statement is a truth of the law of nations, which flattery has on occasion attacked, but which good princes have always defended as a tutelary divinity of their states. How much more legitimate is it to say, with the wise Plato, that the perfect felicity of a kingdom is that a prince be obeyed by his subjects, that the prince obey the law, and that the law be right and always directed to the public good.* I will not stop to investigate whether, with liberty being the most noble of man's faculties, he degrades his nature, places himself on the level of animals enslaved by instinct, offends even his maker, when he unreservedly renounces the most precious of all his gifts, and allows himself to commit all the crimes he forbids us to commit, in order to please a ferocious or crazed master; nor whether this sublime workman should be more irritated at seeing his finest work destroyed rather than at seeing it dishonored. [I will disregard, if you will, the authority of Barbeyrac, who flatly declares, following Locke, that no one can sell his liberty to the point of submitting himself to an arbitrary power that treats him according to its fancy. *For*, he adds, *this would be selling his own life, of which he is not the master.*] I will merely ask by what right those who have not been afraid of debasing themselves to this degree have been able to subject their posterity to the same ignominy and to renounce for it goods that do not depend on their liberality, and without which life itself is burdensome to all who are worthy of it.

Pufendorf says that just as one transfers his goods to another by conventions and contracts, one can also divest himself of his liberty in favor of someone. That, it seems to me, is very bad reasoning; for, in the first place, the goods I give away become something utterly foreign to me, and it is a matter of indifference to me whether or not these goods are abused; but it is important to me that my liberty is not abused, and I cannot expose myself to becoming the instrument of crime without making myself guilty of the evil I will be forced to commit. Moreover, since the right of property is merely the result of convention and human institution, every man can dispose of what he possesses as he sees fit. But it is not the same for the essential gifts of nature such as life and liberty, which everyone is allowed to enjoy, and of which it is at least doubtful that one has the right to divest himself. In giving up the one he degrades his being; in giving up the other he annihilates that being insofar as he can. And because no temporal goods can compensate for the one or the other, it would offend at the same time both nature and reason to renounce them, regardless of the price. But even if one could give away his liberty as he does his goods, the difference would be very great for the children who enjoy the father's goods only by virtue of a transmission of his right; whereas, since liberty is a gift they receive from nature in virtue of being men, their parents had no right to divest them of it. Thus, just as violence had to be done to nature in order to establish slavery, nature had to be changed in order to perpetuate this right. And the jurists, who have gravely pronounced that the child of a slave woman is born a slave, have decided, in other words, that a man is not born a man.

Thus it appears certain to me not only that governments did not begin with arbitrary power, which is but their corruption and extreme limit, and which finally brings them back simply to the law of the strongest, for which they were initially to have been the remedy; but also that even if they had begun thus, this power, being illegitimate by its nature, could not have served as a foundation for the rights of society, nor, as a consequence, for the inequality occasioned by social institutions.

Without entering at present into the investigations that are yet to be made into the nature of the fundamental compact of all government, I restrict myself, in following common opinion, to considering here the establishment of the body politic as a true contract between the populace and the leaders it chooses for itself: a contract by which the two parties obligate themselves to observe the laws that are stipulated in it and that form the bonds of their union. Since, with respect to social relations, the populace has united all its wills into a single one, all the articles on which this will is explicated become so many fundamental laws obligating all the members of the state without exception, and one of these regulates the choice and power of the magistrates charged with watching over the execution of the others. This power extends to everything that can maintain the constitution, without going so far as to change it. To it are joined honors that make the laws and their ministers worthy of respect, and, for the ministers personally, prerogatives that compensate them for the troublesome labors that a good administration requires. The magistrate, for his part, obligates himself to use the power entrusted to him only in accordance with the intention of the constituents, to maintain each one in the peaceful enjoyment of what belongs to him, and to prefer on every occasion the public utility to his own interest.

Before experience had shown or knowledge of the human heart had made men foresee the inevitable abuses of such a constitution, it must have seemed all the better because those who were charged with watching over its preservation were themselves the ones who had the greatest interest in it. For since the magistracy and its rights were established exclusively on fundamental laws, were they to be destroyed, the magistracy would immediately cease to be legitimate; the people would no longer be bound to obey them. And since it was not the magistrate but the law that had constituted the essence of the state, everyone would rightfully return to his natural liberty.

The slightest attentive reflection on this point would confirm this by new reasons, and by the nature of the contract it would be seen that it could not be irrevocable. For were there no superior power that could guarantee the fidelity of the contracting parties or force them to fulfill their reciprocal commitments, the parties would remain sole judges in their own case, and each of them would always have the right to renounce the contract as soon as he should find that the other party violated the conditions of the contract, or as soon as the conditions should cease to suit him. It is on this principle that it appears the right to abdicate can be founded. Now to consider, as we are doing, only what is of human institution, if the magistrate, who has all the power in his hands and who appropriates to himself all the advantages of the contract, nevertheless had the right to renounce the authority, a fortiori the populace, which pays for all the faults of the leaders, should have the right to renounce their dependence. But the horrible dissensions, the infinite disorders that this dangerous power would necessarily bring in its wake, demonstrate more than anything else how much need human governments had for a basis more solid than reason alone, and how necessary it was for public tranquillity that the divine will intervened to give to sovereign authority a sacred and inviolable character which took from the subjects the fatal right to dispose of it. If religion had brought about this good for men, it would be enough to oblige them to cherish and adopt it, even with its abuses, since it spares even more blood than fanaticism causes to be shed. But let us follow the thread of our hypothesis.

The various forms of government take their origin from the greater or lesser differences that were found among private individuals at the moment of institution. If a man were eminent in power, virtue, wealth or prestige, he alone was elected magistrate, and the state became monarchical. If several men, more or less equal among themselves, stood out over all the others, they were elected jointly, and there was an aristocracy. Those whose fortune or talents were less disproportionate, and who least departed from the state of nature, kept the supreme administration and formed a democracy. Time made evident which of these forms was the most advantageous to men. Some remained in subjection only to the laws; the others soon obeyed masters. Citizens wanted to keep their liberty; the subjects thought only of taking it away from their neighbors, since they could not endure others enjoying a good they themselves no longer enjoyed. In a word, on the one hand were riches and conquests, and on the other were happiness and virtue.

In these various forms of government all the magistratures were at first elective; and when wealth did not prevail, preference was given to merit, which gives a natural ascendancy, and to age, which gives experience in conducting business and cool-headedness in deliberation. The elders of the Hebrews, the gerontes of Sparta, the senate of Rome, and even the etymology of our word *seigneur* show how much age was respected in former times. The more elections fell upon men of advanced age, the more frequent elections became, and the more their difficulties were made to be felt. Intrigues were introduced; factions were formed; parties became embittered; civil wars flared up. Finally, the blood of citizens was sacrificed to the alleged happiness of the state, and people were on the verge of falling back into the anarchy of earlier times. The ambition of the leaders profited from these circumstances to perpetuate their offices within their families. The people, already accustomed to dependence, tranquillity and the conveniences of life, and already incapable of breaking their chains, consented to let their servitude increase in order to secure their tranquillity. Thus it was that the leaders, having become hereditary, grew accustomed to regard their magistratures as family property, to regard themselves as the proprietors of the state (of which at first they were but the officers), to call their fellow citizens their slaves, to count them like cattle in the number of things that belonged to them, and to call themselves equals of the gods and kings of kings.

If we follow the progress of inequality in these various revolutions, we will find that the first stage was the establishment of the law and of the right of property, the second stage was the institution of the magistracy, and the third and final stage was the transformation of legitimate power into arbitrary power. Thus the class of rich and poor was authorized by the first epoch, that of the strong and the weak by the second, and that of master and slave by the third: the ultimate degree of inequality and the limit to which all the others finally lead, until new revolutions completely dissolve the government or bring it nearer to its legitimate institution.

To grasp the necessity of this progress, we must consider less the motives for the establishment of the body politic than the form it takes in its execution and the disadvantages that follow in its wake. For the vices that make social institutions necessary are the same ones that make their abuses inevitable. And with the sole exception of Sparta, where the law kept watch chiefly over the education of children, and where Lycurgus established mores that nearly dispensed with having to add laws to them, since laws are generally less strong than passions and restrain men without changing them, it would be easy to prove that any government that always moved forward in conformity with the purpose for which it was founded without being corrupted or altered, would have been needlessly instituted, and that a country where no one eluded the laws and abused the magistrature would need neither magistracy nor laws.

Political distinctions necessarily lend themselves to civil distinctions. The growing inequality between the people and its leaders soon makes itself felt among private individuals, and is modified by them in a thousand ways according to passions, talents and events. The magistrate cannot usurp illegitimate power without producing protégés for himself to whom he is forced to yield some part of it. Moreover, citizens allow themselves to be oppressed only insofar as they are driven by blind ambition; and looking more below than above them, domination becomes more dear to them than independence, and they consent to wear chains in order to be able to give them in turn to others. It is very difficult to reduce to obedience someone who does not seek to command; and the most adroit politician would never succeed in subjecting men who wanted merely to be free. But inequality spreads easily among ambitious and cowardly souls always ready to run the risks of fortune and, almost indifferently, to dominate or serve, according to whether it becomes favorable or unfavorable to them. Thus it is that there must have come a time when the eyes of people were beguiled to such an extent that its leaders merely had to say to the humblest men, "Be great, you and all your progeny," and he immediately appeared great to everyone as well as in his own eyes, and his descendants were elevated even more in proportion as they were at some remove from him. The more remote and uncertain the cause, the more the effect increased; the more loafers one could count in a family, the more illustrious it became.

If this were the place to go into detail, I would easily explain how [even without government involvement] the inequality of prestige and authority becomes inevitable among private individuals,[19] as soon as they are united in one single society and are forced to make comparisons among themselves and to take into account the differences they discover in the continual use they have to make of one another. These differences are of several sorts, but in general, since wealth, nobility or rank, power and personal merit are the principal distinctions by which someone is measured in society, I would prove that the agreement or conflict of these various forces is the surest indication of a well- or ill-constituted state. I would make it apparent that among these four types of inequality, since personal qualities are the origin of all the others, wealth is the last to which they are ultimately reduced, because it readily serves to buy all the rest, since it is the most immediately useful to well-being and the easiest to communicate. This observation enables one to judge rather precisely the extent to which each people is removed from its primitive institution, and of the progress it has made toward the final stage of corruption. I would note how much that universal desire for reputation, honors, and preferences, which devours us all, trains and compares our talents and strengths; how much it excites and multiplies the passions; and, by making all men competitors, rivals, or rather enemies, how many setbacks, successes and catastrophes of every sort it causes every day, by making so many contenders run the same course. I would show that it is to this ardor for making oneself the topic of conversation, to this furor to distinguish oneself which nearly always keeps us outside ourselves, that we owe what is best and worst among men, our virtues and vices, our sciences and our errors, our conquerors and our philosophers, that is to say, a multitude of bad things against a small number of good ones. Finally, I would prove that if one sees a handful of powerful and rich men at the height of greatness and fortune while the mob grovels in obscurity and misery, it is because the former prize the things they enjoy only to the extent that the others are deprived of them; and because, without changing their position, they would cease to be happy, if the people ceased to be miserable.

But these details alone would be the subject of a large work in which one would weigh the advantages and the disadvantages of every government relative to the rights of the state of nature, and where one would examine all the different faces under which inequality has appeared until now and may appear in [future] ages, according to the nature of these governments and the upheavals that time will necessarily bring in its wake. We would see the multitude oppressed from within as a consequence of the very precautions it had taken against what menaced it from without. We would see oppression continually increase, without the oppressed ever being able to know where it would end or what legitimate means would be left for them to stop it. We would see the rights of citizens and national liberties gradually die out, and the protests of the weak treated like seditious murmurs. We would see politics restrict the honor of defending the common cause to a mercenary portion of the people. We would see arising from this the necessity for taxes, the discouraged farmer leaving his field, even during peacetime, and leaving his plow in order to gird himself with a sword. We would see the rise of fatal and bizarre rules in the code of honor. We would see the defenders of the homeland sooner or later become its enemies, constantly holding a dagger over their fellow citizens, and there would come a time when we would hear them say to the oppressor of their country: *"If you order me to plunge my sword into my brother's breast or my father's throat, and into my pregnant wife's entrails, I will do so, even though my right hand is unwilling."*

From the extreme inequality of conditions and fortunes, from the diversity of passions and talents, from useless arts, from pernicious arts, from frivolous sciences there would come a pack of prejudices equally contrary to reason, happiness and virtue. One would see the leaders fomenting whatever can weaken men united together by disuniting them; whatever can give society an air of apparent concord while sowing the seeds of real division; whatever can inspire defiance and hatred in the various classes through the opposition of their rights and interests, and can as a consequence strengthen the power that contains them all.

It is from the bosom of this disorder and these upheavals that despotism, by gradually raising its hideous head and devouring everything it had seen to be good and healthy in every part of the state, would eventually succeed in trampling underfoot the laws and the people, and in establishing itself on the ruins of the republic. The times that would precede this last transformation would be times of troubles and calamities; but in the end everything would be swallowed up by the monster, and the peoples would no longer have leader or laws, but only tyrants. Also, from that moment on, there would no longer be any question of mores and virtue, for wherever despotism, *in which decency affords no hope,* reigns, it tolerates no other master. As soon as it speaks, there is neither probity nor duty to consult, and the blindest obedience is the only virtue remaining for slaves.

Here is the final stage of inequality, and the extreme point that closes the circle and touches the point from which we started. Here all private individuals become equals again, because they are nothing. And since subjects no longer have any law other than the master's will, nor the master any rule other than his passions, the notions of good and the principles of justice again vanish. Here everything is returned solely to the law of the strongest, and consequently to a new state of nature different from the one with which we began, in that the one was the state of nature in its purity, and this last one is the fruit of an excess of corruption. Moreover, there is so little difference between these two states, and the governmental contract is so utterly dissolved by despotism, that the despot is master only as long as he is the strongest; and as soon as he can be ousted, he has no cause to protest against violence. The uprising that ends in the strangulation or the dethronement of a sultan is as lawful an act as those by which he disposed of the lives and goods of his subjects the day before. Force alone maintained him; force alone brings him down. Thus everything happens in accordance with the natural order, and whatever the outcome of these brief and frequent upheavals may be, no one can complain about someone else's injustice, but only of his own imprudence or his misfortune.

In discovering and following thus the forgotten and lost routes that must have led man from the natural state to the civil state; in reestablishing, with the intermediate positions I have just taken note of, those that time constraints on me have made me suppress or that the imagination has not suggested to me, no attentive reader can fail to be struck by the immense space that separates these two states. It is in this slow succession of things that he will see the solution to an infinity of moral and political problems which the philosophers are unable to resolve. He will realize that, since the human race of one age is not the human race of another age, the reason why Diogenes did not find his man is because he searched among his contemporaries for a man who no longer existed. Cato, he will say, perished with Rome and liberty because he was out of place in his age; and this greatest of men merely astonished the world, which five hundred years earlier he would have governed. In short, he will explain how the soul and human passions are imperceptibly altered and, as it were, change their nature; why, in the long run, our needs and our pleasures change their objects; why, with original man gradually disappearing, society no longer offers to the eyes of the wise man anything but an assemblage of artificial men and factitious passions which are the work of all these new relations and have no true foundation in nature. What reflection teaches us on this subject is perfectly confirmed by observation: savage man and civilized man differ so greatly in the depths of their hearts and in their inclinations, that what constitutes the supreme happiness of the one would reduce the other to despair. Savage man breathes only tranquillity and liberty; he wants simply to live and rest easy; and not even the unperturbed tranquillity of the Stoic approaches his profound indifference for any other objects. On the other hand, the citizen is always active and in a sweat, always agitated, and unceasingly tormenting himself in order to seek still more laborious occupations. He works until he dies; he even runs to his death in order to be in a position to live, or renounces life in order to acquire immortality. He pays court to the great whom he hates and to the rich whom he scorns. He stops at nothing to obtain the honor of serving them. He proudly crows about his own baseness and their protection; and proud of his slavery, he speaks with disdain about those who do not have the honor of taking part in it. What a spectacle for the Carib are the difficult and envied labors of the European minister! How many cruel deaths would that indolent savage not prefer to the horror of such a life, which often is not mollified even by the pleasure of doing good. But in order to see the purpose of so many cares, the words *power* and *reputation* would have to have a meaning in his mind; he would have to learn that there is a type of men who place some value on the regard the rest of the world has for them, and who know how to be happy and content with themselves on the testimony of others rather than on their own. Such, in fact, is the true cause of all these differences; the savage lives in himself; the man accustomed to the ways of society is always outside himself and knows how to live only in the opinion of others. And it is, as it were, from their judgment alone that he draws the sentiment of his own existence. It is not pertinent to my subject to show how, from such a disposition, so much indifference for good and evil arises, along with such fine discourse on morality; how, with everything reduced to appearances, everything becomes factitious and bogus: honor, friendship, virtue, and often even our vices, about which we eventually find the secret of boasting; how, in a word, always asking others what we are and never daring to question ourselves on this matter, in the midst of so much philosophy, humanity, politeness, and sublime maxims, we have merely a deceitful and frivolous exterior: honor without virtue, reason without wisdom, and pleasure without happiness. It is enough for me to have proved that this is not the original state of man, and that this is only the spirit of society, and the inequality that society engenders, which thus change and alter all our natural inclinations.

I have tried to set forth the origin and progress of inequality, the establishment and abuse of political societies, to the extent that these things can be deduced from the nature of man by the light of reason alone, and independently of the sacred dogmas that give to sovereign authority the sanction of divine right. It follows from this presentation that, since inequality is practically non-existent in the state of nature, it derives its force and growth from the development of our faculties and the progress of the human mind, and eventually becomes stable and legitimate through the establishment of property and laws. Moreover, it follows that moral inequality, authorized by positive right alone, is contrary to natural right whenever it is not combined in the same proportion with physical inequality: a distinction that is sufficient to determine what one should think in this regard about the sort of inequality that reigns among all civilized people, for it is obviously contrary to the law of nature, however it may be defined, for a child to command an old man, for an imbecile to lead a wise man, and for a handful of people to gorge themselves on superfluities while the starving multitude lacks necessities.

Rousseau's Notes to
Discourse on the Origin of Inequality

1. *(Page 26)* Herodotus relates that after the murder of the false Smerdis, the seven liberators of Persia being assembled to deliberate on the form of government they would give the state, Otanes was fervently in support of a republic: an opinion all the more extraordinary in the mouth of a satrap, since, over and above the claim he could have to the empire, a grandee fears more than death a type of government that forces him to respect men. Otanes, as may readily be believed, was not listened to; and seeing that things were progressing toward the election of a monarch, he, who wanted neither to obey nor command, voluntarily yielded to the other rivals his right to the crown, asking as his sole compensation that he and his descendants be free and independent. This was granted him. If Herodotus did not inform us of the restriction that was placed on this privilege, it would be necessary to suppose it, otherwise Otanes, not acknowledging any sort of law and not being accountable to anyone, would have been all powerful in the state and more powerful than the king himself. But there was hardly any likelihood that a man capable of contenting himself, in similar circumstances, with such a privilege, was capable of abusing it. In fact, there is no evidence that this right ever caused the least trouble in the kingdom, either from wise Otanes or from any of his descendants.

2. *(Page 33)* From the start I rely with confidence on one of those authorities that are respectable for philosophers, because they come from a solid and sublime reason, which they alone know how to find and perceive.

"Whatever interest we may have in knowing ourselves, I do not know whether we do not have a better knowledge of everything that is not us. Provided by nature with organs uniquely destined for our preservation, we use them merely to receive impressions of external things; we seek merely to extend ourselves outward and to exist outside ourselves. Too much taken with multiplying the functions of our senses and with increasing the external range of our being, we rarely make use of that internal sense which reduces us to our true dimensions, and which separates us from all that is not us. Nevertheless, this is the sense we must use if we wish to know ourselves. It is the only one by which we can judge ourselves. But how can this sense be activated and given its full range? How can our soul, in which it resides, be rid of all the illusions of our mind? We have lost the habit of using it; it has remained unexercised in the midst of the tumult of our bodily sensations; it has been dried out by the fire of our passions; the heart, the mind, the senses, everything has worked against it.'' *Hist. Nat.*, Vol. IV: *de la Nat. de l'homme*, p. 151.

3. *(Page 39)* The changes that a long-established habit of walking on two feet could have brought about in the conformation of man, the relations that are still observed between his arms and the forelegs of quadrupeds, and the induction drawn from their manner of walking, could have given rise to doubts about the manner that must have been the most natural to us. All children begin by walking on all fours, and need our example and our lessons to learn to stand upright. There are even savage nations, such as the Hottentots, who, greatly neglecting their children, allow them to walk on their hands for so long that they then have a great deal of trouble getting them to straighten up. The children of the Caribs of the Antilles do the same thing. There are various examples of quadruped men, and I could cite among others that of the child who was found in 1344 near Hesse, where he had been raised by wolves, and who said afterward at the court of Prince Henry that, had the decision been left exclusively to him, he would have preferred to return to the wolves than to live among men. He had embraced to such an extent the habit of walking like those animals, that wooden boards had to be attached to him to force him to stand upright and maintain his balance on two feet. It was the same with the child who was found in 1694, in the forests of Lithuania, and who lived among bears. He did not give, says M. de Condillac, any sign of reason, walked on his hands and feet, had no language, and formed sounds that bore no resemblance whatever to those of a man. The little savage of Hanover, who was brought to the court of England several years ago, had all sorts of trouble getting himself to walk on two feet. And in 1719, two other savages, who were found in the Pyrenees, ran about the mountains in the manner of quadrupeds. As for the objection one might make that this deprives one of the use of one's hands from which we derive so many advantages, over and above the fact that the example of monkeys shows that the hand can be used quite well in both ways, this would prove only that man can give his limbs a destination more congenial than that of nature, and not that nature has destined man to walk otherwise than it teaches him.

But there are, it seems to me, much better reasons to state in support of the claim that man is a biped. First, if it were shown that he could have originally been formed otherwise than we see him and yet finally become what he is, this would not suffice to conclude that this is how it happened; for, after having shown the possibility of these changes, it would still be necessary, prior to granting them, to demonstrate at least their probability. Moreover, if man's arms seem as if they could have served as legs when needed, it is the sole observation favorable to that system, out of a great number of others which are contrary to it. The chief ones are that the manner in which man's head is attached to his body, instead of directing his view horizontally (as is the case for all other animals and for man himself when he walks upright), would have kept him, while walking on all fours, with his eyes fixed directly on the ground, a situation hardly conducive to the preservation of the individual; that the tail he is lacking, and for which he has no use when walking on two feet, is useful to quadrupeds, and none of them is deprived of one; that the breast of a woman, very well located for a biped who holds her child in her arms, is so poorly located for a quadruped that none has it located in that way; that, since the hind part is of an excessive height in proportion to the forelegs (which causes us to crawl on our knees when walking on all fours), the whole would have made an animal that was poorly proportioned and that walked uncomfortably; that if he had placed his foot as well as his hand down flat, he would have had one less articulation in the hind leg than do other animals, namely the one that joins canon to the tibia; and that by setting down only the tip of the foot, as doubtlessly he would have been forced to do, the tarsus (not to mention the plurality of bones that make it up) appears too large to take the place of the canon, and its articulations with the metatarsus and the tibia too close together to give the human leg in this situation the same flexibility as those of quadrupeds. Since the example of children is taken from an age when natural forces are not yet developed nor the members strengthened, it proves nothing whatever. I might just as well say that dogs are not destined to walk because several weeks after their birth they merely crawl. Particular facts also have little force against the universal practice of all men; even nations that have had no communication with others could not have imitated anything about them. A child abandoned in a forest before he is able to walk, and nourished by some beast, will have followed the example of his nurse in training himself to walk like her. Habit could have given him capabilities he did not have from nature, and just as one-armed men are successful, by dint of exercise, at doing with their feet whatever we do with our hands, he will finally have succeeded in using his hands as feet.

4. *(Page 40)* Should there be found among my readers a scientist nasty enough to cause me difficulties regarding the supposition of this natural fertility of the earth, I am going to answer him with the following passage:

"As plants derive much more substance from air and water for their sustenance than they do from the earth, it happens that when they rot they return to the earth more than they have derived from it. Moreover, a forest determines the amount of rainwater by stopping vapors. Thus, in a wooded area that was preserved for a long time without being touched, the bed of earth that serves for vegetation would increase considerably. But since animals return to the soil less than they derive from it, and since men take in huge quantities of wood and plants for fire and other uses, it follows that the bed of vegetative earth of an inhabited country must always diminish and finally become

like the terrain of Arabia Petraea, and like that of so many other provinces of the Orient (which in fact is the region that has been inhabited
from the most ancient times), where only salt and sand are found. For
the fixed salt of plants and animals remains, while all the other parts
are volatized." M. de Buffon, *Hist. Nat.*

To this can be added the factual proof based on the quantity of trees and
plants of every sort, which filled almost all the uninhabited islands that
have been discovered in the last few centuries, and on what history
teaches us about the immense forests all over the earth that had to be cut
down to the degree that it was populated or civilized. On this I will also
make the following three remarks. First, if there is a kind of vegetation
that can make up for the loss of vegetative matter which was occasioned
by animals, according to M. de Buffon's reasoning, it is above all the
wooded areas, where the treetops and the leaves gather and appropriate
more water and vapors than do other plants. Second, the destruction of
the soil, that is, the loss of the substance that is appropriate for vegetation,
should accelerate in proportion as the earth is more cultivated and as the
more industrious inhabitants consume in greater abundance its products
of every sort. My third and most important remark is that the fruits of
trees supply animals with more abundant nourishment than is possible for
other forms of vegetation: an experiment I made myself, by comparing the
products of two land masses of equal size and quality, the one covered
with chestnut trees and the other sown with wheat.

5. *(Page 40)* Among the quadrupeds, the two most universal distinguishing traits of voracious species are derived, on the one hand, from
the shape of the teeth, and, on the other, from the conformation of the
intestines. Animals that live solely on vegetation have all flat teeth, like
the horse, ox, sheep and hare, but voracious animals have pointed
teeth, like the cat, dog, wolf and fox. And as for the intestines, the
frugivorous ones have some, such as the colon, which are not found in
voracious animals. It appears therefore that man, having teeth and intestines like frugivorous animals, should naturally be placed in that
class. And not only do anatomical observations confirm this opinion,
but the monuments of antiquity are also very favorable to it. "Dicaear-
chus," says St. Jerome, "relates in his books on Greek antiquities that
under the reign of Saturn, when the earth was still fertile by itself, no
man ate flesh, but that all lived on fruits and vegetables that grew naturally." *(Adv. Jovinian.,* Bk. II) [This opinion can also be supported by
the reports of several modern travelers. François Corréal, among
others, testifies that the majority of inhabitants of the Lucayes, whom
the Spaniards transported to the islands of Cuba, Santo Domingo, and
elsewhere, died from having eaten flesh.] From this one can see that I
am neglecting several advantageous considerations that I could turn to
account. For since prey is nearly the exclusive subject of fighting
among carnivorous animals, and since frugivorous animals live among
themselves in continual peace, if the human species were of this latter

genus, it is clear that it would have had a much easier time subsisting in the state of nature, and much less need and occasion to leave it.

6. *(Page 41)* All the kinds of knowledge that demand reflection, all those acquired only by the concatenation of ideas and perfected only successively, appear to be utterly beyond the grasp of savage man, owing to the lack of communication with his fellow-men, that is to say, owing to the lack of the instrument which is used for that communication, and to the lack of the needs that make it necessary. His understanding and his industry are limited to jumping, running, fighting, throwing a stone, climbing a tree. But if he knows only those things, in return he knows them much better than we, who do not have the same need for them as he. And since they depend exclusively on bodily exercise and are not capable of any communication or progress from one individual to another, the first man could have been just as adept at them as his last descendants.

The reports of travelers are full of examples of the force and vigor of men of barbarous and savage nations. They praise scarcely less their adroitness and nimbleness. And since eyes alone are needed to observe these things, nothing hinders us from giving credence to what eyewitnesses certify on the matter. I draw some random examples from the first books that fall into my hands.

"The Hottentots," says Kolben, "understand fishing better than the Europeans at the Cape. Their skill is equal when it comes to the net, the hook and the spear, in coves as well as in rivers. They catch fish by hand no less skillfully. They are incomparably good at swimming. Their style of swimming has something surprising about it, something entirely unique to them. They swim with their body upright and their hands stretched out of the water, so that they appear to be walking on land. In the greatest agitation of the sea, when the waves form so many mountains, they somehow dance on the top of the waves, rising and falling like a piece of cork.

"The Hottentots," says the same author further, "are surprisingly good at hunting, and the nimbleness of their running surpasses the imagination." He is amazed that they did not put their agility to ill use more often, which, however, sometimes happens, as can be judged from the example he gives. "A Dutch sailor," he says, "on disembarking at the Cape, charged a Hottentot to follow him to the city with a roll of tobacco that weighed about twenty pounds. When they were both some distance from the crew, the Hottentot asked the sailor if he knew how to run. Run! answered the Dutchman; yes, very well. Let us see, answered the African. And fleeing with the tobacco, he disappeared almost immediately. The sailor, confounded by such marvelous quickness, did not think of following him, and he never again saw either his tobacco or his porter.

"They have such quick sight and such a sure hand that Europeans cannot go near them. At a hundred paces they will hit with a stone a mark the size of a halfpenny. And what is more amazing, instead of fixing their eyes on the target as we do, they make continuous movements and contortions. It appears that their stone is carried by an invisible hand."

Father du Tertre says about the savages of the Antilles nearly the same things that have just been read about the Hottentots of the Cape of Good Hope. He praises, above all, their accuracy in shooting with their arrows birds in flight and swimming fish, which they then catch by diving for them. The savages of North America are no less famous for their strength and adroitness, and here is an example that will lead us to form a judgment about those qualities in the Indians of South America.

In the year 1746, an Indian from Buenos Aires, having been condemned to the galleys of Cadiz, proposed to the governor that he buy back his liberty by risking his life at a public festival. He promised that by himself he would attack the fiercest bull with no other weapon in his hand but a rope; that he would bring him to the ground, seize him with his rope by whatever part they would indicate, saddle him, bridle him, mount him, and so mounted he would fight two other of the fiercest bulls to be released from the Torillo, and that he would put all of them to death, one after the other, the moment they would command him to do so, and without anyone's help. This was granted him. The Indian kept his word and succeeded in everything he had promised. On the way in which he did it and on the details of the fight, one can consult M. Gautier, *Observations sur l'Histoire Naturelle,* Vol. I (in-12°), p. 262, whence this fact is taken.

7. *(Page 42)* "The lifespan of horses," says M. de Buffon, "is, as in all other species of animals, proportionate to the length of their growth period. Man, who takes fourteen years to grow, can live six or seven times as long, that is to say, ninety or a hundred years. The horse, whose growth period is four years, can live six or seven times as long, that is to say, twenty-five or thirty years. The examples that could be contrary to this rule are so rare, that they should not even be regarded as an exception from which conclusions can be drawn. And just as large horses achieve their growth in less time than slender horses, they also have a shorter lifespan and are old from the age of fifteen."

8. *(Page 42)* I believe I see another difference between carnivorous and frugivorous animals still more general than the one I have remarked upon in Note 5, since this one extends to birds. This difference consists in the number of young, which never exceeds two in each litter for the species that lives exclusively on plant life, and which ordinarily exceeds this number for voracious animals. It is easy to know nature's plan in this regard by the number of teats, which is only two in each female of the first species, like the mare, the cow, the goat, the doe, the

ewe, etc., and which is always six or eight in the other females, such as the dog, the cat, the wolf, the tigress, etc. The hen, the goose, the duck, which are all voracious birds (as are the eagle, the sparrow hawk, the screech owl), also lay and hatch a large number of eggs, which never happens to the pigeon, the turtle-dove, or to birds that eat nothing but grain, which lay and hatch scarcely more than two eggs at a time. The reason that can be given for this difference is that the animals that live exclusively on grass and plants, remaining nearly the entire day grazing and being forced to spend considerable time feeding themselves, could not be up to the task of nursing several young; whereas the voracious animals, taking their meal almost in an instant, can more easily and more often return to their young and to their hunting, and can compensate for the loss of so large a quantity of milk. There would be many particular observations and reflections to make on all this, but this is not the place to make them, and it is enough for me to have shown in this part the most general system of nature, a system which furnishes a new reason to remove man from the class of carnivorous animals and to place him among the frugivorous species.

9. *(Page 45)* A famous author, on calculating the goods and evils of human life and comparing the two sums, has found that the latter greatly exceeded the former, and that, all things considered, life was a pretty poor present for man. I am not surprised by his conclusion; he has drawn all of his arguments from the constitution of civil man. Had he gone back as far as natural man, the judgment can be made that he would have found very different results, that he would have realized that man has scarcely any evils other than those he has given himself, and that nature would have been justified. It is not without trouble that we have managed to make ourselves so unhappy. When, on the one hand, one considers the immense labors of men, so many sciences searched into, so many arts invented, and so many forces employed, abysses filled up, mountains razed, rocks broken, rivers made navigable, lands cleared, lakes dug, marshes drained, enormous buildings raised upon the earth, the sea covered with ships and sailors; and when, on the other hand, one searches with a little meditation for the true advantages that have resulted from all this for the happiness of the human species, one cannot help being struck by the astonishing disproportion that obtains between these things, and to deplore man's blindness, which, to feed his foolish pride and who knows what vain sense of self-importance, makes him run ardently after all the miseries to which he is susceptible, and which beneficent nature has taken pains to keep from him.

Men are wicked; a sad and continual experience dispenses us from having to prove it. Nevertheless, man is naturally good; I believe I have demonstrated it. What therefore can have depraved him to this degree, if not the changes that have befallen his constitution, the progress he has made, and the sorts of knowledge he has acquired? Let human society be admired as much as one wants; it will be no less true for it that it necessarily brings men to hate one another to the extent that their interests are at cross-purposes with one another, to render mutually to one another apparent services and in fact do every evil imaginable to one another. What is one to think of an interaction where the reason of each private individual dictates to him maxims directly contrary to those that public reason preaches to the body of society, and where each finds his profit in the misfortune of another? Perhaps there is not a wealthy man whose death is not secretly hoped for by greedy heirs and often by his own children; not a ship at sea whose wreck would not be good news to some merchant; not a firm that a debtor of bad faith would not wish to see burn with all the papers it contains; not a people that does not rejoice at the disasters of its neighbors. Thus it is that we find our advantage in the setbacks of our fellow-men, and that one person's loss almost always brings about another's prosperity. But what is even more dangerous is that public calamities are anticipated and hoped for by a multitude of private individuals. Some want diseases, others death, others war, others famine. I have seen ghastly men weep with the sadness at the likely prospects of a fertile year. And the great and deadly fire of London, which cost the life or the goods of so many unfortunate people, made the fortunes of perhaps more than ten thousand people. I know that Montaigne blames the Athenian Demades for having had a worker punished, who, by selling coffins at a high price, made a great deal from the death of the citizens. But since the reason Montaigne proposes is that everyone would have to be punished, it is evident that it confirms my own. Let us therefore penetrate, through our frivolous demonstration of good will, to what happens at the bottom of our hearts; and let us reflect on what the state of things must be where all men are forced to caress and destroy one another, and where they are born enemies by duty and crooks by interest. If someone answers me by claiming that society is constituted in such a manner that each man gains by serving others, I will reply that this would be very well and good, provided he did not gain still more by harming them. There is no profit, however legitimate, that is not surpassed by one that can be made illegitimately, and wrong done to a neighbor is always more lucrative than services. It is therefore no longer a question of anything but finding the means of being assured of impunity. And this is what the powerful spend all their forces on, and the weak all their ruses.

Savage man, when he has eaten, is at peace with all nature, and the friend of all his fellow-men. Is it sometimes a question of his disputing over his meal? He never comes to blows without having first compared the difficulty of winning with that of finding his sustenance elsewhere. And since pride is not involved in the fight, it is ended by a few swings of the fist. The victor eats; the vanquished is on his way to seek his fortune, and everything is pacified. But for man in society, these are quite different affairs. It is first of all a question of providing for the necessary and then for the superfluous; next come delights, and then immense riches, and then subjects, and then slaves. He has not a moment's respite. What is most singular is that the less natural and pressing the needs, the more the passions increase and, what is worse, the power to satisfy them; so that after long periods of prosperity, after having swallowed up many treasures and ruined many men, my hero will end by butchering everything until he is the sole master of the universe. Such in brief is the moral portrait, if not of human life, then at least of the secret pretensions of the heart of every civilized man.

Compare, without prejudices, the state of civil man with that of savage man and seek, if you can, how many new doors to suffering and death (other than his wickedness, his needs and his miseries) the former has opened. If you consider the emotional turmoil that consumes us, the violent passions that exhaust and desolate us, the excessive labors with which the poor are overburdened, the still more dangerous softness to which the rich abandon themselves, and which cause the former to die of their needs and the latter of their excesses; if you call to mind the monstrous combinations of foods, their pernicious seasonings, the corrupted foodstuffs, tainted drugs, the knavery of those who sell them, the errors of those who administer them, the poison of the vessels in which they are prepared; if you pay attention to the epidemic diseases engendered by the bad air among the multitudes of men gathered together, to the illnesses occasioned by the effeminacy of our lifestyle, by the coming and going from the inside of our houses to the open air, the use of garments put on or taken off with too little precaution, and all the cares that our excessive sensuality has turned into necessary habits, the neglect or privation of which then costs us our life or our health; if you take into account fires and earthquakes, which, in consuming or turning upside down whole cities, cause their inhabitants to die by the thousands; in a word, if you unite the dangers that all these causes continually gather over our heads, you will realize how dearly nature makes us pay for the scorn we have shown for its lessons.

I will not repeat here what I have said elsewhere about war, but I wish that informed men would, for once, want or dare to give the public the detail of the horrors that are committed in armies by provisions and hospital suppliers. One would see that their not too secret maneuvers, on account of which the most brilliant armies dissolve into less than nothing, cause more soldiers to perish than are cut down by enemy swords. Moreover, no less surprising is the calculation of the number of men swallowed up by the sea every year, either by hunger, or scurvy, or pirates, or fire, or shipwrecks. It is clear that we must also put to the account of established property, and consequently to that of society, the assassinations, the poisonings, the highway robberies, and even the punishments of these crimes, punishments necessary to prevent greater ills, but which, costing the lives of two or more for the murder of one man, do not fail really to double the loss to the human species. How many are the shameful ways to prevent the birth of men or to fool nature: either by those brutal and depraved tastes which insult its most charming work, tastes that neither savages nor animals ever knew, and that have arisen in civilized countries only as the result of a corrupt imagination; or by those secret abortions, worthy fruits of debauchery and vicious honor; or by the exposure or the murder of a multitude of infants, victims of the misery of their parents or of the barbarous shame of their mothers; or, finally by the mutilation of those unfortunates, part of whose existence and all of whose posterity are sacrificed to vain songs, or what is worse still, to the brutal jealousy of a few men: a mutilation which, in this last case, doubly outrages nature, both by the treatment received by those who suffer it and by the use to which they are destined.

[But are there not a thousand more frequent and even more dangerous cases where paternal rights overtly offend humanity? How many talents are buried and inclinations are forced by the imprudent constraint of fathers! How many men would have distinguished themselves in a suitable station who die unhappy and dishonored in another station for which they have no taste! How many happy but unequal marriages have been broken or disturbed, and how many chaste wives dishonored by this order of conditions always in contradiction with that of nature! How many other bizarre unions formed by interests and disavowed by love and by reason! How many even honest and virtuous couples cause themselves torment because they were ill-matched! How many young and unhappy victims of their parent's greed plunge into vice or pass their sorrowful days in tears, and moan in indissoluble chains which the heart rejects and which gold alone has formed! Happy sometimes are those whose courage and even virtue tear them from life before a barbarous violence forces them into crime or despair. Forgive me, father and mother forever deplorable. I regrettably worsen your sorrows; but may they serve as an eternal and terrible example to whoever dares, in the name of nature, to violate the most sacred of its rights!

If I have spoken only of those ill-formed relationships that are the result of our civil order, is one to think that those where love and sympathy have presided are themselves exempt from drawbacks?]

What would happen if I were to undertake to show the human species attacked in its very source, and even in the most holy of all bonds, where one no longer dares to listen to nature until after having consulted fortune, and where, with civil disorder confounding virtues and vices, continence becomes a criminal precaution, and the refusal to give life to one's fellow-man an act of humanity? But without tearing away the veil that covers so many horrors, let us content ourselves with pointing out the evil, for which others must supply the remedy.

Let us add to all this that quantity of unwholesome trades which shorten lives or destroy one's health, such as work in mines, various jobs involving the processing of metals, minerals, and especially lead, copper, mercury, cobalt, arsenic, realgar; those other perilous trades which everyday cost the lives of a number of workers, some of them roofers, others carpenters, others masons, others working in quarries; let us bring all of these objects together, I say, and we will be able to see in the establishment and the perfection of societies the reasons for the diminution of the species, observed by more than one philosopher.

Luxury, impossible to prevent among men who are greedy for their own conveniences and for the esteem of others, soon completes the evil that societies have begun; and on the pretext of keeping the poor alive (which it was not necessary to do), luxury impoverishes everyone else, and sooner or later depopulates the state.

Luxury is a remedy far worse than the evil it means to cure; or rather it is itself the worst of all evils in any state, however large or small it may be, and which, in order to feed the hordes of lackeys and wretches it has produced, crushes and ruins the laborer and the citizen—like those scorching south winds that, by covering grass and greenery with devouring insects, take sustenance away from useful animals, and bring scarcity and death to all the places where they make themselves felt.

From society and the luxury it engenders, arise the liberal and mechanical arts, commerce, letters, and all those useless things that make industry flourish, enriching and ruining states. The reason for this decay is quite simple. It is easy to see that agriculture, by its nature, must be the least lucrative of all the arts, because, with its product being of the most indispensable use to all men, its price must be proportionate to the abilities of the poorest. From the same principle can be drawn this rule: that, in general, the arts are lucrative in inverse proportion to their usefulness, and that the most necessary must finally become the most neglected. From this it is clear what must be thought of the true advantages of industry and of the real effect that results from its progress.

Such are the discernible causes of all the miseries into which opulence finally brings down the most admired nations. To the degree that industry and the arts expand and flourish, the scorned farmer, burdened with taxes necessary to maintain luxury and condemned to spend his life between toil and hunger, abandons his fields to go to the cities in search of the bread he ought to be carrying there. The more the capital cities strike the stupid eyes of the people as wonderful, the more it will be necessary to groan at the sight of countrysides abandoned, fields fallow, and main roads jammed with unhappy citizens who have become beggars or thieves, destined to end their misery one day on the rack or on a dung-heap. Thus it is that the state, enriching itself on the one hand, weakens and depopulates itself on the other; and that the most powerful monarchies, after much labor to become opulent and deserted, end by becoming the prey of poor nations which succumb to the deadly temptation to invade them, and which enrich and enfeeble themselves in their turn, until they are themselves invaded and destroyed by others.

Let someone deign to explain to us for once what could have produced those hordes of barbarians which for so many centuries have overrun Europe, Asia and Africa. Was it to the industry of their arts, the wisdom of their laws, the excellence of their civil order that they owed that prodigious population? Would our learned ones be so kind as to tell us why, far from multiplying to that degree, those ferocious and brutal men, without enlightenment, without restraint, without education, did not all kill one another at every moment to argue with one another over their food or game? Let them explain to us how these wretches even had the gall to look right in the eye such capable people as we were, with such fine military discipline, such fine codes, and such wise laws, and why, finally, after society was perfected in the countries of the north, and so many pains were taken there to teach men their mutual duties and the art of living together agreeably and peaceably, nothing more is seen to come from them like those multitudes of men it produced formerly. I am very much afraid that someone might finally get it into his head to reply to me that all these great things, namely the arts, sciences, and laws, have been very wisely invented by men as a salutary plague to prevent the excessive multiplication of the species, out of fear that this world, which is destined for us, might finally become too small for its inhabitants.

What then! Must we destroy societies, annihilate thine and mine, and return to live in the forests with bears?—a conclusion in the style of my adversaries, which I prefer to anticipate, rather than leave to them the shame of drawing it. Oh you, to whom the heavenly voice has not made itself heard, and who recognize for your species no other destination except to end this brief life in peace; you who can leave in the midst of the cities your deadly acquisitions, your troubled minds, your corrupt hearts and your unbridled desires. Since it depends on you, retake your ancient and first innocence; go into the woods to lose sight and memory of the crimes of your contemporaries, and have no fear of cheapening your species in renouncing its enlightenment in order to renounce its vices. As for men like me, whose passions have forever destroyed their original simplicity, who can no longer feed on grass and acorn[s], nor get by without laws and chiefs; those who were honored in their first father with supernatural lessons; those who will see, in the intention of giving human actions from the beginning a morality they would not have acquired for a long time, the reason for a precept indifferent in itself and inexplicable in any other system; those, in a word, who are convinced that the divine voice called the entire human race to the enlightenment and the happiness of the celestial intelligences; all those latter ones will attempt, through the exercise of virtues they oblige themselves to practice while learning to know them, to merit the eternal reward that they ought to expect for them. They will respect the sacred bonds of the societies of which they are members; they will love their fellow-men and will serve them with all their power; they will scrupulously obey the laws and the men who are their authors and their ministers; they will honor above all the good and wise princes who will know how to prevent, cure or palliate that pack of abuses and evils always ready to overpower us; they will animate the zeal of these worthy chiefs by showing them without fear or flattery the greatness of their task and the rigor of their duty. But they will despise no less for it a constitution that can be maintained only with the help of so many respectable people, who are desired more often than they are obtained, and from which, despite all their care, always arise more real calamities than apparent advantages.

10. *(Page 45)* Among the men we know, whether by ourselves, or from historians, or from travelers, some are black, others white, others red. Some wear their hair long; others have merely curly wool. Some are almost entirely covered with hair; others do not even have a beard. There have been and perhaps there still are nations of men of gigantic size; and apart from the fable of the Pygmies (which may well be merely an exaggeration), we know that the Laplanders and above all the Greenlanders are considerably below the average size of man. It is even maintained that there are entire peoples who have tails like quadrupeds. And without putting blind faith in the accounts of Herodotus and Ctesias, we can at least draw from them the very likely opinion that had one been able to make good observations in those ancient times when various peoples followed lifestyles differing more greatly among themselves than do those of today, one would have also noted in the shape and posture of the body, much more striking varieties. All these facts, for which it is easy to furnish incontestable proofs, are capable of surprising only those who are accustomed to look solely at the objects that surround them and who are ignorant of the powerful effects of the diversity of climates, air, foods, lifestyle, habits in general, and especially the astonishing force of the same causes when they act continually for long successions of generations. Today, when commerce, voyages and conquests reunite various peoples further, and their lifestyles are constantly approximating one another through frequent communication, it is evident that certain national differences have diminished; and, for example, everyone can take note of the fact that today's Frenchmen are no longer those large, colorless and blond-haired bodies described by Latin historians, although time, together with the mixture of the Franks and the Normans, themselves colorless and blond-haired, should have reestablished what commerce with the Romans could have removed from the influence of the climate in the natural constitution and complexion of the inhabitants. All of these observations on the varieties that a thousand causes can produce and have in fact produced in the human species cause me to wonder whether the various animals similar to men, taken without much scrutiny by travelers for beasts, either because of some differences they noticed in their outward structure or simply because these animals did not speak, would not in fact be veritable savage men, whose race, dispersed in the woods during olden times, had not had an occasion to

develop any of its virtual faculties, had not acquired any degree of perfection, and was still found in the primitive state of nature. Let us give an example of what I mean.

"There are found in the kingdom of the Congo," says the translator of the *Histoire des Voyages,* "many of those large animals called *orangutans* in the East Indies, which occupy a middle ground between the human species and the baboons. Battel relates that in the forests of Mayomba, in the kingdom of Loango, one sees two kinds of monsters, the larger of which are called *pongos* and the others *enjocos.* The former bear an exact resemblance to man, except they are much larger and very tall. With a human face, they have very deep-set eyes. Their hands, cheeks and ears are without hair, except for their eyebrows, which are very long. Although the rest of their body is quite hairy, the hair is not very thick; the color of the hair is brown. Finally, the only part that distinguishes them from men is their leg, which has no calf. They walk upright, grasping the hair of their neck with their hand. Their retreat is in the woods. They sleep in the trees, and there they make a kind of roof which offers them shelter from the rain. Their foods are fruits or wild nuts; they never eat flesh. The custom of the Negroes who cross the forests is to light fires during the night. They note that in the morning, at their departure, the pongos take their place around the fire, and do not withdraw until it is out; because, for all their cleverness, they do not have enough sense to lay wood on the fire to keep it going.

"They occasionally walk in groups and kill the Negroes who cross the forests. They even fall upon elephants who come to graze in the places they inhabit, and they irritate the elephants so much with punches or with whacks of a stick that they force them howling to take flight. Pongos are never taken alive, because they are so strong that ten men would not be enough to stop them. But the Negroes take a good many young ones after having killed the mother, to whose body the young stick very closely. When one of these animals dies, the others cover its body with a pile of branches or leaves. Purchass adds that, in the conversations he has had with Battel, he had learned from him also that a pongo abducted a little Negro who passed an entire month in the society of these animals, for they do not harm men they take by surprise, at least when these men do not pay any attention to them, as the little Negro had observed. Battel had not described the second species of monster.

"Dapper confirms that the kingdom of the Congo is filled with those animals which in the Indies bear the name orangutans, that is to say, inhabitants of the woods, and which the Africans call *quojas-morros.* This beast, he says, is so similar to man, that it has occurred to some travelers that it could have issued from a woman and a monkey: a myth which even the Negroes reject. One of these animals was transported from the Congo to Holland and presented to the Prince of Orange, Frederick Henry. It was the height of a three-year old child, moderately stocky, but square and well-proportioned, very agile and lively;

its legs fleshy and robust; the entire front of the body naked, but the
rear covered with black hairs. At first sight, its face resembled that of a
man, but it had a flat and turned up nose; its ears were also those of the
human species; its breast (for it was a female), was plump, its navel
sunken, its shoulders very well joined, its hands divided into fingers
and thumbs, its calves and heels fat and fleshy. It often walked upright
on its legs; it was capable of lifting and carrying heavy burdens. When
it wanted to drink, it took the cover of the pot in one hand, and held
the base with the other; afterward it graciously wiped its lips. It lay
down to sleep with its head on a cushion, covering itself with such skill
that it would have been taken for a man in bed. The Negroes tell
strange stories about this animal. They assert not only that it takes
women and girls by force, but that it dares to attack armed men. In a
word, there is great likelihood that it is the satyr of the ancients.
Perhaps Merolla is speaking only of these animals whom he relates that
Negroes sometimes lay hold of savage men and women in their hunts.''

These species of anthropomorphic animals are again discussed in the
third volume of the same *Histoire des Voyages* under the name of *beg-
gos* and *mandrills*. But sticking to the preceding accounts, we find in
the description of these alleged monsters striking points of conformity
with the human species and lesser differences than those that would be
assigned between one man and another. From these pages it is not
clear what the reasons are that the authors have for refusing to give the
animals in question the name ''savage men''; but it is easy to conjecture that it is on account of their stupidity and also because they did
not speak—feeble reasons for those who know that although the organ
of speech is natural to man, nevertheless speech itself is not natural to
him, and who knows to what point his perfectibility can have elevated
civil man above his original state. The small number of lines these descriptions contain can cause us to judge how badly these animals have
been observed and with what prejudices they have been viewed. For
example, they are categorized as monsters, and yet there is agreement
that they reproduce. In one place, Battel says that the pongos kill the
Negroes who cross the forests; in another place, Purchass adds that
they do not do any harm, even when they surprise them, at least when
the Negroes do not fix their gaze upon them. The pongos gather around
fires lit by the Negroes upon the Negroes' withdrawal, and withdraw in
their turn when the fire is out. There is the fact. Here now is the com-
mentary of the observer: *because, for all their cleverness, they do not
have enough sense to lay wood on the fire to keep it going.* I would like
to hazard a guess how Battel, or Purchass, his compiler, could have
known that the withdrawal of the pongos was an effect of their stupidity rather than their will. In a climate such as Loango, fire is not something particularly necessary for the animals; and if the Negroes light a
fire, it is less against the cold than to frighten ferocious beasts. It is
therefore a very simple matter that, after having been for some time
delighted with the flame or being well warmed, the pongos grow tired
of always remaining in the same place and go off to graze, which re-

quires more time than if they ate flesh. Moreover, we know that most animals, man not excluded, are naturally lazy, and that they refuse all sorts of cares which are not absolutely necessary. Finally, it seems very strange that pongos, whose adroitness and strength are praised, the pongos who know how to bury their dead and to make themselves roofs out of branches, should not know how to push fagots into the fire. I recall having seen a monkey perform the same maneuver that people deny the pongos can do. It is true that since my ideas were not oriented in this direction, I myself committed the mistake for which I reproach our travelers; I neglected to examine whether the intention of the monkey was actually to sustain the fire or simply, as I believe is the case, to imitate the actions of a man. Whatever the case may be, it is well demonstrated that the monkey is not a variety of man: not only because he is deprived of the faculty of speech, but above all because it is certain that his species does not have the faculty of perfecting itself, which is the specific characteristic of the human species: experiments that do not seem to have been made on the pongos and the orangutan with sufficient care to enable one to draw the same conclusion in their case. However, there would be a means by which, if the orangutan or others were of the human species, even the least sophisticated observers could assure themselves of it by means of demonstration. But beyond the fact that a single generation would not be sufficient for this experiment, it should pass as unworkable, since it would be necessary that what is merely a supposition be demonstrated to be true, before the test that should establish the fact could be innocently tried.

Precipitous judgments, which are not the fruit of an enlightened reason, are prone to be excessive. Without any fanfare, our travelers made into beasts, under the names *pongos, mandrills, orangutans,* the same beings that the ancients, under the names *satyrs, fauns, sylvans,* made into divinities. Perhaps, after more precise investigations it will be found that they are [neither beasts nor gods but] men. Meanwhile, it would seem to me that there is as much reason to defer on this point to Merolla, an educated monk, an eyewitness, and one who, with all his naïveté, did not fail to be a man of wit, as to the merchant Battel, Dapper, Purchass, and the other compilers.

What judgment do we think such observers would have made regarding the child found in 1694, of whom I have spoken before, who gave no indication of reason, walked on his feet and hands, had no language, and made sounds that bore no resemblance whatever to those of a man? It took a long time, continues the same philosopher who provided me with this fact, before he could utter a few words, and then he did it in a barbarous manner. Once he could speak, he was questioned about his first state, but he did not recall it any more than we recall what happened to us in the cradle. If, unhappily* for him, this child had

---

*In the copy of the Discourse sent to Richard Davenport, Rousseau inserts here: or perhaps happily.

fallen into the hands of our travelers, there can be no doubt that after
having observed his silence and stupidity, they would have resolved to
send him back to the woods or lock him up in a menagerie; after which
they would have spoken eruditely about him in their fine accounts as a
very curious beast who looked rather like a man.

For the three or four hundred years since the inhabitants of Europe
inundated the other parts of the world and continually published new
collections of travels and stories, I am convinced that we know no
other men but the Europeans alone. Moreover, it would appear, from
the ridiculous prejudices that have not been extinguished even among
men of letters, that everybody does hardly anything under the pompous
name of "the study of man" except study the men of his country. Individuals may well come and go; it seems that philosophy travels
nowhere; moreover, the philosophy of one people is little suited to another. The reason for this is manifest, at least for distant countries.
There are hardly more than four sorts of men who make long voyages:
sailors, merchants, soldiers, and missionaries. Now we can hardly expect the first three classes to provide good observers; and as for those
in the fourth, occupied by the sublime vocation that calls them, even if
they were not subject to the prejudices of social position as are all the
rest, we must believe that they would not voluntarily commit themselves to investigations that would appear to be sheer curiosity, and
which would sidetrack them from the more important works to which
they are destined. Besides, to preach the Gospel in a useful manner,
zeal alone is needed, and God gives the rest. But to study men, talents
are needed which God is not required to give anyone, and which are
not always the portion of saints. One does not open a book of voyages
where one does not find descriptions of characters and mores. But one
is utterly astonished to see that these people who have described so
many things have said merely what everyone already knew, that, at the
end of the world, they knew how to understand only what it was for
them to notice without leaving their street; and that those true qualities
which characterize nations and strike eyes made to see have almost
always escaped theirs. Whence this fine moral slogan, so bandied about
by the philosophizing rabble: that men are everywhere the same; that,
since everywhere they have the same passions and the same vices, it is
rather pointless to seek to characterize different peoples—which is
about as well reasoned as it would be for someone to say that Peter and
James cannot be distinguished from one another, because they both
have a nose, a mouth and eyes.

Will we never see those happy days reborn when the people did not
dabble in philosophizing, but when a Plato, a Thales, a Pythagoras,
taken with an ardent desire to know, undertook the greatest voyages
merely to inform themselves, and went far away to shake off the yoke
of national prejudices, in order to learn to know men by their
similarities and their differences, and to acquire those sorts of universal
knowledge that are exclusively those of a single century or country, but

which, since they are of all times and all places, are, as it were, the common science of the wise?

We admire the splendor of some curious men who, at great expense, made or caused to be made voyages to the Orient with learned men and painters, in order to sketch hovels and to decipher or copy inscriptions. But I have trouble conceiving how, in a century where people take pride in fine sorts of knowledge, there are not to be found two closely united men—rich, one in money, the other in genius, both loving glory and aspiring for immortality—one of whom sacrifices twenty thousand crowns of his goods and the other ten years of his life for a famous voyage around the world, in order to study, not always rocks and plants, but, for once, men and mores, and who, after so many centuries used to measure and examine the house, would finally be of a mind to want to know its inhabitants.

The academicians who have traveled through the northern parts of Europe and the southern parts of America had for their object to visit them more as geometers than as philosophers. Nevertheless, since they were both simultaneously, we cannot regard as utterly unknown the regions that have been seen and described by La Condamine and Maupertuis. The jeweler Chardin, who has traveled like Plato, has left nothing to be said about Persia. China appeared to have been well observed by the Jesuits. Kempfer gives a passable idea of what little he has seen in Japan. Except for these reports, we know nothing about the peoples of the East Indies, who have been visited exclusively by Europeans interested more in filling their purses than their heads. All of Africa and its numerous inhabitants, as unique in character as in color, are yet to be examined. The entire earth is covered with nations of which we know only the names, and we dabble in judging the human race! Let us suppose a Montesquieu, a Buffon, a Diderot, a Duclos, a d'Alembert, a Condillac, or men of that ilk traveling in order to inform their compatriots, observing and describing as they know how to do, Turkey, Egypt, Barbary, the empire of Morocco, Guinea, the land of the Bantus, the interior of Africa and its eastern coastlines, the Malabars, Mogul, the banks of the Ganges, the kingdoms of Siam, Pegu, and Ava, China, Tartary, and especially Japan; then in the other hemisphere, Mexico, Peru, Chile, the straits of Magellan, not to forget the Patagonias true or false, Tucuman, Paraguay (if possible), Brazil; finally the Caribbean Islands, Florida, and all the savage countries— the most important voyage of all and the one that should be embarked upon with the greatest care. Let us suppose that these new Hercules, back from these memorable treks, then wrote at leisure the natural, moral, and political history of what they would have seen; we ourselves would see a new world sally forth from their pen, and we would thus learn to know our own. I say that when such observers will affirm of an animal that it is a man and of another that it is a beast, we will have to believe them. But it would be terribly simpleminded to defer in this to unsophisticated travelers, concerning whom we will sometimes be tempted to put the same question that they dabble at resolving concerning other animals.

11. *(Page 46)* That appears utterly evident to me and I am unable to conceive whence our philosophers can derive all the passions they ascribe to natural man. With the single exception of the physically necessary which nature itself demands, all our other needs are such merely out of habit (previous to which they were not needs), or by our own desires; and we do not desire what we are not in a position to know. Whence it follows that since savage man desires only the things he knows and knows only those things whose possession is in his power or easily acquired, nothing should be so tranquil as his soul and nothing so limited as his mind.

12. *(Page 48)* I find in Locke's *Civil Government* an objection which seems to me too specious for me to be permitted to hide it. "Since the purpose of the society between male and female," says this philosopher, "is not merely to procreate, but to continue the species, this society should last, even after procreation, at least as long as it is necessary for the nurture and support of the procreated, that is to say, until they are capable of seeing to their needs on their own. This rule, which the infinite wisdom of the creator has established upon the works of his hands, we see creatures inferior to man observing constantly and strictly. In those animals which live on grass, the society between male and female lasts no longer than each act of copulation, because, the teats of the mother being sufficient to feed the young until they are able to feed on grass, the male is content to beget and no longer mingles with the female or the young, to whose sustenance he has nothing to contribute. But as far as beasts of prey are concerned, the society lasts longer, because, with the mother being unable to see to her own sustenance and at the same time feed her young by means of her prey alone (which is a more laborious and more dangerous way of taking in nourishment than by feeding on grass), the assistance of the male is utterly necessary for the maintenance of their common family (if one may use that term), which is able to subsist to the point where it can go hunt for prey only through the efforts of the male and the female. We note the same thing in all the birds (with the exception of some domestic birds which are found in places where the continual abundance of nourishment exempts the male from the effort of feeding the young). It is clear that when the young in their nest need food, the male and female bring it to them until the young there are capable of flying and seeing to their own sustenance.

"And, in my opinion, herein lies the principal, if not the only reason why the male and the female in mankind are bound to a longer period of society than is undertaken by other creatures: namely, that the female is capable of conceiving and is ordinarily pregnant again and has a new child long before the previous child is in a position to do without the help of its parents and can take care of itself. Thus, since the father is bound to take care of those he has produced, and to take that care for a long time, he is also under an obligation to continue in conjugal society with the same woman by whom he has had them, and to remain in that society much longer than other creatures, whose young being capable of subsisting by themselves before the time comes for a new procreation, the bond of the male and female breaks of its own accord, and they are both at complete liberty, until such time as that season, which usually solicits the animals to join with one another, obliges them to choose new mates. And here we cannot help admiring the wisdom of the creator, who, having given to man the qualities needed to provide for the future as well as for the present, has willed and has brought it about that the society of man should last longer than that of the male and female among other creatures, so that thereby the industry of man and woman might be stimulated more, and that their interests might be better united, with a view to making provisions for their children and to leaving them their goods—nothing being more to the detriment of the children than an uncertain and vague conjunction, or an easy and frequent dissolution of the conjugal society."*

The same love of truth which has made me to set forth sincerely this objection, moves me to accompany it with some remarks, if not to resolve it, at least to clarify it.

1. I will observe first that moral proofs do not have great force in matters of physics, and that they serve more to explain existing facts than to establish the real existence of those facts. Now such is the type of proof that M. Locke employs in the passage I have just quoted; for although it may be advantageous to the human species for the union between man and woman to be permanent, it does not follow that it has been thus established by nature; otherwise it would be necessary to say that it also instituted civil society, the arts, commerce, and all that is asserted to be useful to men.

2. I do not know where M. Locke has found that among animals of prey, the society of the male and female lasts longer than does the society of those that live on grass, and that the former assists the latter to feed the young; for it is not manifest that the dog, the cat, the bear, or the wolf recognize their female better than the horse, the ram, the bull, the stag, or all the other quadruped animals do theirs. On the contrary, it seems that if the assistance of the male were necessary to the female to preserve her young, it would be particularly in the species that live only on grass, because a long period of time is needed by the mother to graze, and during that entire interval she is forced to neglect her brood, whereas the prey of a female bear or wolf is devoured in an instant, and, without suffering hunger, she has more time to nurse her young. This line of reasoning is confirmed by an observation upon the relative number of teats and young which distinguishes carnivorous

*Translator's note: This is a translation of the French rendering of Locke's text.

from frugivorous species, and of which I have spoken in Note 8. If this observation is accurate and general, since a woman has only two teats and rarely has more than one child at a time, this is one more strong reason for doubting that the human species is naturally carnivorous. Thus it seems that, in order to draw Locke's conclusion, it would be necessary to reverse completely his reasoning. There is no more solidity in the same distinction when it is applied to birds. For who could be persuaded that the union of the male and the female is more durable among vultures and crows than among turtle-doves? We have two species of domestic birds, the duck and the pigeon, which furnish us with examples directly contrary to the system of this author. The pigeon, which lives solely on grain, remains united to its female, and they feed their young in common. The duck, whose voraciousness is known, recognizes neither his female nor his young, and provides no help in their sustenance. And among hens, a species hardly less carnivorous, we do not observe that the rooster bothers himself in the least with the brood. And if in the other species the male shares with the female the care of feeding the young, it is because birds, which at first are unable to fly and which the mother cannot nurse, are much less in a position to get along without the help of the father than are quadrupeds, for which the mother's teat is sufficient, at least for a time.

3. There is much uncertainty about the principal fact that serves as a basis for all of M. Locke's reasoning; for in order to know whether, as he asserts, in the pure state of nature the female ordinarily is pregnant again and has a new child long before the preceding one could see to its needs for itself, it would be necessary to perform experiments that M. Locke surely did not perform and that no one is in a position to perform. The continual cohabitation of husband and wife is so near an occasion for being exposed to a new pregnancy that it is very difficult to believe that the chance encounter or the mere impulsion of temperament produced such frequent effects in the pure state of nature as in that of conjugal society: a slowness that would contribute perhaps toward making the children more robust, and that, moreover, might be compensated by the power to conceive, prolonged to a greater age in the women who would have abused it less in their youth. As to children, there are several reasons for believing that their forces and their organs develop much later among us than they did in the primitive state of which I am speaking. The original weakness which they derive from the constitution of the parents, the cares taken to envelop and constrain all of their members, the softness in which they are raised, perhaps the use of milk other than that of their mother, everything contradicts and slows down in them the initial progress of nature. The heed they are forced to pay to a thousand things on which their attention is continually fixed, while no exercise is given to their bodily forces, can also bring about considerable deflection from their growth. Thus, if, instead of first overworking and exhausting their minds in a thousand ways, their bodies were allowed to be exercised by the con-

tinual movements that nature seems to demand of them, it is to be believed that they would be in a much better position to walk and to provide for their needs by themselves.

4. Finally, M. Locke at most proves that there could well be in a man a motive for remaining attached to a woman when she has a child but in no way does he prove that the man must have been attached to her before the childbirth and during the nine months of pregnancy. If a given woman is indifferent to the man during those nine months, if she even becomes unknown to him, why will he help her after childbirth? Why will he help her to raise a child that he does not know belongs to him alone, and whose birth he has neither decided upon nor foreseen? Evidently M. Locke presumes what is in question, for it is not a matter of knowing why the man will remain attached to the woman after childbirth, but why he will be attached to her after conception. Once his appetite is satisfied, the man has no further need for a given woman, nor the woman for a given man. The man does not have the least care or perhaps the least idea of the consequences of his action. The one goes off in one direction, the other in another, and there is no likelihood that at the end of nine months they have the memory of having known one another. For this type of memory, by which one individual gives preference to another for the act of generation, requires, as I prove in the text, more progress or corruption in human understanding than may be supposed in man in the state of animality we are dealing with here. Another woman can therefore satisfy the new desires of the man as congenially as the one he has already known, and another man in the same manner satisfy the woman, supposing she is impelled by the same appetite during the time of pregnancy, about which one can reasonably be in doubt. And if in the state of nature the woman no longer feels the passion of love after the conception of the child, the obstacle to her society with the man thus becomes much greater still, since she then has no further need either for the man who has made her pregnant or for anyone else. There is not, therefore, in the man any reason to seek the same woman, or in the woman any reason to seek the same man. Thus Locke's reasoning falls in ruin, and all the dialectic of this philosopher has not shielded him from the mistake committed by Hobbes and others. They had to explain a fact of the state of nature, that is to say, of a state where men lived in isolation and where a given man did not have any motive for living in proximity to another given man, nor perhaps did a given group of men have a motive for living in proximity to another given group of men, which is much worse. And they gave no thought to transporting themselves beyond the centuries of society, that is to say, of those times when men always have a reason for living in proximity to one another, and when a given man often has a reason for living in proximity to a given man or woman.

13. *(Page 49)* I will hold back from embarking on the philosophical reflections that there would be to engage in concerning the advantages and disadvantages of this institution of languages. It is not for me to be permitted to attack vulgar errors; and educated people respect their prejudices too much to abide patiently my alleged paradoxes. Let us therefore allow men to speak, to whom it has not been made a crime to risk sometimes taking the part of reason against the opinion of the multitude. *Nor would anything disappear from the happiness of the human race, if, when the disaster and confusion of so many languages has been cast out, mortals should cultivate one art, and if it should be allowed to explain anything by means of signs, movements and gestures. But now it has been so established that the condition of animals commonly believed to be brutes is considerably better than ours in this respect, inasmuch as they articulate their feelings and their thoughts without an interpreter more readily and perhaps more felicitously than any mortals can, especially if they use `a foreign language.** Is. Vossius *de Poëmat. Cant. et Viribus Rythmi,* p. 66.

14. *(Page 51)* In showing how ideas of discrete quantity and its relationships are necessary in the humblest of the arts, Plato mocks with good reason the authors of his time who alleged that Palamedes had invented numbers at the siege of Troy, as if, says this philosopher, Agamemnon could have been ignorant until then of how many legs he had. In fact, one senses the impossibility that society and the arts should have arrived at the point where they already were at the time of the siege of Troy, unless men had the use of numbers and arithmetic. But the necessity for knowing numbers, before acquiring other types of knowledge, does not make their invention easier to imagine. Once the names of the numbers are known, it is easy to explain their meaning and to elicit the ideas which these names represent; but in order to invent them, it was necessary, prior to conceiving of these same ideas, to be, as it were, on familiar terms with philosophical meditations, to be trained to consider beings by their essence alone and independently of all other perception—a very difficult, very metaphysical, hardly natural abstraction, and yet one without which these ideas could never have been transported from one species or genus to another, nor could numbers have become universal. A savage could consider separately his right leg and his left leg, or look at them together under the indivisible idea of a pair without ever thinking that he had two of them; for the representative idea that portrays for us an object is one thing, and the numerical idea which determines it is another. Even less was he able to count to five. And although, by placing his hands one on top of the other, he could have noticed that the fingers corresponded exactly, he was far from thinking of their numerical equality. He did not know the

*Translator's note: Rousseau here quotes the Latin text.

sum of his fingers any more than that of his hairs. And if, after having made him understand what numbers are, someone had said to him that he had as many fingers as toes, he perhaps would have been quite surprised, in comparing them, to find that this was true.

15. *(Page 53)* We must not confuse egocentrism with love of oneself, two passions very different by virtue of both their nature and their effects. Love of oneself is a natural sentiment which moves every animal to be vigilant in its own preservation and which, directed in man by reason and modified by pity, produces humanity and virtue. Egocentrism is merely a sentiment that is relative, artificial and born in society, which moves each individual to value himself more than anyone else, which inspires in men all the evils they cause one another, and which is the true source of honor.

With this well understood, I say that in our primitive state, in the veritable state of nature, egocentrism does not exist; for since each particular man regards himself as the only spectator who observes him, as the only being in the universe that takes an interest in him, as the only judge of his own merit, it is impossible that a sentiment which has its source in comparisons that he is not in a position to make could germinate in his soul. For the same reason, this man could not have either hatred or desire for revenge, passions which can arise only from the belief that offense has been received. And since what constitutes the offense is scorn or the intention to harm and not the harm, men who know neither how to appraise nor to compare themselves can do considerable violence to one another when it returns them some advantage for doing it, without ever offending one another. In a word, on seeing his fellow-men hardly otherwise than he would see animals of another species, each man can carry away the prey of the weaker or yield his own to the stronger, viewing these lootings as merely natural events, without the least stirring of insolence or resentment, and without any other passion but the sadness or the joy of a good or bad venture.

16. *(Page 65)* It is something extremely remarkable that, for the many years that the Europeans torment themselves in order to acclimate the savages of various countries to their lifestyle, they have not yet been able to win over a single one of them, not even by means of Christianity; for our missionaries sometimes turn them into Christians, but never into civilized men. Nothing can overcome the invincible repugnance they have against appropriating our mores and living in our way. If these poor savages are as unhappy as is alleged, by what inconceivable depravity of judgment do they constantly refuse to civilize themselves in imitation of us, or to learn to live happily among us; whereas one reads in a thousand places that the French and other Europeans have voluntarily taken refuge among those nations, and have spent their entire lives there, no longer able to leave so strange a lifestyle; and whereas we even see level-headed missionaries regret

with tenderness the calm and innocent days they have spent among those much scorned peoples? If one replies that they do not have enough enlightenment to make a sound judgment about their state and ours, I will reply that the reckoning of happiness is less an affair of reason than of sentiment. Moreover, this reply can be turned against us with still greater force; for there is a greater distance between our ideas and the frame of mind one needed to be in in order to conceive the taste which the savages find in their lifestyle, than between the ideas of savages and those that can make them conceive our lifestyle. In fact, after a few observations it is easy for them to see that all our labors are directed toward but two objects: namely, the conveniences of life for oneself and esteem among others. But what are the means by which we are to imagine the sort of pleasure a savage takes in spending his life alone amidst the woods, or fishing, or blowing into a sorry-looking flute, without ever knowing how to derive a single tone from it and without bothering himself to learn?

Savages have frequently been brought to Paris, London and other cities; people have been eager to display our luxury, our wealth, and all our most useful and curious arts. None of this has ever excited in them anything but a stupid admiration, without the least stirring of covetousness. I recall, among others, the story of a chief of some North Americans who was brought to the court of England about thirty years ago. A thousand things were made to pass before his eye in an attempt to give him some present that could please him, but nothing was found about which he seemed to care. Our weapons seemed heavy and cumbersome to him, our shoes hurt his feet, our clothes restricted him; he rejected everything. Finally, it was noticed that, having taken a wool blanket, he seemed to take some pleasure in wrapping it around his shoulders. You will agree at least, someone immediately said to him, on the usefulness of this furnishing? Yes, he replies, this seems to me to be nearly as good as an animal skin. However, he would not have said that, had he worn them both in the rain.

Perhaps someone will say to me that it is habit which, in attaching everyone to his lifestyle, prevents savages from realizing what is good in ours. And at that rate, it must at least appear quite extraordinary that habit has more force in maintaining the savages in the taste for their misery than the Europeans in the enjoyment of their felicity. But to give to this last objection a reply to which there is not a word to make in reply, without adducing all the young savages that people have tried in vain to civilize, without speaking of the Greenlanders and the inhabitants of Iceland, whom people have tried to raise and feed in Denmark, and all of whom sadness and despair caused to perish, whether from languor or in the sea when they attempted to regain their homeland by swimming back to it, I will be content to cite a single, well-documented example, which I give to the admirers of European civilization to examine.

"All the efforts of the Dutch missionaries at the Cape of Good Hope have never been able to convert a single Hottentot. Van der Stel, Governor of the Cape, having taken one from infancy, had raised him in the principles of the Christian religion and in the practice of the customs of Europe. He was richly clothed; he was taught several languages and his progress corresponded very closely to the care that was taken for his education. Having great hopes for his wit, the Governor sent him to the Indies with a commissioner general who employed him usefully in the affairs of the company. He returned to the Cape after the death of the commissioner. A few days after his return, on a visit he made to some of his Hottentot relatives, he made the decision to strip himself of his European dress in order to clothe himself with a sheepskin. He returned to the fort in this new outfit, carrying a bundle containing his old clothes, and, on presenting them to the Governor, he made the following speech to him: *Please, sir, be so kind as to pay heed to the fact that I forever renounce this clothing. I also renounce the Christian religion for the rest of my life. My resolution is to live and die in the religion, ways and customs of my ancestors. The only favor I ask of you is that you let me keep the necklace and cutlass I am wearing. I will keep them for love of you.* Thereupon, without waiting for Van der Stel's reply, he escaped by taking flight and was never seen again at the Cape." *Histoire des Voyages,* Vol. V, p. 175.

17. *(Page 68)* One could raise against me the objection that, in such a disorder, men, instead of willfully murdering one another, would have dispersed, had there been no limits to their dispersion. But first, these limits would at least have been those of the world. And if one thinks about the excessive population that results from the state of nature, one will judge that the earth in that state would not have taken long to be covered with men thus forced to keep together. Besides, they would have dispersed, had the evil been rapid, and had it been an overnight change. But they were born under the yoke; they were in the habit of carrying it when they felt its weight, and they were content to wait for the opportunity to shake it off. Finally, since they were already accustomed to a thousand conveniences which forced them to keep together, dispersion was no longer so easy as in the first ages, when, since no one had need for anyone but himself, everyone made his decision without waiting for someone else's consent.

18. *(Page 70)* Marshal de V∗∗∗ related that, on one of his campaigns, when the excessive knavery of a provisions supplier had made the army suffer and complain, he gave him a severe dressing down and threatened to have him hanged. "This threat has no effect on me," the knave boldly replied to him, "and I am quite pleased to tell you that nobody hangs a man with a hundred thousand crowns at his disposal." I do not know how it happened, the Marshal added naïvely, but in fact he was not hanged, even though he deserved to be a hundred times over.

19. *(Page 77)* Distributive justice would still be opposed to this rigorous equality of the state of nature, if it were workable in civil society. And since all the members of the state owe it services proportionate to their talents and forces, the citizens for their part should be distinguished and favored in proportion to their services. It is in this sense that one must understand a passage of Isocrates, in which he praises the first Athenians for having known well how to distinguish which of the two sorts of equality was the more advantageous, one of which consists in portioning out indifferently to all citizens the same advantages, and the other in distributing them according to each one's merit. These able politicians, adds the orator, in banishing that unjust equality that makes no differentiation between wicked and good men, adhered inviolably to that equality which rewards and punishes each according to one's merit. But first, no society has ever existed, regardless of the degree of corruption they could have achieved, in which no differentiation between wicked and good men was made. And in the matter of mores, where the law cannot set a sufficiently precise measurement to serve as a rule for the magistrate, the law very wisely prohibits him from the judgment of persons, leaving him merely the judgment of actions, in order not to leave the fate or the rank of citizens to his discretion. Only mores as pure as those of the ancient Romans could withstand censors; such tribunals would soon have overturned everything among us. It is for public esteem to differentiate between wicked and good men. The magistrate is judge only of strict law [*droit*]; but the populace is the true judge of mores—an upright and even enlightened judge on this point, occasionally deceived but never corrupted. The ranks of citizens ought therefore to be regulated not on the basis of their personal merit, which would be to leave to the magistrate the means of making an almost arbitrary application of the law, but upon the real services which they render to the state and which lend themselves to a more precise reckoning.

DISCOURSE ON POLITICAL ECONOMY

Rousseau's third and least known Discourse, that on Political Economy, was first published in 1755, in the fifth volume of Diderot's Encyclopédie, *and appeared as a separate volume three years later. Once again, as in the great second Discourse—on the Origin of Inequality—Rousseau adverts to the creation of private property as a decisive moment in human history. But this third Discourse looks ahead far more than backward. In passage after passage, Rousseau foreshadows, sometimes in rather elementary form, principles and arguments he would state fully in his political masterpiece,* On the Social Contract, *published some seven years later. While the present Discourse contains some striking and persuasive proposals on taxation and public education, it is most profitably read as a kind of rehearsal for the* Social Contract—*for it suggests, in its references to the general will and to sovereignty, how long and how carefully Rousseau had meditated those crucial ideas for which he must remain a permanent fixture in the pantheon enshrining the leading political theorists of all time.*

P. G.

ECONOMY or OECONOMY, (*Moral and Political*). This word is derived from οἶκος, *house,* and νόμος, *law,* and originally signified merely the wise and legitimate government of the household for the common good of the entire family. The meaning of this term was later extended to the government of the large family which is the state. To distinguish these two usages, in the latter case it is called *general* or *political economy,* and in the former case it is called *domestic* or *private economy.* Only the first of these is the subject of this article. Regarding *domestic economy,* see FATHER OF THE FAMILY.

Even if there were as much similarity between the state and the family as many authors would have us believe, it would not follow as a consequence that the rules of conduct proper to one of these societies would be suitable to the other. They differ too much in size to be capable of being administered in the same fashion. Moreover, there will always be an extreme difference between domestic government, where the father can see everything for himself, and civil government, where the leader sees hardly anything unless through someone else's eyes. For things to become equal in this regard, the talents, force and all the faculties of the father would have to increase in proportion to the size of his family, and the soul of a powerful monarch would have to be, in comparison with that of an ordinary man, what the size of his empire is to that of the private individual's patrimony.

But how could the government of the state be similar to that of the family, whose basis is so different? With the father being physically stronger than his children, paternal power is reasonably said to be established by nature for as long as his help is needed by them. In the large family all of whose members are naturally equal, political authority, purely arbitrary as far as its establishment is conceived, can be founded only upon conventions, and the magistrate can command others only by virtue of the laws. The duties of the father are dictated to him by natural feelings, and in a manner that seldom allows him to be disobedient. Leaders have no such similar rule and are not really bound to the people except in regard to what they have promised to do for them and which the people can rightfully demand they carry out. Another even more important difference is that, since everything children have they receive from their father, it is obvious that all property rights belong to or emanate from him. It is quite the contrary in the case of the large family, where the general administration is established merely to assure private property, which is antecedent to it. The chief purpose of the entire household's labors is to maintain and increase the father's patrimony, so that he can someday disperse it among his children without reducing them to poverty. On the other hand, the wealth of the public treasury is merely a means—often very much misunderstood—of maintaining private individuals in peace and prosperity. In a word, the small family is destined to die off and to be dissolved someday into many other families; on the other hand, the large family was made to last forever in the same condition, whereas not only is it enough that the large family maintains itself, it is easily proved that any increase does it more harm than good.

For several reasons derived from the nature of things, in the family it is the father who should command. First, the authority of the father and mother ought not be equal; on the contrary, there must be a single government and when there are differences of opinion there must be one dominant voice which decides. Second, however slight we regard the handicaps that are peculiar to a wife, since they always occasion a period of inactivity for her, this is a sufficient reason for excluding her from this primacy. For when the balance is perfectly equal, a straw is enough to tip the scales. Moreover, a husband should oversee his wife's conduct, for it is important to him to be assured that the children he is forced to recognize and nurture belong to no one but himself. The wife, who has nothing like this to fear, does not have the same right over her husband. Third, children ought to obey their father—initially out of necessity, later out of gratitude. After having their needs met by him for half their lives, they ought to devote the other half to seeing to his needs. Fourth, as far as domestic servants are concerned, they too owe him their services in exchange for the livelihood he provides them, unless they cancel their arrangement once it ceases to be to their advantage. I say nothing here of slavery, since it is contrary to nature and no right can authorize it.

None of this is to be found in political society. Far from the leader's having a natural interest in the happiness of private individuals, it is not uncommon for him to seek his own happiness in the misery of others. If the magistracy is hereditary, often it is a child that is in command of men. If it is elective, a thousand inconveniences make themselves to be felt in the elections. In either case one loses all the advantages of paternity. Were you to have but one leader, you are at the discretion of a master who has no reason to love you. Were you to have several, you must endure both their tyranny and their disagreements. In short, abuses are inevitable and their consequences devastating in every society where the public interest and the laws have no natural force, and are constantly attacked by the personal interest and passions of the ruler and the members.

Although the functions of the father of a family and those of a chief magistrate ought to tend toward the same goal, their paths are so different, their duty and rights so unlike, that one cannot confound them without forming false ideas about the fundamental laws of society and without falling into errors that are fatal to the human race. In effect, though nature's voice is the best advice a good father could listen to in the fulfillment of his duty, for the magistrate it is merely a false guide which works constantly to divert him from his duties and which sooner or later leads to his downfall or to that of the state, unless he is restrained by the most sublime virtue. The only precaution necessary to the father of a family is that he protect himself from depravity and prevent his natural inclinations from becoming corrupt, whereas it is these very inclinations that corrupt the magistrate. To act properly, the former need only consult his heart; the latter becomes a traitor as soon as he listens to his. Even his own reason ought to be suspect to him, and the only rule he should follow is the public reason, which is the law. Thus nature has made a multitude of good fathers of families, but it is doubtful that, since the beginning of the world, human wisdom has ever produced ten men capable of governing their peers.

It follows from all I have just put forward that one has good reason to distinguish *public* from *private economy* and that, since the state has nothing in common with the family except the obligation their respective leaders bear to render each of them happy, the same rules of conduct could not be suitable to both. I thought these few lines would suffice to overturn the odious system that Sir [Robert] Filmer attempted to establish in a work entitled *Patriarcha*, to which two famous men have already done too much honor by writing books to refute it. Besides, this error is very old, since Aristotle himself saw fit to combat it with arguments which can be found in Book One of his *Politics*.

I ask my readers also to distinguish carefully between the *public economy* about which I have been speaking and which I call *government,* and the supreme authority which I call *sovereignty*. This distinction consists in the one having the right of legislation and, in certain cases, in placing an obligation on the very body of the nation, while the other has only executive power and can place an obligation only upon private individuals. See POLITICS and SOVEREIGNTY.

Permit me to use for a moment a common comparison, inaccurate in many respects, but useful to making myself better understood.

The body politic, taken individually, can be considered to be like a body that is organized, living and similar to that of a man. The sovereign power represents the head; the laws and customs are the brain, source of the nerves and seat of the understanding, the will and the senses, of which the judges and magistrates are the organs; the commerce, industry and agriculture are the mouth and stomach which prepare the common subsistence; the public finances are the blood that is discharged by a wise *economy,* performing the functions of the heart, in order to distribute nourishment and life throughout the body; the citizens are the body and members that make the machine move, live and work, and that cannot be harmed in any part without a painful impression immediately being transmitted to the brain, if the animal is in a state of good health.

The life of both is the *self* common to the whole, the reciprocal sensibility and the internal coordination of all the parts. What if this communication were to cease, if the formal unity were to disappear, and if contiguous parts were to be related to one another solely by their juxtaposition? The man is dead and the state is dissolved.

The body politic, therefore, is also a moral being which possesses a will; and this general will, which always tends toward the conservation and well-being of the whole and of each part, and which is the source of the laws, is for all the members of the state, in their relations both to one another and to the state, the rule of what is just and what is unjust. This, by the way, is a truth which shows how absurd many writers have been for regarding as theft the subtlety prescribed to the children of Sparta for obtaining their frugal meal, as if everything prescribed by law could fail to be lawful. See the word RIGHT for the source of this great and luminous principle, of which this article is an elucidation.

It is important to observe that this rule of justice, on a firm footing with all citizens, can be defective with regard to foreigners; and the reason for this is obvious. For the will of the state, however general it may be in relation to its members, is no longer so in relation to other states and to their members, but becomes for them a private and individual will which has its rule of justice in the law of nature, which enters equally into the principle established. For then the great city of the world becomes the political body whose law of nature is always the general will, and whose states and diverse peoples are merely private individuals.

From these same distinctions, applied to each political society and to its members, are derived the most universal and most secure rules on whose basis one could judge a government to be good or bad, and in general of the morality of all human actions.

Every political society is composed of other smaller and different societies, each of which has its interests and maxims. But these societies, which everyone perceives (since they have an external and authorized form), are not the only ones really existing in the state. All the private individuals who are united by a common interest make up as many others, permanent or transitory, whose force is no less real for being less apparent, and the proper observation of whose various relationships is the true knowledge of mores. It is all these tacit or formal associations which modify in so many ways the appearances of the public will by the influence of their will. The will of these particular societies always has two relations: for the members of the association it is the general will; for the large society it is a particular will, which is quite often found to be upright in the first respect and vice-ridden in the second. Someone could be a devout priest or a brave soldier or a zealous man of action but a bad citizen. A deliberation can be advantageous to the small community and quite pernicious to the large community. It is true that, since some particular societies are always subordinated to those which contain them, one should obey the latter rather than the former; the duties of the citizen take precedence over those of the senator, and those of the man over those of the citizen. But unfortunately private interest is always found in inverse proportion to duty, and it increases to the extent that the association becomes narrower and the commitment less sacred. This is irrefutable proof that the most general will is also always the most just, and that the voice of the populace is, in effect, the voice of God.

It does not thence follow that public deliberations are always equitable; they could fail to be so when it is a question of matters involving foreigners. I have stated the reason for this. Thus it is not possible for a well-governed republic to wage an unjust war. Nor is it any less impossible for the council of a democracy to pass bad decrees and to condemn the innocent. But this will never happen unless the populace is seduced by private interests which certain clever men have managed to substitute for those of the state by means of personal trust and eloquence. Then the public resolution will be one thing and the general will another. Please do not offer me the democracy of Athens as a counter-instance, because Athens was not really a democracy but a highly tyrannical aristocracy, governed by learned men and orators. Examine carefully what goes on in any deliberation and you will see that the general will is always for the common good; however, quite often there is a secret schism, a tacit confederation, which causes the natural disposition of the assembly to be lost sight of for the sake of private purposes. Then the social body really is divided into other bodies whose members take on a general will that is good and just as regards these new bodies, and bad as regards the whole from which each of them has cut itself off.

We see how easy it is to explain by means of these principles the apparent contradictions one notices in the conduct of many men who are filled with scruple and honor in some respects, while deceitful and unprincipled in others. They trample underfoot the most sacred duties and are faithful to the death to illegal commitments. Thus the most corrupt of men always pay some sort of homage to the public faith. Thus (as is noted in the article entitled RIGHT) even bandits, who are the enemies of virtue in the large society, worship something like virtue in their lairs.

In establishing the general will as the first principle of public *economy* and as the fundamental rule of government, I did not believe it necessary to examine seriously whether the magistrates belong to the populace or the populace to the magistrates, and whether in public affairs one should keep in mind the good of the state or that of the leaders. This question was decided long ago in one way by usage and in another by reason; and in general it would be great folly to hope that those who are in fact masters would prefer some interest other than their own. It would therefore be appropriate to divide public *economy* once again into popular and tyrannical. The former is that of every state where there reigns a unity of interest and will between the populace and the leaders. The latter necessarily exists wherever the government and the populace have different interests and, consequently, opposing wills. The maxims of the latter are inscribed at some length in the archives of history and in the satires of Machiavelli. The maxims of the former are found only in the writings of philosophers who dare to reclaim the rights of humanity.

I. The first and most important maxim of legitimate or popular government, that is to say, of a government that has the good of the populace for its object, is therefore, as I have said, to follow the general will in all things. But to follow the general will one must know it, and, above all, properly distinguish it from the private will, beginning with oneself: a distinction that is always most difficult to make and only the most sublime virtue is capable of shedding enough light on it. Since one must be free in order to will, another no less formidable difficulty is how to secure both the public liberty and the authority of the government. Examine the motives that have brought men, united by their mutual needs in the large society, to unite themselves more closely by means of civil societies. You will find no other motive than that of securing the goods, life and liberty of each member through the protection of all. For how can men be forced to defend the liberty of one of their number without infringing on the liberty of others? And how can the public needs be attended to without altering the private property of those who are forced to contribute to it? Whatever sophisms one uses to whitewash all this, it is certain that I am no longer free if someone can constrain my will, and that I am no longer master of my estate if someone else can get his hands on it. This difficulty, which must have seemed insurmountable, was removed with the first inspiration which taught man to imitate here below the immutable decrees of the divinity. By what inconceivable art could one have found the means to place men in subjection in order to make them free? To use the goods, the manual labor, even the very life of all its members in the service of the state without forcing them and without consulting them? To bind their will by their own consent? To force them to punish themselves when they do what they did not want to do? How is it possible that they obey and no one commands, that they serve and have no master, and yet are actually more free because, under what appears to be subjection, no one loses any of his liberty except what can be harmful to the liberty of another? These wonders are the work of the law. It is to the law alone that men owe justice and liberty. It is this healthy tool of the will of all which reestablishes as a civil right the natural equality among men. This is the heavenly way that dictates to each citizen the precepts of public reason, and teaches him to act in accordance with the maxims of his own judgment and not to be at odds with himself. It is also with this voice alone that leaders should speak when they command; for no sooner does a man claim, independently of the laws, to subject another to his private will, than he at once leaves the civil state, and, in relation to the other man, places himself in the pure state of nature, where obedience is never prescribed except out of necessity.

The leader's most pressing concern, as well as his most indispensable duty, is therefore to keep watch over the observance of the laws of which he is the minister, and upon which all his authority is based. If he must make others observe them, then a fortiori he ought to observe them himself, since he enjoys all their favor. For his example is so powerful that even if the populace were willing to allow him to free himself from the yoke of the law, he ought to avoid taking advantage of such a dangerous prerogative—a prerogative others would in turn try to usurp, and often to his disadvantage. At bottom, since all the commitments of society are reciprocal in nature, it is impossible to put oneself outside the law without renouncing its advantages, and no one owes anything to someone who claims to owe nothing to anyone. For the same reason, no exception from the law will ever be accorded for any reason whatever in a well policed government. Even the citizens who are most deserving of something from the homeland should be rewarded with honors but never with privileges. For the republic is on the verge of its ruin at the very moment someone can think it is a fine thing not to obey the laws. But if the nobility or the military or some other order within the state were ever to adopt such a maxim, everything would be irretrievably lost.

The power of the laws depends even more on the ministers' wisdom rather than on their severity, and the public will draws its greatest weight from the reason which dictated it. It is for this reason that Plato regards it as a very important precaution always to place at the beginning of an edict a well-reasoned preamble which shows their justice and usefulness. In effect, the first of the laws is to respect the laws. Harshness of punishments is merely a vain expedient dreamed up by small minds to substitute terror for the respect they cannot obtain. It has always been remarked that the countries where punishments are the most severe are also those where they are the most frequent, so that the cruelty of punishments is indicative of nothing but the multitude of lawbreakers, and when everything is punished with equal severity, those culpable are forced to commit crimes to escape punishment for their faults.

But although the government is not the master of the law, it is not an insignificant thing to be its guarantor and to have a thousand ways of making people love it. The talent for reigning consists of nothing else but this. When one has force at hand, there is no art to making everyone tremble and not even very much to winning over people's hearts, for experience has long taught the populace to be deeply grateful to its leaders for all the evils they do not do to it and to worship them when not despised by its leaders. An imbecile can, like anyone else, punish crimes; the real statesman knows how to prevent them. He extends his venerable rule over wills even more than over actions. If he could bring it about that everyone behaved correctly, he himself would have nothing left to do, and the masterpiece of his works would be to remain at his ease. At least it is certain that the greatest talent of leaders is to disguise their power in order to render it less odious and to manage the state so peacefully that it seems to have no need of managers.

I conclude therefore that just as the legislator's first duty is to conform the laws to the general will, the first rule of the public *economy* is that the administration should be in conformity with the laws. This will be sufficient even to keep the state from being poorly governed, if the legislator has paid the attention he should to everything that is required by the locale, climate, soil, mores, and surrounding areas, and all the relationships he had to institute which were peculiar to the populace. This is not to say that there does not still remain an infinity of administrative and *economic* details that are left to the wisdom of the government. But it always has two infallible rules for behaving correctly in these occasions. The one is the spirit of the law which should help decide cases the law could not have foreseen. The other is the general will, source and supplement of all the laws and which ought always be consulted for want of them. How, I will be asked, does one go about knowing the general will in the situation where it is not expressed? Must the whole nation be assembled at each unforeseen event? It ought the less to be assembled, because it is not sure its decision would be the expression of the general will; because this means is unworkable for a large populace; because it is rarely necessary when the government is well intentioned. For the leaders know very well that the general will is always on the side most favorable to the public interest, that is, the most equitable, so that it is necessary simply to be just to be assured of following the general will. Often, when this is flouted too openly, it makes its presence known despite the terrible restraint of the public authority. I look as close to home as I can for examples to follow in such a case. In China, the prince has as an unshaking maxim that he should side against his officials in every dispute that rises between them and the populace. Is bread expensive in one province? The intendant of that province is thrown in prison. Is there a civil disturbance in another? The governor is dismissed and each mandarin answers with his life for all the unpleasantness that takes place in his department. This is not to say that there is no subsequent examination of the affair in a regular trial. But long experience has made the judgment thus to be anticipated. One rarely has any injustice to rectify in this; and the emperor, convinced that public clamor never arises without cause, always discerns among the seditious cries he punishes, some just grievances that he remedies.

It is no mean feat to have made peace and order reign in all parts of the republic; it is no small matter that the state is tranquil and the law is respected. But if one does nothing more, the government would have a difficult time making itself obeyed if it limits itself to obedience. If it is good to know how to use men as they are, it is better still to turn them into what one needs them to be. The most absolute authority is that which penetrates to the inner part of a man and is exerted no less on his will than on his actions. It is certain that in the long run people are what the government makes them. Warriors, citizens, men when it so wishes; rabble and riff-raff when it so pleases. And every prince who belittles his subjects dishonors himself by showing that he did not know how to turn them into something worthy of respect. Therefore train men if you want to command them. If you want the laws obeyed, make them beloved, so that to get men to do what they should, they need only consider that they ought to do it. That was the great art of governments of old, in those remote times when philosophers gave laws to the peoples and merely used their authority to make them wise and happy. From this came the many sumptuary laws, the many regulations concerning mores, the many public maxims accepted or rejected with the greatest of care. Even the tyrants did not forget this important part of administration, and they took as many pains in corrupting the mores of their slaves as did the magistrates in correcting the mores of their fellow citizens. But our modern governments, which are under the impression they have done all there is to do when they have raised money, never imagine it to be either necessary or possible to go that far.

II. The second essential rule of public economy is no less important than the first. Do you want the general will to be accomplished? Make all private wills be in conformity with it. And since virtue is merely this conformity of the private to the general will, in a word, make virtue reign.

If politicians were less blinded by their ambitions, they would see how impossible it is for any establishment whatever to act in accordance with the law of duty. They would be aware of the fact that the greatest support for public authority lies in the hearts of the citizens, and that nothing can take the place of mores in the maintenance of the government. Not only is it just men of good character who know how to administer the laws, but it is essentially only upright men who know how to obey them. Anyone who gets the upper hand on remorse will not put off defying punishments which are less severe, less continuous forms of chastisement and from which there is at least some hope of escape. And whatever precautions one takes, those who are on the lookout for impunity in order to do wrong hardly lack the means of eluding the law or escaping a penalty. Then, since all private interests are joined together against the general interest which is no longer that of anyone, public vices have greater power to enervate the laws than the laws have to repress vices. And the corruption of the populace and the leaders at length extends to the government, however wise it may be. The worst of all abuses is to obey the laws in appearance only to transgress them with security. Eventually the best laws become the most baneful. It would have been a hundred times better had they never existed. It would be one resource that would be available when nothing else remains. In such a situation it is pointless to add edicts upon edicts, regulations upon regulations. All that seems merely to introduce additional abuse without correcting the abuses with which one began. The more you multiply laws, the more contemptible you make them. All the overseers you put in place are merely the latest crop of lawbreakers, who are destined either to join in with the veteran lawbreakers or to do their pillaging on their own. In time the price of virtue becomes that of brigandage. Men of the vilest character are the ones held in the highest regard. The greater they are the more contemptible they are. Their infamy is manifest in their dignities, and they are dishonored by their honors. If they buy off the votes of leaders or the protection of women, it is so that they in their turn can sell justice, duty and the state. And the populace, which fails to see that its own vices are the primary cause of its troubles, mutters and cries, groaning: "All my troubles come from no one but those I pay to protect me."

At times like this, in place of the voice of duty which no longer speaks in men's hearts, the leaders are forced to substitute the cry of terror or the lure of an apparent interest with which they deceive their dependents. At times like this, one must have recourse to all the disgusting little tricks they call "state maxims" and "cabinet mysteries." Whatever vigor there remains to the government is used by its members to bring down and to replace one another, while day-to-day business continues to be neglected or is dealt with only to the extent that personal interest demands it and in accordance with its dictates. Finally, the entire skill of these great politicians consists in so mesmerizing the eyes of those whose help they need, that each individual believes he is working for his own interest while he is working for *theirs*. I say "theirs," if indeed it actually is the real interest of the leaders to annihilate the populace in order to place it in subjection and to destroy their own estate in order to secure its possession.

But when the citizens love their duty, and when those entrusted with public authority sincerely apply themselves to nurturing this love through their example and efforts, all difficulties vanish and administration takes on an easiness which enables it to dispense with that shady art whose baseness constitutes its entire mystery. Those ambitious minds, so dangerous and so admired, all the great ministers whose glory is mingled with the people's troubles, are not missed any more. Public mores supplant the genius of the leaders; and the more virtue reigns the less talents are needed. Ambition itself is better served by duty rather than by usurpation. Convinced that its leaders work exclusively for its happiness, the populace exempts them by its deference from working to strengthen their power. And history shows us in a thousand ways that the authority the populace accords to those it loves and by whom it is loved is a hundred times more absolute than all the tyranny of usurpers. This does not mean that the government should fear using its power, but that it should use it only in a legitimate manner. There are a thousand examples in history of ambitious or pusillanimous leaders who were ruined either by softness or pride, but there are no examples of someone for whom things went badly simply because he was equitable. But negligence should not be confused with moderation, nor mildness with weakness. To be just one must be severe. Putting up with wickedness when one has the right and the power to repress it is being wicked oneself.

It is not enough to say to the citizens: be good. They must be taught to be so; and example itself, which is in this respect the first lesson, is not the only means to be used. Love of country is the most effective, for as I have already said, every man is virtuous when his private will is in conformity with the general will in all things, and we willingly want what is wanted by the people we love.

It seems that the sentiment of humanity evaporates and weakens in being extended over the entire world, and that we cannot be affected by the calamities in Tartary or Japan the way we are by those of a European people. Interest and commiseration must somehow be limited and restrained to be active. For since this inclination in us can be useful only to those with whom we have to live, it is a good thing that the humanity concentrated among fellow citizens takes on a new force through the habit of seeing each other and through the common interest that unites them. It is certain that the greatest miracles of virtue have been produced by the love of country. In joining together the force of self-love and all the beauty of virtue, this sweet and lively sentiment takes on an energy that, without disfiguring it, makes it the most heroic of all the passions. This is the passion that produced so many immortal actions whose radiance dazzles our feeble eyes, and so many great men whose ancient virtues were thought to be fables once the love of country became the object of derision. We should not find this surprising. The ecstasies of tender hearts appear utterly fanciful to anyone who has not felt them. And the love of country, a hundred times more ardent and delightful than that of a mistress, likewise cannot be conceived except by being felt. But it is easy to observe, in all the hearts it inflames and in all the actions it inspires, that fiery and sublime ardor which the purest virtue is lacking when it is separated from the love of country. Let us dare to compare Socrates himself to Cato. The one was more a philosopher; the other more a citizen. Athens was already lost, and Socrates had no other country but the whole world. Cato always carried his country in the bottom of his heart. He lived only for it and could not outlive it. The virtue of Socrates is that of the wisest of men. But compared with Caesar and Pompey, Cato seems like a god among mortals. One teaches a few individuals, combats the sophists and dies for the truth. The other defends the state, liberty and the laws against the conquerors of the world, and finally leaves the earth when he no longer sees a country to serve. A worthy student of Socrates would be the most virtuous of his contemporaries. A worthy imitator of Cato would be the greatest. The virtue of the first would constitute his happiness; the second would seek his happiness in that of others. We ought to be taught by the one and led by the other, and that alone would decide our preference. For a people consisting of wise men has never been produced; however, it is not impossible to make a people happy.

Do we want people to be virtuous? Let us begin then by making them love their country. But how can they love it, if their country means nothing more to them than it does to foreigners, allotting to them only what it cannot refuse to anyone? It would be worse still if they did not enjoy even civil welfare, and if their goods, their life or their liberty were at the discretion of powerful men, without it being possible or permitted for them to dare to invoke the laws. In such circumstances, subjected to the duties of the civil state without enjoying even the rights of the state of nature and without being able to use their strength to defend themselves, they would as a result be in the worst condition in which free men can find themselves, and the word "country" could have only an odious or ridiculous meaning for them. There is no point to believing that one can strike or cut off an arm without pain being transmitted to the head. And it is no more believable that the general will would permit a member of the state, whoever he might be, to injure or destroy another member than that the fingers of a man in his right mind would put out his eyes. Individual welfare is so closely linked to the public confederation that, were it not for the attention one should pay to human frailty, this convention would be dissolved by right if just one citizen were to perish who could have been saved, if just one citizen were wrongly held in prison, and if a single litigation were to be lost because of an obvious injustice. For when these fundamental conventions are violated, it is no longer apparent what right or what interest could maintain the populace in the social union, unless it is restrained by force alone, which brings about the dissolution of the civil state.

In effect, is it not the commitment of the body of the nation to provide for the maintenance of the humblest of its members with as much care as for that of all others? And is the welfare of a citizen any less the common cause than the welfare of the entire state? If someone were to tell us that it is good that one person should perish for all, I would admire this saying when it comes from the lips of a worthy and virtuous patriot who dedicates himself willingly and out of duty to die for the welfare of his country. But if this means that the government is permitted to sacrifice an innocent person for the welfare of the multitude, I hold this maxim to be one of the most despicable that tyranny has ever invented, the most false that one might propose, the most dangerous one might accept, and the most directly opposed to the fundamental laws of society. For far from it being the case that one individual should die for all, all have committed their goods and their lives in defense of each of them, so that individual weakness would always be protected by public force, and each member by the entire state. After conjuring up an image of the attrition of the people, one after another, press the partisans of this maxim to explain better what they mean by *the body of the state,* and you will see that eventually they will reduce it to a small number of men who are not the people, but the officers of the people, and who, having obliged themselves by a personal oath to perish for its welfare, maintain they prove by this that it is the people's place to die for them.

Does anyone want to find examples of the protection that the state owes its members, and of the respect it owes their persons? These examples are to be found only among the world's most illustrious and courageous nations, and it is exclusively among free peoples where one knows what a man is worth. It is commonly known how great was the perplexity in which the whole republic in Sparta found itself, when there arose the question of punishing a guilty citizen. In Macedonia, a human life was such an important matter that, in all his grandeur, Alexander, that powerful monarch, would not have dared to put to death in cold blood a Macedonian criminal unless the accused had appeared to defend himself before his fellow citizens and had been condemned by them. But the Romans were preeminent among all the peoples of the earth for the government's deference toward private individuals and for its scrupulous attention to respecting the inviolable rights of all the members of the state. Nothing was as sacred as the life of the simple citizens. There needed to be no less than the assembly of the entire people in order to condemn one of them. Neither the senate itself nor the consuls, in all their majesty, had the right to do this. And among the most powerful people in the world the crime and punishment of a citizen was a public affliction. It also appeared so harsh to shed blood for any crime whatever, that by the *Lex Porcia* the death penalty converted to exile for all those who wished to outlive the loss of so sweet a country. Everything in Rome and in the armies betokened that love of fellow citizens for one another, and that respect for the Roman name which stirred up the courage and animated the virtue of whoever had the honor to bear it. The hat of a citizen freed from slavery, the civic crown of him who had saved the life of another: these were things that were viewed with the greatest pleasure in the midst of the celebrations of their military triumphs. And it is worth noting that of the crowns with which in time of war one honors noble actions, only the civic crown and that of the victors were made of grass and leaves, all the rest being made of gold. Thus it was that Rome was virtuous and became the mistress of the world. Ambitious leaders! A shepherd governs his dogs and his flocks, and he is but the humblest of men. If it is a fine thing to command, it is when those who obey us can honor us. Therefore respect your fellow citizens and you will make yourselves respectable. Respect liberty and your power will increase daily. Never go beyond your rights, and eventually they will be limitless.

Let the homeland, therefore, show itself as the common mother of all citizens. Let the advantages they enjoy in their homeland endear it to them. Let the government leave them a large enough part of the public administration so that they can feel that they are at home. And let the laws be in their sight merely the guarantees of the common liberty. These rights, fine as they all are, belong to all men. But without appearing to attack them directly, the bad will of the leaders easily reduces their effect to nothing. The law that is abused at the same time serves the powerful as an offensive weapon and as a shield against the weak, and the pretext of the public good is always the most dangerous scourge of the people. What is most necessary and perhaps the most difficult in the government is rigorous integrity in dispensing justice to all and especially in protecting the poor against the tyranny of the rich. The greatest evil is already done when there are poor people to defend and rich ones to keep in check. It is only at intermediate levels of wealth that the full force of the laws is exerted. Laws are equally powerless against the treasures of the rich and against the wretched state of the poor. The first eludes them; the second escapes them. The one breaks the webbing and the other slips through.

It is one of the most important items of business for the government to prevent extreme inequality of fortunes, not by appropriating treasures from their owners, but by denying everyone the means of acquiring them, and not by building hospitals for the poor but by protecting citizens from becoming poor. Men unequally distributed over the territory and crowded into one place while other areas are underpopulated; arts of pleasure and pure industry favored over useful and demanding crafts; agriculture sacrificed to commerce; the publican made necessary by the bad administration of state funds; finally, venality pushed to such excess that esteem is measured in gold coins and the virtues themselves are sold for money: such are the most readily apparent causes of opulence and poverty, of the substitution of private interest for the public interest, of the mutual hatred of citizens, of their indifference to the common cause, of the corruption of the people, and of the enfeebling of all of governmental power. Such, as a consequence, are the ills that are difficult to treat once they make themselves felt, but which a wise administration ought to prevent in order to maintain, along with good mores, respect for the laws, love of country and the vitality of the general will.

But all these precautions will be insufficient without going further still. I end this part of the public *economy* where I ought to have started it. A country cannot subsist without liberty, nor can liberty without virtue, nor can virtue without citizens. You will have everything if you train citizens; without this you will merely have wicked slaves, beginning with the leaders of the state. But training citizens is not to be accomplished in one day, and turning them into men requires that they be taught as children. Somebody will say to me that anyone who has men to govern should not seek outside their nature a perfection of which they are incapable, that he should not desire to destroy their passions, and that the execution of such a project should be no more desirable than it is possible. I will agree more strongly with all of this because a man who had no passion would certainly be a very bad citizen. But one must agree that even though men cannot be taught to love nothing, it is not impossible for them to learn to love one object more than another and what is truly beautiful more than what is deformed. If, for example, they are trained early enough never to consider their own persons except in terms of being related to the body of the state, and not to perceive their own existence except as part of the state's existence, they will eventually come to identify themselves in some way with this larger whole, to feel themselves to be members of the country, to love it with that exquisite sentiment that every isolated man feels only for himself, to elevate their soul perpetually toward this great object, and thus to transform into a sublime virtue this dangerous disposition from which arises all our vices. Not only does philosophy demonstrate the possibility of these new directions, but history furnishes us with a thousand striking examples. If they are so rare among us, it is because no one is concerned about whether there are any citizens, and still less does anyone give any thought to take steps early enough to train them. It is too late to alter our natural inclinations when they have taken their course and habit has been joined with self-love. It is too late to draw us out of ourselves, once the *human self* concentrated in our hearts has acquired that disreputable activity which absorbs all virtue and constitutes the life of meanspirited people. How could love of country develop in the midst of so many other passions which choke it? And what is left for fellow citizens of a heart already dividing its affections among greed, a mistress and vanity?

It is from the first moment of life that one must learn to deserve to live; and since at birth one shares the rights of citizens, the moment of our own birth should be the beginning of the exercise of our duties. If there are laws for those of mature age, there should also be some for the very young which teach them to obey others. And since each man's reason cannot be allowed to be the sole arbiter of his duties, a fortiori the education of children cannot be abandoned to the lights and prejudices of their fathers, since it is of even more importance to the state than it is to their fathers. For according to the natural course of things, the death of the father often strips him of the last fruits of this education, but sooner or later the country feels its effects. The state remains; the family dissolves. Now if the public authority, in taking the fathers' place and charging itself with this important function, acquires their rights by fulfilling their duties, the fathers have that much less reason to complain, because strictly speaking, in this regard, they are merely changing a name, and will have in common, under the name "citizens," the same authority over their children they exercised separately under the name "fathers," and will be obeyed no less well when they speak in the name of the law than they were when they spoke in the name of nature. Public education under the rules prescribed by the government and under the magistrates put in place by the sovereign, is therefore one of the fundamental maxims of popular or legitimate government. If children are raised in common and in the bosom of equality, if they are imbued with the laws of the state and the maxims of the general will, if they are instructed to respect them above all things, if they are surrounded by examples and objects that constantly speak to them of the tender mother who nourishes them, of the love she bears for them, of the inestimable benefits they receive from her, and in turn of the debt they owe her, doubtlessly they thus will learn to cherish one another as brothers, never to want anything but what the society wants, never to substitute the actions of men and of citizens for the sterile and vain babbling of sophists, and to become one day the defenders and the fathers of the country whose children they will have been for so long.

I will not discuss the magistrates destined to preside over this education, which certainly is the state's most important business. Clearly, if such marks of public confidence were lightly granted, if this sublime function were not, for those who had honorably fulfilled all the others, the reward for their labors, the honorable and sweet repose of their old age and the high point of all their honors, the entire undertaking would be useless and the education unsuccessful. For wherever the lesson is unsupported by authority, or the precept by example, instruction remains fruitless, and virtue itself loses its influence in the mouth of him who does not practice it. But let the illustrious warriors bent under the weight of their laurels preach courage; let upright magistrates, whitened in the wearing of purple and in service at the tribunals, teach justice. Both of these groups will thus train virtuous successors and will transmit from age to age to the generations that follow the experience and talents of leaders, the courage and virtue of citizens and the emulation common to all of living and dying for one's country.

I know of but three peoples who in an earlier era practiced public education, namely, the Cretans, the Lacedemonians, and the ancient Persians. Among all three it was the greatest success and brought about marvels among the latter two. Since the time the world was divided into nations too large to be governed well, this method has not been practicable. And other reasons the reader can easily see have also prevented it from being tried by any modern people. It is quite remarkable that the Romans were able to do without it. But Rome was for five hundred years a continual miracle that the world cannot hope to see again. The virtue of the Romans, engendered by the horror of tyranny and the crimes of tyrants and by an inborn love of country, made all their homes into as many schools for citizens. And the unlimited power of fathers over their children placed so much severity in private enforcement that the father, more feared than the magistrates, was the censor of mores and the avenger of laws in his domestic tribunal.

In this way an attentive and well-intentioned government, constantly vigilant to maintain or restore love of country and good mores among the people, anticipates far in advance the evils that sooner or later result from citizens' indifference to the fate of the republic, and restricts within narrow limits that personal interest which so isolates private individuals that the state is weakened by their power and has nothing to hope for from their good will. Anywhere the populace loves its country, respects its laws and lives simply, little else remains to do to make it happy. And in public administration, where fortune plays less of a role than it does in the lot of private individuals, wisdom is so close to happiness that these two objects are confounded.

III. It is not enough to have citizens and to protect them; it is also necessary to give some thought to their subsistence. And seeing to the public needs is an obvious consequence of the general will, and the third essential duty of the government. This duty is not, as should be apparent, to fill the granaries of private individuals and to exempt these people from working, but rather to maintain abundance so within their reach that to acquire it, labor is always necessary and never useless. It also extends to all the operations regarding the preservation of the public treasury and the expenditures of the public administration. Thus, after having discussed the general *economy* in relation to the government of persons, it remains for us to consider it in relation to the administration of goods.

This part offers no fewer difficulties to resolve or contradictions to overcome than the preceding one. Certainly the right to property is the most sacred of all the citizens' rights, and more important in certain respects than liberty itself, either because it is more intimately linked with the preservation of life, or because, being easier to usurp and more difficult to defend than one's person, more respect needs to be given to what can more easily be stolen, or finally because property is the true foundation of civil society and the true guarantee of the citizens' commitments. For if goods were not answerable for persons, nothing would be so easy as eluding one's duties and scoffing at the laws. On the other hand, it is no less certain that the maintenance of the state and of the government demands costs and expenditures. And since anyone granting the end cannot refuse the means, it follows that the members of the society should contribute their goods toward its preservation. Moreover, it is difficult on the one hand to maintain the security of the property of private individuals without attacking it on the other. And it is impossible for all the regulations bearing on inheritance, wills, and contracts not to restrict the citizens in certain respects regarding the disposition of their estate, and consequently regarding their right to property.

But besides what I have already said about the unanimity which reigns between the authority of the law and the liberty of the citizen, there is, in relation to the disposition of goods, an important point to be made which eliminates several difficulties. It is, as Pufendorf has shown, that by the nature of the right to property, it does not extend beyond the life of the property owner, and the moment a man dies his estate no longer belongs to him. Thus, prescribing to him the conditions under which he can dispose of them is actually less an apparent alteration of his right than it is a real extension of it.

In general, although the institution of the laws which govern the power of private individuals in the disposition of their own estate belongs only to the sovereign, the spirit of the laws which the government must follow in carrying them out is that, from father to son and from relative to relative, the family's goods should leave the family and be alienated as little as possible. There is good reason for this in favor of children, to whom the right to property would be quite useless, were the father to leave them nothing, and who, moreover, having often contributed by their labor to the acquisition of the father's goods, are associated in their own right with his right. But another reason, more remote and no less important, is that nothing is more baneful to mores and to the republic than continual changes of status and fortune among the citizens, changes that are the proof and the source of a thousand disorders which overturn and confuse everything, and because of which neither those who were raised for one thing and find themselves destined for another nor those who rise nor those who fall can adopt the maxims or the lights suitable to their new status, and much less fulfill its duties. I turn now to the matter of public finances.

If the populace were to govern itself and there were nothing interposed between the administration of the state and the citizens, they would have to assess themselves on occasion, in proportion to the public needs and the abilities of private individuals. And since no one would ever lose sight of the payment or the use of funds, neither fraud nor abuse could slip into the management of them. The state would never be weighed down with debts, nor would the populace be crushed by taxes; or at least the assurance of how it would be used would console the people for hardship of the tax. But things cannot happen this way; and however limited a state may be, the civil society is always too populous to be capable of being governed by all its members. Public funds must necessarily pass through the hands of the leaders who all have over and above the interest of the state, their own private interest, which is not the last to be heard. The populace, for its part, perceiving the leaders' greed and ridiculous expenditures more than public needs, grumbles about seeing itself despoiled of necessity to furnish someone else with superfluities. And when once these manoeuvres have embittered it to a certain degree, the most honorable administration would utterly fail to reestablish confidence. In such circumstances, if contributions are voluntary, they produce nothing. If they are forced, they are illegitimate. And the difficulty of a just and wise *economy* lies in the cruel alternatives of allowing the state to perish or attacking the sacred right to property which is its underpinning.

The first thing to be done by the founder of the republic, after the establishment of the laws, is to find a sufficient fund for the maintenance of the magistrates and other officers, and for all public expenditures. This fund is called *aerarium* or *fisc,* if it consists of money, and *public domain,* if it consists of lands. And the latter is far preferable to the former for reasons that are not hard to see. Anyone who has reflected enough on this matter could hardly be of any other opinion than that of Bodin, who views the public domain as the most upright and the most secure of all the means of providing for the needs of the state. It is worth noting that Romulus' first concern in the division of lands was to set aside a third of the land for this use. I confess that it is not impossible for the proceeds of a badly administered state to be reduced to nothing. But it is not of the essence of the domain to be administered poorly.

Prior to any use of that fund, it ought to be assigned or accepted by the assembly of the people or the estates of the country, which should then determine its use. After this solemnity which renders this fund inalienable, it changes its nature, as it were, and its revenues become so sacred that diverting the least amount to the detriment of its destination is not only the most infamous of all thefts but a crime of high treason. It is a great dishonor for Rome that the integrity of the quaestor Cato had been a subject of conversation, and that an emperor, on rewarding a singer's talent with a few crowns, needed to add that the money came from his family's estate and not from the state's. But if there are not many like Galba, where will we find Catos? And once vice is no longer a cause for dishonor, what leaders will be scrupulous enough to refrain from getting their hands on the public funds left to their discretion, and not eventually fool themselves by pretending to confuse their vain and scandalous dissipations with the glory of the state, and the means of extending their authority with those of increasing its power? It is above all in this delicate part of the administration that virtue is the only effective instrument, and that the integrity of the magistrate is the only restraint capable of containing his greed. Books and all the ledgers of managers seem less to reveal their infidelities than to cover them up. And prudence is never as prompt at imagining new precautions as knaves are at eluding them. Therefore forget about the ledgers and papers, and place the finances in faithful hands; this is the only way to have them faithfully administered.

Once the public fund is established, the leaders of the state are rightfully its administrators, for this administration constitutes a part of the government, always essential, though not always equally so. Its influence increases in proportion to the decrease of the influence of the other parts of the government. One could say that a government has reached its final degree of corruption when the only thing left of its sinews is money. For since every government constantly tends toward diminution, this reason alone shows why no state can subsist if its revenues do not constantly increase.

The first experience of the necessity of this argument is also the first sign of the interior disorder of the state. And the wise administrator, in giving thought to finding money in order to see to present need, does not neglect to seek the distant cause of this new need, just as a sailor, on seeing water flood his vessel, does not forget, while working the pumps, to take steps to find and plug the leak.

From this rule flows the most important maxim of the administration of finances, which is to work with much greater care to prevent needs than to augment revenues. However diligent one might be, help that comes only after the misfortune took place, and more slowly, always leaves the state in distress. While one gives thought to the remedy for one problem, another problem is already making itself felt, and the resources themselves produce new difficulties. Thus in the end the nation is thrown into debt, the populace is downtrodden, the government loses all its vigor and it spends a great deal of money doing not much of anything. I believe it was from this great and well established maxim that the marvels of ancient governments flowed, which did more with their parsimony than ours do with all their treasures. And it is perhaps from this that the standard meaning of the word *economy* is derived, which denotes more the wise management of what one has, than the means of acquiring what one does not have.

Independently of the public domain, which remits to the state in proportion to the probity of those who supervise it, were one to have had sufficient knowledge of the whole force of the general administration, especially when it is limited to legitimate means, one would be astonished at the resources leaders have for anticipating all the public needs without touching the goods of private individuals. Since they are the masters of the state's entire commerce, nothing is easier for them than to direct it in a manner that provides for everything, often without them appearing to have been involved. The distribution of commodities, money and merchandise in just proportions according to time and place is the true secret of finances, and the source of their riches, provided those who administer them know how to be far-sighted enough and on occasion to take an apparent present loss so as really to obtain immense profits at some time in the distant future. When one sees a government paying duties instead of receiving them for the export of grain in years of plenty and for its import in years of scarcity, one needs to have such facts before one's eyes to think them true; and they would have merited being classed with novels if they had happened long ago. Suppose that, to prevent scarcity in bad years, one were to propose the establishment of public warehouses. In many countries, would not the maintenance of so useful an establishment serve as a pretext for new taxes? In Geneva, such granaries, established and maintained by a wise administration, are a public resource in bad years and the state's chief revenue at all times. *Alit et ditat* [*it nourishes and enriches*] is the fine and just inscription one reads on the facade of the building. To show here the economic system of a good government, I have often turned my eyes toward the wisdom and happiness I would like to see reign in every country.

If one examines how the needs of a state grow, one will find that this often arises in the same way as do those of private individuals: less by a true necessity than by an increase in useless desires, and that expenditures are increased for the sole reason of having a pretext for increasing income. Thus, the state would occasionally gain from not being rich, and such apparent wealth is essentially more burdensome than poverty itself. It is true one can hope to hold peoples in a stricter dependence by giving them with one hand what one has taken away from them with the other, and this was the style of politics Joseph used with the Egyptians. But this vain sophism is all the more fatal to the state in that the money does not return to the same hands it left. Such maxims only serve to enrich the idle with spoils taken from useful men.

The taste for conquests is one of the most obvious and dangerous causes of this increase. This taste, often engendered by another sort of ambition than the one it seems to proclaim, is not always what it appears to be, and its true motive is not the seeming desire to increase the nation but rather the hidden desire to increase the authority of the leaders at home, with the help of the increase in the size of the troops and under the cover of the diversion created in the minds of citizens by wartime objectives.

What is at least very certain is that nothing is as oppressed or as miserable as conquering peoples, and even their successes serve only to increase their miseries. Even if history did not teach us this, reason would suffice to show us that the larger a state is, the heavier and more burdensome will its expenditures become. For all the provinces are required to furnish their share of the expenses of the general administration, and, in addition, each province is required to spend the same amount for its own particular administration that it would if it were independent. Add to this the fact that all fortunes are made in one place and consumed in another. This eventually upsets the equilibrium of production and consumption, impoverishing a great deal of the country to enrich a single town.

Another source of the increase in public needs is linked to the preceding one. There may come a time when the citizens, no longer considering themselves interested in the common cause, would cease to be the defenders of the homeland, and when the magistrates would prefer to command mercenaries rather than free men, if only to use the former at a suitable time and place to subjugate the latter more effectively. Such was the state of Rome at the end of the Republic and under the emperors. For all the victories of the first Romans, just like those of Alexander, had been won by brave citizens who knew how to give their blood to their country in time of need, but never sold it. Marius was the first who, in the Jugurthine War, dishonored the legions by introducing free men, vagabonds and other mercenaries. Having become enemies of the peoples whom they were assigned to make happy, the tyrants established regular standing armies, in appearance to contain foreigners and in actual fact to oppress the inhabitants. To raise these troops, farmers had to be taken away from their land; the lack of their services decreased the quality of the provisions, and maintaining these troops required the imposition of taxes which in turn increased food prices. The first disorder caused the people to murmur. Repressing them required the troops to be multiplied, and consequently the misery. And the more despair increased, the more one was constrained to increase it again to prevent its effects. On the other hand, these mercenaries, whose value could be determined on the basis of the price at which they sold themselves, were proud of their debasement, held in contempt the laws by which they were protected, as well as their comrades whose bread they ate, and believed it a greater honor to be Caesar's satellites than Rome's defenders. And given as they were to blind obedience, their task was to have their swords raised against their fellow citizens, ready to slaughter them all at the first signal. It would not be difficult to show that this was one of the principal causes of the ruin of the Roman Empire.

The invention of artillery and fortifications has in our times forced the sovereigns of Europe to reestablish the use of regular standing troops to guard their fortresses. Yet however legitimate the motives, there is reason to fear that the effect will be no less fatal. It will be no less necessary to depopulate the rural areas in order to raise armies and garrisons. To maintain them it will be no less necessary to oppress the peoples. And these dangerous establishments have in recent times been growing so rapidly in all of our part of the world, that no one can foresee anything but the imminent depopulation of Europe, and, sooner or later, the ruin of the people who inhabit it.

Be that as it may, it should be noted that such institutions necessarily subvert the public domain, leaving only the wearisome resource of subsidies and taxes, which remain for me to discuss.

It should be remembered here that the foundation of the social compact is property, together with its first condition that each person should be maintained in the peaceful enjoyment of what belongs to him. It is true that by the same treaty each person at least tacitly obliges himself to be assessed for public needs. But since this commitment cannot harm the fundamental law and presumes that contributors acknowledge the evidence of need, it is clear that to be legitimate, this assessment should be voluntary. It is not based on a private will, as if it were necessary to have the consent of each citizen, who should pay only as much as he pleases. This would be directly contrary to the spirit of the confederation. Rather, it should be through the general will, by majority vote, and on the basis of proportional rates that leave no room for an arbitrary imposition of taxes.

This truth (that taxes can be legitimately established only by the general consent of the people or its representatives) has generally been recognized by all the philosophers and jurists who have any reputation in matters of political right, including even Bodin. While some of them have established maxims that appear contrary, it is easy to see the private motives that moved them to do so. They stipulate so many conditions and restrictions that it all boils down to exactly the same thing. For whether the people can refuse it or whether the sovereign should not demand it, is a matter of indifference as far as right is concerned. And if it is only a question of force, it is utterly pointless to inquire what is or is not legitimate.

The contributions levied on the people are of two kinds: real taxes (levied on things) and personal taxes (paid by the head). Both are called *taxes* or *subsidies*. When the people sets the amount it pays, it is called a *subsidy;* when it grants the entire proceeds of an assessment, it is a *tax.* In *The Spirit of the Laws* we find that a head tax is more in keeping with servitude, while a real tax is more suited to liberty. This would be incontestable, were everyone's head share equal. For nothing would be more disproportionate than such a tax. It is especially in an exacting observance of proportions that the spirit of liberty consists. But if a head tax is exactly proportioned to the means of private individuals (as the tax in France known as the *capitation* could be) and is thus at once both real and personal, it is the most equitable and, as a result, the one best suited to free men. At first these proportions appear quite easy to observe, because, being relative to each person's position, the indications are always public. But besides the fact that greed, influence-peddling, and fraud know how to leave no evidence behind, it is rare that an account is taken of all the elements that should enter into these calculations. First, one ought to consider the relationship of quantities according to which, all things being equal, someone who has ten times more goods than someone else should pay ten times more. Second, one ought to consider the relationship of use, that is, the distinction between what is necessary and what is super-fluous. Someone who has only the bare necessities of life should not pay anything at all. Taxing someone who has superfluities can, in time of need, be extended to everything over and above the necessities of life. To this he will declare that, given his rank, what would be superfluous for a man of inferior standing is a necessity for him. But that is a lie. For a man of superior standing has two legs, just like a cowherd, and, like the cowherd, has only one stomach. Moreover, this alleged necessity of life is so little necessary to his standing that, if he knew how to renounce these things for some worthy cause, he could only be respected more. The people would prostrate themselves before a minister who would go on foot to the council because he had sold his carriages when the state had a pressing need. Finally, the law does not demand magnificence of anyone, and propriety is never a reason against right.

A third relationship that is never taken into account, although it always ought to be reckoned the chief concern is that of the utility each person derives from the social confederation which provides powerful protection for the immense possessions of the rich and hardly allows a poor wretch to enjoy the cottage he built with his own hands. Are not the advantages of society for the powerful and the rich? Are not all the lucrative posts filled by them alone? Are not all the privileges and exemptions reserved for them alone? And is not the public authority entirely in their favor? When a man of high standing steals from his creditors or commits other acts of knavery, is he not always certain of impunity? Are not the assaults, the acts of violence he commits, even the murders and assassinations he is guilty of, are not these things hushed up and after six months not given a thought? If this same man were robbed, the entire police force is im-mediately put in motion, and woe to the innocent persons he suspects. Does he have to pass through a dangerous area? He has escorts in rural areas. Is the axle of his chaise about to break? Everyone flies to his aid. Is there a noisy disturbance outside his door? He says one word and every-one is silent. Does a crowd aggravate him? He makes a gesture and every-one steps aside for him. And better that fifty honest pedestrians going about their business should be crushed than that some lazy scoundrel's coach should be delayed. All this respect costs him not a penny; it is the right of a rich man, not the price of riches. How different a picture is to be painted of the poor man! The more humanity owes him, the more society refuses him. All doors are closed to him, even when he has a right to open them. And if sometimes he obtains justice, it is with greater difficulty than the rich man would have obtaining a pardon. If there is an unpleasant job to do or troops to be raised, he is given preference. Besides his own burden, he always bears the one from which his more wealthy neighbor has the influence to get himself exempted. At the least accident that happens to him, everyone avoids him. If his humble cart tips over, far from being helped by anyone, I count him lucky if he avoids the insults of the smart-aleck servants of some young duke who is passing by. In short, any free assistance escapes him when he needs it, precisely because he has nothing with which to pay for it. But I take him for a lost man, if he has the misfortune of having an honest soul, a beautiful daughter and a powerful neighbor.

Another no less important point to make is that the losses of poor men are much more difficult to recoup than those of the rich, and that the difficulty of acquiring always grows in proportion to need. Nothing comes from nothing: it is just as true in business as it is in physics. Money breeds money, and the first *pistole* is sometimes harder to earn than the second million. But there is still more. Everything the poor man pays for is forever lost to him, and remains in or returns to the hands of the rich. And since the proceeds of the taxes sooner or later pass only to those men who take part in the government or who are closely connected with it, they have, even in paying their share, a clear interest in increasing taxes.

Let us summarize in a few words the social part of the two estates. *You need me, for I am rich and you are poor. Let us come to an agreement between ourselves. I will permit you to have the honor of serving me, provided you give me what little you have for the trouble I will be taking to command you.*

If all these things are carefully combined, we will find that in order to levy taxes in an equitable and truly proportionate way, the imposition should not be made merely in proportion to the goods belonging to the contributors, but in a proportion consisting in the difference of their conditions and of the superfluity of their goods. This terribly important and difficult operation is accomplished everyday by multitudes of honest clerks who know their arithmetic; but a Plato or a Montesquieu would not have dared to undertake such a task without trembling and imploring heaven for enlightenment and integrity.

Another disadvantage of the personal tax is that it makes itself felt too much and is levied with too much severity. This does not prevent its being subject to many instances of nonpayment, since it is much easier to hide one's head than one's possessions from the tax rolls and prosecution.

Of all the other kinds of tax assessment, the land tax or real tax has always passed for the most advantageous in countries where more thought is given to both the quantity of the proceeds and the certainty of recovering the funds, than to causing the least annoyance to the people. Some people have even dared to say that the peasant must be burdened in order to rouse him from his idleness, and that he would do nothing if he did not have to pay anything. But among all the peoples of the world experience contradicts this ridiculous maxim. It is in Holland and England, where the farmer pays very little, and above all in China, where he pays nothing, that the land is best cultivated. On the other hand, wherever the worker finds himself taxed in proportion to the product of his fields, he lets them lie fallow or else reaps just as much from them as he needs in order to live. For to him who loses the fruit of his labors gaining means doing nothing. Imposing a fine on work is a rather unusual method of abolishing idleness.

Taxes on land or on grain, especially when they are excessive, result in two disadvantages that are so terrible that they cannot in the long run avoid depopulating and ruining every country where they are established.

The first comes from the lack of circulation of currency, for commerce and industry draw all the money from the rural areas into the capitals; and because the tax destroys the proportion that might still obtain between the needs of farmers and the price of his grain, money constantly leaves and never returns. The richer the city, the more miserable the rural areas. The proceeds from the tax pass from the hands of the prince or the financier into those of artists and merchants. And the farmer, who never receives anything more than the smallest part of the proceedings, is eventually exhausted by always paying the same amount and always receiving less. How could a man live if he had veins and no arteries, or if the arteries carried blood only to within four inches of his heart? Chardin says that in Persia the king's duties on commodities are also paid in commodities. This custom, which, Herodotus tells us, was practiced previously in the same country until the time of Darius, could prevent the evil of which I have been speaking. But unless the intendents, directors, commissioners and warehouse attendants in Persia are a breed apart from what they are everywhere else, I am hard pressed to believe that the smallest part of all these products reaches the king, that the grain does not rot in the granaries, and that fire does not consume the greater part of the warehouses.

The second disadvantage comes from an apparent advantage, which lets the problems become aggravated before they are noticed: namely that grain is a commodity whose price is not increased by taxes in the countries where it is produced, so that despite its absolute necessity, the quantity is diminished without the price being increased. This is what causes many people to die of hunger, even though grain remains cheap, and the farmer is the only one to bear the burden of the tax, which he has been unable to recoup in his selling price. It must be noted that one should not reason about a real tax the way one would about duties on all merchandise which in turn raise the price on all these goods and which are paid not so much by the sellers as by the buyers. For these duties, however heavy they may be, are still voluntary and are paid by the seller only in proportion to the quantity he buys. And since he buys only in proportion to his sales, he applies the law to private individuals. But the farmer, who is required to pay, whether he sells or not, at a fixed rate for the land he cultivates, is not in a position to wait until he gets the price he wants for his produce. And even if he were not to sell it to support himself, he would be forced to sell it to be able to pay the tax, so that sometimes it is the enormity of the assessment that keeps the produce at a low price.

Note too that the resources of commerce and industry, far from making the tax more endurable through an abundance of money, only make it more burdensome. I will not dwell upon a very obvious point, namely that, although a greater or lesser quantity of money in a state can give it more or less credit outside the state, it in no way alters the real fortune of the citizens and does not make them any more or less comfortable. But I must make two important remarks. First, unless the state has extra commodities and the abundance of money comes from export trade, only the commercial towns are aware of this abundance, and the peasant only becomes relatively poorer. Second, since the price of everything increases with the increase in money, taxes must be increased proportionately, so that the farmer finds himself under a greater burden without having greater resources.

It should be noted that the tax on lands is actually a tax on its product. While everyone agrees that nothing is so dangerous as a tax on grain paid by the buyer, how is it we do not see that it is a hundred times worse if this tax is paid by the farmer himself? Is this not an attack on the very source of the state's subsistence? Is it not the most direct method possible of depopulating the homeland, and thus in the long run of ruining it? For there is no worse scarcity for a nation than that of men.

Only the true statesman can raise his sights above the financial objectives of imposing greater taxes. Only he can transform onerous burdens into useful regulations of public administration. Only he can make the people wonder whether such establishments have for their purpose the good of the nation rather than the production of taxes.

Duties on the importation of foreign merchandise which the local people are eager to have but which the homeland does not need; on the exportation of domestically produced merchandise of which the homeland has none to spare and which foreigners cannot do without; on the product of useless and excessively lucrative arts; on the entry into towns of pure luxuries, and in general on all luxury items will all achieve this twofold purpose. It is by means of such taxes, which ease the burden of poverty and place the onus on wealth, that one must prevent the continual increase in the inequality of fortunes, the subjection of a multitude of workers and useless servants to the rich, the multiplication of idle people in the cities, and the desertion of rural areas.

It is important to place a proportion between the price of things and the duties imposed on them such that the greediness of private individuals is not too strongly tempted by the size of the profits to commit fraud. Moreover, smuggling must be made difficult by singling out merchandise that is more difficult to conceal. Finally, it is appropriate for the tax to be paid by the one who uses the thing taxed rather than the one who sells it, to whom the quantity of the duties with which he is charged would provide greater temptations and means of committing fraud. This is the usual practice in China, the country where the taxes are the heaviest and the best paid in the world. The merchant pays nothing. Only the buyer pays the duty, without any murmuring or sedition resulting, for since the provisions necessary for life, such as rice and grain, are completely exempt, the people are not oppressed and the tax falls only on the wealthy. Moreover, all these precautions ought to be dictated not so much by the fear of smuggling as by the attention the government ought to pay to protecting private individuals from the seduction of illegitimate profits, which, after having turned them into bad citizens, would waste no time turning them into dishonest people.

Let heavy taxes be levied on livery servants, carriages, mirrors, chandeliers and furnishings, on fabrics and gilding, on the courtyards and gardens of large homes, on public entertainment of all kinds, on the idle professions, such as those of buffoons, singers, and actors, and, in short, on that group of objects of luxury, amusement and idleness that catch everyone's eye and that can scarcely be hidden, since their whole purpose is to be on display, and they would be useless if they should fail to be seen. There is no cause for fear that the proceeds of such taxes would be arbitrary, since they are imposed only on things that are not absolutely necessary. It shows a poor knowledge of men to believe that men who have once been seduced by luxury can never renounce it. They would a hundred times rather renounce necessities, preferring to die of hunger than of shame. The increase in their expense is only a new reason for sustaining it, when the vanity of displaying oneself as wealthy will reap its reward from the price of the thing as well as the expense of the tax. As long as there are rich people, they will want to distinguish themselves from poor people, and the state cannot contrive a revenue less onerous and more secure than one based on this distinction.

For some reason, industry would have nothing to suffer from an economic order that enriched the public finances, revitalized agriculture by relieving the farmer, and imperceptibly brought all fortunes closer to that intermediate level of wealth which constitutes the true force of a state. I confess it could happen that these taxes might contribute to making some fashions come and go more quickly; but it would never happen without substituting others on which the worker would earn a profit without the public treasury taking a loss. In short, suppose the spirit of the government was constantly to levy all taxes on the superfluities of the rich, one of two things must happen. Either the rich would remove their superfluities to turn them into something useful, which would redound to the profit of the state, in which case, the imposition of taxes would have produced the effect of the best sumptuary laws. The expenses of the state will of necessity have diminished with those of private individuals; and the public treasury in this way would not receive less than it would thereby gain for having to pay out less. Or, if the rich do not cut back on any of their extravagances, the public treasury would have, in tax proceeds on these extravagances, the resources it was seeking in order to provide for the real needs of the state. In the first case, the public treasury is enriched by reducing expenditures. In the second case, it is enriched by the useless expenditures of private individuals.

Let us add to all this an important distinction in the matter of political right, and to which governments, jealous of doing everything by themselves, should pay great attention. I have said that since personal taxes and taxes on absolute necessities attack the right to property and consequently the true foundation of public society, they are always subject to dangerous consequences, if they are not established with the express consent of the people or its representatives. It is not the same for duties on things whose use can be forbidden. For then, since the private individual is absolutely constrained to pay, his contribution can be reckoned as voluntary. Thus the individual consent of each of the contributors takes the place of the general consent, and even presupposes it in a certain way. For why would the people be opposed to any tax levy that falls only on whoever wants to pay it? It would appear to me certain that whatever is not prescribed by the laws or not contrary to mores and that the government can forbid, it can permit on payment of a duty. If, for example, the government can forbid the use of carriages, a fortiori it can impose a tax on carriages, a wise and useful way to blame their use without terminating it. Then one can view the tax as a type of fine, whose proceeds compensate for the abuse it punishes.

Someone may perhaps object that since those whom Bodin calls *impostors*, that is, those who impose or invent the taxes, are in the class of the rich, they will not take care to spare others at their own expense and to burden themselves in order to relieve the poor. But such ideas must be rejected. If in each nation those to whom the sovereign commits the government of the peoples were, in virtue of their position, the enemies of the state, it would not be worth the trouble to inquire what they should do to make people happy.

ON THE

SOCIAL CONTRACT,

OR

PRINCIPLES

OF

POLITICAL RIGHT

By J.-J. Rousseau,
Citizen of Geneva

–foederis aequas
Dicamus leges

—*Aeneid,* XI

FOREWORD

This little treatise is part of a longer work I undertook some time ago without taking stock of my abilities, and have long since abandoned. Of the various selections that could have been drawn from what had been completed, this is the most considerable, and, it appears to me, the one least unworthy of being offered to the public. The rest no longer exists.

ON THE SOCIAL CONTRACT

BOOK I

I want to inquire whether there can be some legitimate and sure rule of administration in the civil order, taking men as they are and laws as they might be. I will always try in this inquiry to bring together what right permits with what interest prescribes, so that justice and utility do not find themselves at odds with one another.

I begin without demonstrating the importance of my subject. It will be asked if I am a prince or a legislator that I should be writing about politics. I answer that I am neither, and that is why I write about politics. Were I a prince or a legislator, I would not waste my time saying what ought to be done. I would do it or keep quiet.

Born a citizen of a free state and a member of the sovereign, the right to vote is enough to impose upon me the duty to instruct myself in public affairs, however little influence my voice may have in them. Happy am I, for every time I meditate on governments, I always find new reasons in my inquiries for loving that of my country.

CHAPTER I
Subject of the First Book

Man is born free, and everywhere he is in chains. He who believes himself the master of others does not escape being more of a slave than they. How did this change take place? I have no idea. What can render it legitimate? I believe I can answer this question.

Were I to consider only force and the effect that flows from it, I would say that so long as a people is constrained to obey and does obey, it does well. As soon as it can shake off the yoke and does shake it off, it does even better. For by recovering its liberty by means of the same right that stole it, either the populace is justified in getting it back or else those who took it away were not justified in their actions. But the social order is a sacred right which serves as a foundation for all other rights. Nevertheless, this right does not come from nature. It is therefore founded upon convention. Before coming to that, I ought to substantiate what I just claimed.

CHAPTER II
Of the First Societies

The most ancient of all societies and the only natural one, is that of the family. Even so children remain bound to their father only so long as they need him to take care of them. As soon as the need ceases, the natural bond is dissolved. Once the children are freed from the obedience they owed the father and their father is freed from the care he owed his children, all return equally to independence. If they continue to remain united, this no longer takes place naturally but voluntarily, and the family maintains itself only by means of convention.

This common liberty is one consequence of the nature of man. Its first law is to see to his maintenance; its first concerns are those he owes himself; and, as soon as he reaches the age of reason, since he alone is the judge of the proper means of taking care of himself, he thereby becomes his own master.

The family therefore is, so to speak, the prototype of political societies; the leader is the image of the father, the populace is the image of the children, and, since all are born equal and free, none give up their liberty except for their utility. The entire difference consists in the fact that in the family the love of the father for his children repays him for the care he takes for them, while in the state, where the leader does not have love for his peoples, the pleasure of commanding takes the place of this feeling.

Grotius denies that all human power is established for the benefit of the governed, citing slavery as an example. His usual method of reasoning is always to present fact as a proof of right.[1] A more logical method could be used, but not one more favorable to tyrants.

According to Grotius, it is therefore doubtful whether the human race belongs to a hundred men, or whether these hundred men belong to the human race. And throughout his book he appears to lean toward the former view. This is Hobbes' position as well. On this telling, the human race is divided into herds of cattle, each one having its own leader who guards it in order to devour it.

Just as a herdsman possesses a nature superior to that of his herd, the herdsmen of men who are the leaders, also have a nature superior to that of their peoples. According to Philo, Caligula reasoned thus, concluding quite properly from this analogy that kings were gods, or that the peoples were beasts.

Caligula's reasoning coincides with that of Hobbes and Grotius. Aristotle, before all the others, had also said that men are by no means equal by nature, but that some were born for slavery and others for domination.

Aristotle was right, but he took the effect for the cause. Every man born in slavery is born for slavery; nothing is more certain. In their chains slaves

---

1. "Learned research on public right is often nothing more than the history of ancient abuses, and taking a lot of trouble to study them too closely gets one nowhere." *Treatise on the Interests of France Along With Her Neighbors,* by the Marquis d'Argenson. This is just what Grotius has done.

lose everything, even the desire to escape. They love their servitude the way the companions of Ulysses loved their degradation.[2] If there are slaves by nature, it is because there have been slaves against nature. Force has produced the first slaves; their cowardice has perpetuated them.

I have said nothing about King Adam or Emperor Noah, father of three great monarchs who partitioned the universe, as did the children of Saturn, whom some have believed they recognize in them. I hope I will be appreciated for this moderation, for since I am a direct descendent of these princes, and perhaps of the eldest branch, how am I to know whether, after the verification of titles, I might not find myself the legitimate king of the human race? Be that as it may, we cannot deny that Adam was the sovereign of the world, just as Robinson Crusoe was sovereign of his island, so long as he was its sole inhabitant. And the advantage this empire had was that the monarch, securely on his throne, had no rebellions, wars or conspirators to fear.

CHAPTER III
On the Right of the Strongest

The strongest is never strong enough to be master all the time, unless he transforms force into right and obedience into duty. Hence the right of the strongest, a right that seems like something intended ironically and is actually established as a basic principle. But will no one explain this word to me? Force is a physical power; I fail to see what morality can result from its effects. To give in to force is an act of necessity, not of will. At most, it is an act of prudence. In what sense could it be a duty?

Let us suppose for a moment that there is such a thing as this alleged right. I maintain that all that results from it is an inexplicable mish-mash. For once force produces the right, the effect changes places with the cause. Every force that is superior to the first succeeds to its right. As soon as one can disobey with impunity, one can do so legitimately; and since the strongest is always right, the only thing to do is to make oneself the strongest. For what kind of right is it that perishes when the force on which it is based ceases? If one must obey because of force, one need not do so out of duty; and if one is no longer forced to obey one is no longer obliged. Clearly then, this word "right" adds nothing to force. It is utterly meaningless here.

Obey the powers that be. If that means giving in to force, the precept is sound, but superfluous. I reply it will never be violated. All power comes from God—I admit it—but so does every disease. Does this mean that calling in a physician is prohibited? If a brigand takes me by surprise at the edge of a wooded area, is it not only the case that I must surrender my purse, but even that I am in good conscience bound to surrender it, if I were able to withhold it? After all, the pistol he holds is also a power.

2. See a short treatise of Plutarch entitled "That Animals Reason."

Let us then agree that force does not bring about right, and that one is obliged to obey only legitimate powers. Thus my original question keeps returning.

CHAPTER IV
On Slavery

Since no man has a natural authority over his fellow man, and since force does not give rise to any right, conventions therefore remain the basis of all legitimate authority among men.

If, says Grotius, a private individual can alienate his liberty and turn himself into the slave of a master, why could not an entire people alienate its liberty and turn itself into the subject of a king? There are many equivocal words here which need explanation, but let us confine ourselves to the word *alienate*. To alienate is to give or to sell. A man who makes himself the slave of someone else does not give himself; he sells himself, at least for his subsistence. But why does a people sell itself? Far from furnishing his subjects with their subsistence, a king derives his own from them alone, and, according to Rabelais, a king does not live cheaply. Do subjects then give their persons on the condition that their estate will also be taken? I fail to see what remains for them to preserve.

It will be said that the despot assures his subjects of civil tranquility. Very well. But what do they gain, if the wars his ambition drags them into, if his insatiable greed, if the oppressive demands caused by his ministers occasion more grief for his subjects than their own dissensions would have done? What do they gain, if this very tranquility is one of their miseries? A tranquil life is also had in dungeons; is that enough to make them desirable? The Greeks who were locked up in the Cyclops' cave lived a tranquil existence as they awaited their turn to be devoured.

To say that a man gives himself gratuitously is to say something absurd and inconceivable. Such an act is illegitimate and null, if only for the fact that he who commits it does not have his wits about him. To say the same thing of an entire populace is to suppose a populace composed of madmen. Madness does not bring about right.

Even if each person can alienate himself, he cannot alienate his children. They are born men and free. Their liberty belongs to them; they alone have the right to dispose of it. Before they have reached the age of reason, their father can, in their name, stipulate conditions for their maintenance and for their well-being. But he cannot give them irrevocably and unconditionally, for such a gift is contrary to the ends of nature and goes beyond the rights of paternity. For an arbitrary government to be legitimate, it would therefore be necessary in each generation for the people to be master of its acceptance or rejection. But in that event this government would no longer be arbitrary.

Renouncing one's liberty is renouncing one's dignity as a man, the rights of humanity and even its duties. There is no possible compensation for anyone who renounces everything. Such a renunciation is incompatible with the nature of man. Removing all morality from his actions is tanta-mount to taking away all liberty from his will. Finally, it is a vain and contradictory convention to stipulate absolute authority on one side and a limitless obedience on the other. Is it not clear that no commitments are made to a person from whom one has the right to demand everything? And does this condition alone not bring with it, without equivalent or exchange, the nullity of the act? For what right would my slave have against me, given that all he has belongs to me, and that, since his right is my right, my having a right against myself makes no sense?

Grotius and others derive from war another origin for the alleged right of slavery. Since, according to them, the victor has the right to kill the vanquished, these latter can repurchase their lives at the price of their liberty—a convention all the more legitimate, since it turns a profit for both of them.

But clearly this alleged right to kill the vanquished does not in any way derive from the state of war. Men are not naturally enemies, for the sim-ple reason that men living in their original state of independence do not have sufficiently constant relationships among themselves to bring about either a state of peace or a state of war. It is the relationship between things and not that between men that brings about war. And since this state of war cannot come into existence from simple personal relations, but only from real [proprietary] relations, a private war between one man and another can exist neither in the state of nature, where there is no con-stant property, nor in the social state, where everything is under the authority of the laws.

Fights between private individuals, duels, encounters are not acts which produce a state. And with regard to private wars, authorized by the ordi-nances of King Louis IX of France and suspended by the Peace of God, they are abuses of feudal government, an absurd system if there ever was one, contrary to the principles of natural right and to all sound polity.

War is not therefore a relationship between one man and another, but a relationship between one state and another. In war private individuals are enemies only incidentally: not as men or even as citizens,[3] but as soldiers; not as members of the homeland but as its defenders. Finally,

3. [*At this point the following passage was added to the 1782 edition:* The Romans, who had a better understanding of and a greater respect for the right of war than any other nation, carried their scruples so far in this regard that a citizen was not allowed to serve as a volunteer unless he had expressly committed himself against the enemy and against a specifically named enemy. When a legion in which Cato the Younger first served had been reorganized, Cato the Elder wrote Popilius that if he wanted his son to continue to serve under him, he would have to make him swear the military oath afresh, since, with the first one having been annulled, he could no longer take up arms against the enemy. And this very same Cato wrote his son to take care to avoid going into battle without swearing this military oath afresh. I know the siege of Clusium and other specific cases can be raised as counter-examples to this, but for my part I cite laws and customs. The Romans were the ones who transgressed their laws least often, and are the only ones to have had such noble laws.]

each state can have as enemies only other states and not men, since there can be no real relationship between things of disparate natures.

This principle is even in conformity with the established maxims of all times and with the constant practice of all civilized peoples. Declarations of war are warnings not so much to powers as to their subjects. The foreigner (be he king, private individual, or a people) who robs, kills or detains subjects of another prince without declaring war on the prince, is not an enemy but a brigand. Even in the midst of war a just prince rightly appropriates to himself everything in an enemy country belonging to the public, but respects the person and goods of private individuals. He respects the rights upon which his own rights are founded. Since the purpose of war is the destruction of the enemy state, one has the right to kill the defenders of that state so long as they bear arms. But as soon as they lay down their arms and surrender, they cease to be enemies or instruments of the enemy. They return to being simply men; and one no longer has a right to their lives. Sometimes a state can be killed without a single one of its members being killed. For war does not grant a right that is unnecessary to its purpose. These principles are not those of Grotius. They are not based on the authority of poets. Rather they are derived from the nature of things; they are based on reason.

As to the right of conquest, the only basis it has is the law of the strongest. If war does not give the victor the right to massacre the vanquished peoples, this right (which he does not have) cannot be the basis for the right to enslave them. One has the right to kill the enemy only when one cannot enslave him. The right to enslave him does not therefore derive from the right to kill him. Hence it is an iniquitous exchange to make him buy his life, to which no one has any right, at the price of his liberty. In establishing the right of life and death on the right of slavery, and the right of slavery on the right of life and death, is it not clear that one falls into a vicious circle?

Even if we were to suppose that there were this terrible right to kill everyone, I maintain that neither a person enslaved during wartime nor a conquered people bears any obligation whatever toward its master, except to obey him for as long as it is forced to do so. In taking the equivalent of his life, the victor has done him no favor. Instead of killing him unprofitably he kills him usefully. Hence, far from the victor having acquired any authority over him beyond force, the state of war subsists between them just as before. Their relationship itself is the effect of war, and the usage of the right to war does not suppose any peace treaty. They have made a convention. Fine. But this convention, far from destroying the state of war, presupposes its continuation.

Thus, from every point of view, the right of slavery is null, not simply because it is illegitimate, but because it is absurd and meaningless. These words, *slavery* and *right,* are contradictory. They are mutually exclusive. Whether it is the statement of one man to another man, or one man to a people, the following sort of talk will always be equally nonsensical. *I make a convention with you which is wholly at your expense and wholly*

*to my advantage; and, for as long as it pleases me, I will observe it and so
will you.*

CHAPTER V
That It Is Always Necessary to Return
to a First Convention

Even if I were to grant all that I have thus far refuted, the supporters
of despotism would not be any better off. There will always be a great
difference between subduing a multitude and ruling a society. If scattered
men, however many they may be, were successively enslaved by a single
individual, I see nothing there but a master and slaves; I do not see a
people and its leader. It is, if you will, an aggregation, but not an association. There is neither a public good nor a body politic there. Even if that
man had enslaved half the world, he is always just a private individual.
His interest, separated from that of others, is never anything but a private
interest. If this same man is about to die, after his passing his empire
remains scattered and disunited, just as an oak tree dissolves and falls
into a pile of ashes after fire has consumed it.

A people, says Grotius, can give itself to a king. According to Grotius,
therefore, a people is a people before it gives itself to a king. This gift itself is a civil act; it presupposes a public deliberation. Thus, before examining the act whereby a people chooses a king, it would be well to examine
the act whereby a people is a people. For since this act is necessarily prior
to the other, it is the true foundation of society.

In fact, if there were no prior convention, then, unless the vote were
unanimous, what would become of the minority's obligation to submit to
the majority's choice, and where do one hundred who want a master get
the right to vote for ten who do not? The law of majority rule is itself an
established convention, and presupposes unanimity on at least one
occasion.

CHAPTER VI
On the Social Compact

I suppose that men have reached the point where obstacles that are
harmful to their maintenance in the state of nature gain the upper hand
by their resistance to the forces that each individual can bring to bear to
maintain himself in that state. Such being the case, that original state
cannot subsist any longer, and the human race would perish if it did not
alter its mode of existence.

For since men cannot engender new forces, but merely unite and direct
existing ones, they have no other means of maintaining themselves but to
form by aggregation a sum of forces that could gain the upper hand over
the resistance, so that their forces are directed by means of a single moving
power and made to act in concert.

This sum of forces cannot come into being without the cooperation of
many. But since each man's force and liberty are the primary instruments
of his maintenance, how is he going to engage them without hurting him-

self and without neglecting the care that he owes himself? This difficulty, seen in terms of my subject, can be stated in the following terms:

"Find a form of association which defends and protects with all common forces the person and goods of each associate, and by means of which each one, while uniting with all, nevertheless obeys only himself and remains as free as before?" This is the fundamental problem for which the social contract provides the solution.

The clauses of this contract are so determined by the nature of the act that the least modification renders them vain and ineffectual, that, although perhaps they have never been formally promulgated, they are everywhere the same, everywhere tacitly accepted and acknowledged. Once the social compact is violated, each person then regains his first rights and resumes his natural liberty, while losing the conventional liberty for which he renounced it.

These clauses, properly understood, are all reducible to a single one, namely the total alienation of each associate, together with all of his rights, to the entire community. For first of all, since each person gives himself whole and entire, the condition is equal for everyone; and since the condition is equal for everyone, no one has an interest in making it burdensome for the others.

Moreover, since the alienation is made without reservation, the union is as perfect as possible, and no associate has anything further to demand. For if some rights remained with private individuals, in the absence of any common superior who could decide between them and the public, each person would eventually claim to be his own judge in all things, since he is on some point his own judge. The state of nature would subsist and the association would necessarily become tyrannical or hollow.

Finally, in giving himself to all, each person gives himself to no one. And since there is no associate over whom he does not acquire the same right that he would grant others over himself, he gains the equivalent of everything he loses, along with a greater amount of force to preserve what he has.

If, therefore, one eliminates from the social compact whatever is not essential to it, one will find that it is reducible to the following terms. *Each of us places his person and all his power in common under the supreme direction of the general will; and as one we receive each member as an indivisible part of the whole.*

At once, in place of the individual person of each contracting party, this act of association produces a moral and collective body composed of as many members as there are voices in the assembly, which receives from this same act its unity, its common *self,* its life and its will. This public person, formed thus by union of all the others formerly took the name *city,*[4] and at present takes the name *republic* or *body politic,* which is

---

4. The true meaning of this word is almost entirely lost on modern men. Most of them mistake a town for a city and a townsman for a citizen. They do not know that houses make a town but citizens make a city. Once this mistake cost the Carthagin-

called *state* by its members when it is passive, *sovereign* when it is active, *power* when compared to others like itself. As to the associates, they collectively take the name *people;* individually they are called *citizens,* insofar as participants in the sovereign authority, and *subjects,* insofar as they are subjected to the laws of the state. But these terms are often confused and mistaken for one another. It is enough to know how to distinguish them when they are used with absolute precision.

CHAPTER VII
On the Sovereign

This formula shows that the act of association includes a reciprocal commitment between the public and private individuals, and that each individual, contracting, as it were, with himself, finds himself under a twofold commitment: namely as a member of the sovereign to private individuals, and as a member of the state toward the sovereign. But the maxim of civil law that no one is held to commitments made to himself cannot be applied here, for there is a considerable difference between being obligated to oneself, or to a whole of which one is a part.

It must be further noted that the public deliberation that can obligate all the subjects to the sovereign, owing to the two different relationships in which each of them is viewed, cannot, for the opposite reason, obligate the sovereign to itself, and that consequently it is contrary to the nature of the body politic that the sovereign impose upon itself a law it could not break. Since the sovereign can be considered under but one single relationship, it is then in the position of a private individual contracting with himself. Whence it is apparent that there neither is nor can be any type of fundamental law that is obligatory for the people as a body, not even the social contract. This does not mean that the whole body cannot perfectly well commit itself to another body with respect to things that do not infringe on this contract. For in regard to the foreigner, it becomes a simple being, an individual.

However, since the body politic or the sovereign derives its being exclusively from the sanctity of the contract, it can never obligate itself, not even to another power, to do anything that derogates from the original act,

---

ians dearly. I have not found in my reading that the title of *citizen* has ever been given to the subjects of a prince, not even in ancient times to the Macedonians or in our own time to the English, although they are closer to liberty than all the others. Only the French adopt this name *citizen* with complete familiarity, since they have no true idea of its meaning, as can be seen from their dictionaries. If this were not the case, they would become guilty of treason for using it. For them, this name expresses a virtue and not a right. When Bodin wanted to speak about our citizens and townsmen, he committed a terrible blunder when he mistook the one group for the other. M. d'Alembert was not in error, and in his article entitled *Geneva* he has carefully distinguished the four orders of men (even five, counting ordinary foreigners) who are in our towns, and of whom only two make up the republic. No other French author I am aware of has grasped the true meaning of the word *citizen.*

such as alienating some portion of itself or submitting to another sovereign. Violation of the act whereby it exists would be self-annihilation, and whatever is nothing produces nothing.

As soon as this multitude is thus united in a body, one cannot harm one of the members without attacking the whole body. It is even less likely that the body can be harmed without the members feeling it. Thus duty and interest equally obligate the two parties to come to one another's aid, and the same men should seek to combine in this two-fold relationship all the advantages that result from it.

For since the sovereign is formed entirely from the private individuals who make it up, it neither has nor could have an interest contrary to theirs. Hence, the sovereign power has no need to offer a guarantee to its subjects, since it is impossible for a body to want to harm all of its members, and, as we will see later, it cannot harm any one of them in particular. The sovereign, by the mere fact that it exists, is always all that it should be.

But the same thing cannot be said of the subjects in relation to the sovereign, for which, despite their common interest, their commitments would be without substance if it did not find ways of being assured of their fidelity.

In fact, each individual can, as a man, have a private will contrary to or different from the general will that he has as a citizen. His private interest can speak to him in an entirely different manner than the common interest. His absolute and naturally independent existence can cause him to envisage what he owes the common cause as a gratuitous contribution, the loss of which will be less harmful to others than its payment is burdensome to him. And in viewing the moral person which constitutes the state as a being of reason because it is not a man, he would enjoy the rights of a citizen without wanting to fulfill the duties of a subject, an injustice whose growth would bring about the ruin of the body politic.

Thus, in order for the social compact to avoid being an empty formula, it tacitly entails the commitment—which alone can give force to the others—that whoever refuses to obey the general will will be forced to do so by the entire body. This means merely that he will be forced to be free. For this is the sort of condition that, by giving each citizen to the homeland, guarantees him against all personal dependence—a condition that produces the skill and the performance of the political machine, and which alone bestows legitimacy upon civil commitments. Without it such commitments would be absurd, tyrannical and subject to the worst abuses.

CHAPTER VIII
On the Civil State

This passage from the state of nature to the civil state produces quite a remarkable change in man, for it substitutes justice for instinct in his behavior and gives his actions a moral quality they previously lacked. Only then, when the voice of duty replaces physical impulse and right replaces appetite, does man, who had hitherto taken only himself into account, find himself forced to act upon other principles and to consult his reason before listening to his inclinations. Although in this state he deprives himself of several of the advantages belonging to him in the state of nature, he regains such great ones. His faculties are exercised and developed, his ideas are broadened, his feelings are ennobled, his entire soul is elevated to such a height that, if the abuse of this new condition did not often lower his status to beneath the level he left, he ought constantly to bless the happy moment that pulled him away from it forever and which transformed him from a stupid, limited animal into an intelligent being and a man.

Let us summarize this entire balance sheet so that the credits and debits are easily compared. What man loses through the social contract is his natural liberty and an unlimited right to everything that tempts him and that he can acquire. What he gains is civil liberty and the proprietary ownership of all he possesses. So as not to be in error in these compensations, it is necessary to draw a careful distinction between natural liberty (which is limited solely by the force of the individual involved) and civil liberty (which is limited by the general will), and between possession (which is merely the effect of the force or the right of the first occupant) and proprietary ownership (which is based solely on a positive title).

To the preceding acquisitions could be added the acquisition in the civil state of moral liberty, which alone makes man truly the master of himself. For to be driven by appetite alone is slavery, and obedience to the law one has prescribed for oneself is liberty. But I have already said too much on this subject, and the philosophical meaning of the word *liberty* is not my subject here.

CHAPTER IX

On the Real [i.e., Proprietary] Domain

Each member of the community gives himself to it at the instant of its constitution, just as he actually is, himself and all his forces, including all the goods in his possession. This is not to say that by this act possession changes its nature as it changes hands and becomes property in the hands of the sovereign. Rather, since the forces of the city are incomparably greater than those of a private individual, public possession is by that very fact stronger and more irrevocable, without being more legitimate, at least to strangers. For with regard to its members, the state is master of all their goods in virtue of the social contract, which serves in the state as the basis of all rights. But with regard to other powers, the state is master only in virtue of the right of the first occupant, which it derives from private individuals.

The right of first occupant, though more real than the right of the strongest, does not become a true right until after the establishment of the right of property. Every man by nature has a right to everything he needs; however, the positive act whereby he becomes a proprietor of some goods excludes him from all the rest. Once his lot has been determined, he should limit himself thereto, no longer having any right against the community. This is the reason why the right of the first occupant, so weak in the state of nature, is able to command the respect of every man living in the civil state. In this right, one respects not so much what belongs to others as what does not belong to oneself.

In general, the following rules must obtain in order to authorize the right of the first occupant on any land. First, this land may not already be occupied by anyone. Second, no one may occupy more than the amount needed to subsist. Third, one is to take possession of it not by an empty ceremony, but by working and cultivating it—the only sign of property that ought, in the absence of legal titles, to be respected by others.

In fact, by according to need and work the right of the first occupant, is it not extended as far as it can go? Is it possible to avoid setting limits to this right? Will setting one's foot on a piece of common land be sufficient to claim it at once as one's own? Will having the force for a moment to drive off other men be sufficient to deny them the right ever to return? How can a man or a people seize a vast amount of territory and deprive the entire human race of it except by a punishable usurpation, since this seizure deprives all other men of the shelter and sustenance that nature gives them in common? When Nuñez Balboa stood on the shoreline and took possession of the South Sea and all of South America in the name of crown of Castille, was this enough to dispossess all the inhabitants and to exclude all the princes of the world? On that basis, those ceremonies would be multiplied quite in vain. All the Catholic King had to do was to take possession of the universe all at once from his private room, excepting afterwards from his empire only what already belonged to other princes.

One can imagine how the combined and contiguous lands of private individuals became public territory; and how the right of sovereignty, extending from subjects to the land they occupied, becomes at once real and personal. This places its owners in a greater dependence, turning their very own forces into guarantees of their loyalty. This advantage does not seem to have been fully appreciated by the ancient monarchs, who, calling themselves merely King of the Persians, the Scythians, and the Macedonians, appeared to regard themselves merely as the leaders of men rather than the masters of the country. Today's monarchs more shrewdly call themselves King of France, Spain, England, and so on. In holding the land thus, they are quite sure of holding the inhabitants.

What is remarkable about this alienation is that, in accepting the goods of private individuals, the community is far from despoiling them; rather, in so doing, it merely assures them of legitimate possession, changing usurpation into a true right, and enjoyment into proprietary ownership. In that case, since owners are considered trustees of the public good, and since their rights are respected by all members of the state and maintained with all its force against foreigners, through an advantageous surrender to the public and still more so to themselves, they have, so to speak, acquired all they have given. This paradox is easily explained by the distinction between the rights of the sovereign and those of the proprietor to the same store, as will be seen later.

It can also happen, as men begin to unite before possessing anything and later appropriate a piece of land sufficient for everyone, that they enjoy it in common or divide it among themselves either in equal shares or according to proportions laid down by the sovereign. In whatever way this acquisition is accomplished, each private individual's right to his very own store is always subordinate to the community's right to all, without which there could be neither solidity in the social fabric nor real force in the exercise of sovereignty.

I will end this chapter and this book with a remark that should serve as a basis for every social system. It is that instead of destroying natural equality, the fundamental compact, on the contrary, substitutes a moral and legitimate equality to whatever physical inequality nature may have been able to impose upon men, and that, however, unequal in force or intelligence they may be, men all become equal by convention and by right.[5]

END OF THE FIRST BOOK

BOOK II

CHAPTER I

That Sovereignty Is Inalienable

The first and most important consequence of the principles established above is that only the general will can direct the forces of the state according to the purpose for which it was instituted, which is the common good. For if the opposition of private interests made necessary the establishment of societies, it is the accord of these same interests that made it possible. It is what these different interests have in common that forms the social bond, and, were there no point of agreement among all these interests, no society could exist. For it is utterly on the basis of this common interest that society ought to be governed.

I therefore maintain that since sovereignty is merely the exercise of the general will, it can never be alienated, and that the sovereign, which is only a collective being, cannot be represented by anything but itself. Power can perfectly well be transmitted, but not the will.

In fact, while it is not impossible for a private will to be in accord on some point with the general will, it is impossible at least for this accord to be durable and constant. For by its nature the private will tends toward

---

5. Under bad governments this equality is only apparent and illusory. It serves merely to maintain the poor man in his misery and the rich man in his usurpation. In actuality, laws are always useful to those who have possessions and harmful to those who have nothing. Whence it follows that the social state is advantageous to men only insofar as they all have something and none of them has too much.

having preferences, and the general will tends toward equality. It is even more impossible for there to be a guarantee of this accord even if it ought always to exist. This is not the result of art but of chance. The sovereign may well say, "Right now I want what a certain man wants or at least what he says he wants." But it cannot say, "What this man will want tomorrow I too will want," since it is absurd for the will to tie its hands for the future and since it does not depend upon any will's consenting to anything contrary to the good of the being that wills. If, therefore, the populace promises simply to obey, it dissolves itself by this act, it loses its standing as a people. The very moment there is a master, there no longer is a sovereign, and thenceforward the body politic is destroyed.

This is not to say that the commands of the leaders could not pass for manifestations of the general will, so long as the sovereign, who is free to oppose them, does not do so. In such a case, the consent of the people ought to be presumed on the basis of universal silence. This will be explained at greater length.

CHAPTER II
That Sovereignty Is Indivisible

Sovereignty is indivisible for the same reason that it is inalienable. For either the will is general,[1] or it is not. It is the will of either the people as a whole or of only a part. In the first case, this declared will is an act of sovereignty and constitutes law. In the second case, it is merely a private will, or an act of magistracy. At most it is a decree.

However, our political theorists, unable to divide sovereignty in its principle, divide it in its object. They divide it into force and will, into legislative and executive power, into rights of imposing taxes, of justice and of war, into internal administration and power to negotiate with foreigners. Occasionally they confuse all these parts and sometimes they separate them. They turn the sovereign into a fantastic being made of interconnected pieces. It is as if they built a man out of several bodies, one of which had eyes, another had arms, another feet, and nothing more. Japanese sleight-of-hand artists are said to dismember a child before the eyes of spectators, then, throwing all the parts in the air one after the other, they make the child fall back down alive and all in one piece. These conjuring acts of our political theorists are more or less like these performances. After having taken apart the social body by means of a sleight-of-hand worthy of a carnival, they put the pieces back together who knows how.

This error comes from not having formed precise notions of sovereign authority, and from having taken for parts of that authority what were

1. For a will to be general, it need not always be unanimous; however, it is necessary for all the votes to be counted. Any formal exclusion is a breach of generality.

merely emanations from it. Thus, for example, the acts of declaring war and making peace have been viewed as acts of sovereignty, which they are not, since each of these acts is not a law but merely an application of the law, a particular act determining the legal circumstances, as will be clearly seen when the idea attached to the word *law* comes to be defined.

In reviewing the other divisions in the same way, one would find that one is mistaken every time one believes one sees sovereignty divided, and that the rights one takes to be the parts of this sovereignty are all subordinated to it and always presuppose supreme wills which these rights merely put into effect.

It would be impossible to say how much this lack of precision has obscured the decisions of authors who have written about political right when they wanted to judge the respective rights of kings and peoples on the basis of the principles they had established. Anyone can see, in Chapters III and IV of Book I of Grotius, how this learned man and his translator, Barbeyrac, become entangled and caught up in their sophisms, for fear of either saying too much or too little according to their perspectives, and of offending the interests they needed to reconcile. Grotius, taking refuge in France, unhappy with his homeland and desirous of paying court to Louis XIII (to whom his book is dedicated), spares no pain to rob the people of all their rights and to invest kings with them by every possible artifice. This would also have been the wish of Barbeyrac, who dedicated his translation to King George I of England. But unfortunately the expulsion of James II (which he calls an abdication) forced him to be evasive and on his guard and to beat around the bush, in order to avoid making William out to be a usurper. If these two writers had adopted the true principles, all their difficulties would have been alleviated and they would always have been consistent. However, sad to say, they would have told the truth and paid court only to the people. For truth does not lead to fortune, and the populace grants neither ambassadorships, university chairs nor pensions.

CHAPTER III
Whether the General Will Can Err

It follows from what has preceded that the general will is always right and always tends toward the public utility. However, it does not follow that the deliberations of the people always have the same rectitude. We always want what is good for us, but we do not always see what it is. The populace is never corrupted, but it is often tricked, and only then does it appear to want what is bad.

There is often a great deal of difference between the will of all and the general will. The latter considers only the general interest, whereas the former considers private interest and is merely the sum of private wills. But remove from these same wills the pluses and minuses that cancel each other out,[2] and what remains as the sum of the differences is the general will.

If, when a sufficiently informed populace deliberates, the citizens were to have no communication among themselves, the general will would always result from the large number of small differences, and the deliberation would always be good. But when intrigues and partial associations come into being at the expense of the large association, the will of each of these associations becomes general in relation to its members and particular in relation to the state. It can be said, then, that there are no longer as many voters as there are men, but merely as many as there are associations. The differences become less numerous and yield a result that is less general. Finally, when one of these associations is so large that it dominates all the others, the result is no longer a sum of minor differences, but a single difference. Then there is no longer a general will, and the opinion that dominates is merely a private opinion.

For the general will to be well articulated, it is therefore important that there should be no partial society in the state and that each citizen make up his own mind.[3] Such was the unique and sublime institution of the great Lycurgus. If there are partial societies, their number must be multiplied and inequality among them prevented, as was done by Solon, Numa and Servius. These precautions are the only effective way of bringing it about that the general will is always enlightened and that the populace is not tricked.

CHAPTER IV
On the Limits of Sovereign Power

If the state or the city is merely a moral person whose life consists in the union of its members, and if the most important of its concerns is that of its own conservation, it ought to have a universal compulsory force to move and arrange each part in the manner best suited to the whole. Just as nature gives each man an absolute power over all his members, the social compact gives the body politic an absolute power over all its members, and it is the same power which, as I have said, is directed by the general will and bears the name sovereignty.

2. *Each interest,* says the Marquis d'Argenson, *has different principles. The accord of two private interests is formed in opposition to that of a third.* He could have added that the accord of all the interests is found in the opposition to that of each. If there were no different interests, the common interest, which would never encounter any obstacle, would scarcely be felt. Everything would proceed on its own and politics would cease being an art.

3. *"It is true,"* says Machiavelli, *"that some divisions are harmful to the republic while others are helpful to it. Those that are accompanied by sects and partisan factions are harmful. Since, therefore, a ruler of a republic cannot prevent enmities from arising within it, he at least ought to prevent them from becoming sects,"* The History of Florence, Book VII. [Rousseau here quotes the Italian.]

But over and above the public person, we need to consider the private persons who make it up and whose life and liberty are naturally independent of it. It is, therefore, a question of making a rigorous distinction between the respective rights of the citizens and the sovereign,[4] and between the duties the former have to fulfill as subjects and the natural right they should enjoy as men.

We grant that each person alienates, by the social compact, only that portion of his power, his goods, and liberty whose use is of consequence to the community; but we must also grant that only the sovereign is the judge of what is of consequence.

A citizen should render to the state all the services he can as soon as the sovereign demands them. However, for its part, the sovereign cannot impose on the subjects any fetters that are of no use to the community. It cannot even will to do so, for under the law of reason nothing takes place without a cause, any more than under the law of nature.

The commitments that bind us to the body politic are obligatory only because they are mutual, and their nature is such that in fulfilling them one cannot work for someone else without also working for oneself. Why is the general will always right, and why do all constantly want the happiness of each of them, if not because everyone applies the word *each* to himself and thinks of himself as he votes for all? This proves that the quality of right and the notion of justice it produces are derived from the preference each person gives himself, and thus from the nature of man; that the general will, to be really such, must be general in its object as well as in its essence; that it must derive from all in order to be applied to all; and that it loses its natural rectitude when it tends toward any individual, determinate object. For then, judging what is foreign to us, we have no true principle of equity to guide us.

In effect, once it is a question of a state of affairs or a particular right concerning a point that has not been regulated by a prior, general convention, the issue becomes contentious. It is a suit in which the interested private individuals are one of the parties and the public the other, but in which I fail to see either what law should be followed or what judge should render the decision. In these circumstances it would be ridiculous to want to defer to an express decision of the general will, which can only be the conclusion reached by one of its parts, and which, for the other party, therefore, is merely an alien, particular will, inclined on this occasion to injustice and subject to error. Thus, just as a private will cannot represent the general will, the general will, for its part, alters its nature when it has a particular object; and as general, it is unable to render a decision on either a man or a state of affairs. When, for example, the populace of Athens appointed or dismissed its leaders, decreed that honors be bestowed on one or inflicted penalties on another, and by a

---

4. Attentive readers, please do not rush to accuse me of contradiction here. I have been unable to avoid it in my choice of words, given the poverty of the language. But wait.

multitude of particular decrees, indiscriminately exercised all the acts of government, the people in this case no longer had a general will in the strict sense. It no longer functioned as sovereign but as magistrate. This will appear contrary to commonly held opinions, but I must be given time to present my own.

It should be seen from this that what makes the will general is not so much the number of votes as the common interest that unites them, for in this institution each person necessarily submits himself to the conditions he imposes on others, an admirable accord between interest and justice which bestows on common deliberations a quality of equity that disappears when any particular matter is discussed, for lack of a common interest uniting and identifying the role of the judge with that of the party.

From whatever viewpoint one approaches this principle, one always arrives at the same conclusion, namely that the social compact establishes among the citizens an equality of such a kind that they all commit themselves under the same conditions and should all enjoy the same rights. Thus by the very nature of the compact, every act of sovereignty (that is, every authentic act of the general will) obligates or favors all citizens equally, so that the sovereign knows only the nation as a body and does not draw distinctions between any of those members that make it up. Strictly speaking, then, what is an act of sovereignty? It is not a convention between a superior and an inferior, but a convention of the body with each of its members. This convention is legitimate, because it has the social contract as a basis; equitable, because it is common to all; useful, because it can have only the general good for its object; and solid, because it has the public force and the supreme power as a guarantee. So long as the subjects are subordinated only to such convention, they obey no one but their own will alone. And asking how far the respective rights of the sovereign and the citizens extend is asking how far the latter can commit themselves to one another, each to all and all to each.

We can see from this that the sovereign power, absolute, wholly sacred and inviolable as it is, does not and cannot exceed the limits of general conventions, and that every man can completely dispose of such goods and freedom as has been left to him by these conventions. This results in the fact that the sovereign never has the right to lay more charges on one subject than on another, because in that case the matter becomes particular, no longer within the range of the sovereign's competence.

Once these distinctions are granted, it is so false that there is, in the social contract, any genuine renunciation on the part of private individuals that their situation, as a result of this contract, is really preferable to what it was beforehand; and, instead of an alienation, they have merely made an advantageous exchange of an uncertain and precarious mode of existence for another that is better and surer. Natural independence is exchanged for liberty; the power to harm others is exchanged for their own security; and their force, which others could overcome, for a right which the social union renders invincible. Their life itself, which they have devoted to the state, is continually protected by it; and when they risk their lives for its defense, what are they then doing but returning to the state what they have received from it? What are they doing, that they did not do more frequently and with greater danger in the state of nature, when they would inevitably have to fight battles, defending at the peril of their lives the means of their preservation? It is true that everyone has to fight, if necessary, for the homeland; but it also is the case that no one ever has to fight on his own behalf. Do we not still gain by running, for something that brings about our security, a portion of the risks we would have to run for ourselves once our security is taken away?

CHAPTER V
On the Right of Life or Death

The question arises how private individuals who have no right to dispose of their own lives can transfer to the sovereign this very same right which they do not have. This question seems difficult to resolve only because it is poorly stated. Every man has the right to risk his own life in order to preserve it. Has it ever been said that a person who jumps out a window to escape a fire is guilty of committing suicide? Has this crime ever been imputed to someone who perishes in a storm, unaware of its danger when he embarked?

The social treaty has as its purpose the conservation of the contracting parties. Whoever wills the end also wills the means, and these means are inseparable from some risks, even from some losses. Whoever wishes to preserve his life at the expense of others should also give it up for them when necessary. For the citizen is no longer judge of the peril to which the law wishes he be exposed, and when the prince has said to him, "it is expedient for the state that you should die," he should die. Because it is under this condition alone that he has lived in security up to then, and because his life is not only a kindess of nature, but a conditional gift of the state.

The death penalty inflicted on criminals can be viewed from more or less the same point of view. It is in order to avoid being the victim of an assassin that a person consents to die, were he to become one. According to this treaty, far from disposing of his own life, one thinks only of guaranteeing it. And it cannot be presumed that any of the contracting parties is then planning to get himself hanged.

Moreover, every malefactor who attacks the social right becomes through his transgressions a rebel and a traitor to the homeland; in violating its laws, he ceases to be a member, and he even wages war with it. In that case the preservation of the state is incompatible with his own. Thus one of the two must perish; and when the guilty party is put to death, it is less as a citizen than as an enemy. The legal proceeding and the judgment are the proofs and the declaration that he has broken the social treaty, and consequently that he is no longer a member of the state. For since he has acknowledged himself to be such, at least by his living there, he ought to be removed from it by exile as a violator of the compact, or by death as a public enemy. For such an enemy is not a moral person, but a man, and in this situation the right of war is to kill the vanquished.

But it will be said that the condemnation of a criminal is a particular act. Fine. So this condemnation is not a function of the sovereign. It is a right the sovereign can confer without itself being able to exercise it. All of my opinions are consistent, but I cannot present them all at once.

In addition, frequency of physical punishment is always a sign of weakness or of torpor in the government. There is no wicked man who could not be made good for something. One has the right to put to death, even as an example, only someone who cannot be preserved without danger.

With regard to the right of pardon, or of exempting a guilty party from the penalty decreed by the law and pronounced by the judge, this belongs only to one who is above the judge and the law, that is, to the sovereign. Still its right in this regard is not clearly defined, and the cases in which it is used are quite rare. In a well governed state, there are few punishments, not because many pardons are granted, but because there are few criminals. When a state is in decline, the sheer number of crimes insures impunity. Under the Roman Republic, neither the senate nor the consuls ever tried to grant pardons. The people itself did not do so, even though it sometimes revoked its own judgment. Frequent pardons indicate that transgressions will eventually have no need of them, and everyone sees where that leads. But I feel that my heart murmurs and holds back my pen. Let us leave these questions to be discussed by a just man who has not done wrong and who himself never needed pardon.

CHAPTER VI

On Law

Through the social compact we have given existence and life to the body politic. It is now a matter of giving it movement and will through legislation. For the primitive act whereby this body is formed and united still makes no determination regarding what it should do to preserve itself.

Whatever is good and in conformity with order is such by the nature of things and independently of human conventions. All justice comes from God; he alone is its source. But if we knew how to receive it from so exalted a source, we would have no need for government or laws. Undoubtedly there is a universal justice emanating from reason alone; but this justice, to be admitted among us, ought to be reciprocal. Considering things from a human standpoint, the lack of a natural sanction causes the laws of justice to be without teeth among men. They do nothing but good to the wicked and evil to the just, when the latter observes them in his dealings with everyone while no one observes them in their dealings with him. There must therefore be conventions and laws to unite rights and duties and to refer justice back to its object. In the state of nature where everything is commonly held, I owe nothing to those to whom I have promised nothing. I recognize as belonging to someone else only what is not useful to me. It is not this way in the civil state where all rights are fixed by law.

But what then is a law? So long as we continue to be satisfied with attaching only metaphysical ideas to this word, we will continue to reason without coming to any understanding. And when they have declared what a law of nature is, they will not thereby have a better grasp of what a law of the state is.

I have already stated that there is no general will concerning a particular object. In effect, this particular object is either within or outside of the state. If it is outside of the state, a will that is foreign to it is not general in relation to it. And if this object is within the state, that object is part of it; in that case, a relationship is formed between the whole and its parts which makes two separate beings, one of which is the part, and the other is the whole less that same part. But the whole less a part is not the whole, and so long as this relationship obtains, there is no longer a whole, but rather two unequal parts. Whence it follows that the will of the one is not more general in relation to the other.

But when the entire populace enacts a statute concerning the entire populace, it considers only itself, and if in that case a relationship is formed, it is between the entire object seen from one perspective and the entire object seen from another, without any division of the whole. Then the subject matter about which a statute is enacted is general like the will that enacts it. It is this act that I call a law.

When I say that the object of the laws is always general, I have in mind that the law considers subjects as a body and actions in the abstract, never a man as an individual or a particular action. Thus the law can perfectly well enact a statute to the effect that there be privileges, but it cannot bestow them by name on anyone. The law can create several classes of citizens, and even stipulate the qualifications that determine membership in these classes, but it cannot name specific persons to be admitted to them. It can establish a royal government and a hereditary line of succession, but it cannot elect a king or name a royal family. In a word, any function that relates to an individual does not belong to the legislative power. On this view, it is immediately obvious that it is no longer necessary to ask who is to make the laws, since they are the acts of the general will; nor whether the prince is above the laws, since he is a member of the state; nor whether the law can be unjust, since no one is unjust to himself; nor how one is both free and subject to the laws, since they are merely the record of our own wills.

Moreover, it is apparent that since the law combines the universality of the will and that of the object, what a man, whoever he may be, decrees on his own authority is not a law. What even the sovereign decrees concerning a particular object is no closer to being a law; rather, it is a decree. Nor is it an act of sovereignty but of magistracy.

I therefore call every state ruled by laws a republic, regardless of the form its administration may take. For only then does the public interest govern, and only then is the "public thing" [in Latin: *res publica*] something real. Every legitimate government is republican.[5] I will explain later on what government is.

Strictly speaking, laws are merely the conditions of civil association. The populace that is subjected to the laws ought to be their author. The regulating of the conditions of a society belongs to no one but those who are in association with one another. But how will they regulate these conditions? Will it be by a common accord, by a sudden inspiration? Does the body politic have an organ for making known its will? Who will give it the necessary foresight to formulate acts and to promulgate them in advance, or how will it announce them in time of need? How will a blind multitude, which often does not know what it wants (since it rarely knows what is good for it), carry out on its own an enterprise as great and as difficult as a system of legislation? By itself the populace always wants the good, but by itself it does not always see it. The general will is always right, but the judgment that guides it is not always enlightened. It must be made to see objects as they are, and sometimes as they ought to appear to it. The good path it seeks must be pointed out to it. It must be made safe from the seduction of private wills. It must be given a sense of time and place. It must weigh present, tangible advantages against the danger of distant, hidden evils. Private individuals see the good they reject. The public wills the good that it does not see. Everyone is equally in need of guides. The former must be obligated to conform their wills to their reason; the latter must learn to know what it wants. Then public enlightenment results in the union of the understanding and the will in the social body; hence the full cooperation of the parts, and finally the greatest force of the whole. Whence there arises the necessity of having a legislator.

CHAPTER VII
On the Legislator

Discovering the rules of society best suited to nations would require a superior intelligence that beheld all the passions of men without feeling any of them; who had no affinity with our nature, yet knew it through and through; whose happiness was independent of us, yet who never-

5. By this word I do not have in mind merely an aristocracy or a democracy, but in general every government guided by the general will, which is the law. To be legitimate, the government need not be made indistinguishable from the sovereign, but it must be its minister. Then the monarchy itself is a republic. This will become clear in the next Book.

theless was willing to concern itself with ours; finally, who, in the passage of time, procures for himself a distant glory, being able to labor in one age and find enjoyment in another.[6] Gods would be needed to give men laws.

The same reasoning used by Caligula regarding matters of fact was used by Plato regarding right in defining the civil or royal man he looks for in his dialogue *The Statesman*. But if it is true that a great prince is a rare man, what about a great legislator? The former merely has to follow the model the latter should propose to him. The latter is the engineer who invents the machine; the former is merely the workman who constructs it and makes it run. At the birth of societies, says Montesquieu, it is the leaders of republics who bring about the institution, and thereafter it is the institution that forms the leaders of the republic.

He who dares to undertake the establishment of a people should feel that he is, so to speak, in a position to change human nature, to transform each individual (who by himself is a perfect and solitary whole), into a part of a larger whole from which this individual receives, in a sense, his life and his being; to alter man's constitution in order to strengthen it; to substitute a partial and moral existence for the physical and independent existence we have all received from nature. In a word, he must deny man his own forces in order to give him forces that are alien to him and that he cannot make use of without the help of others. The more these natural forces are dead and obliterated, and the greater and more durable are the acquired forces, the more too is the institution solid and perfect. Thus if each citizen is nothing and can do nothing except in concert with all the others, and if the force acquired by the whole is equal or superior to the sum of the natural forces of all the individuals, one can say that the legislation has achieved the highest possible point of perfection.

The legislator is in every respect an extraordinary man in the state. If he ought to be so by his genius, he is no less so by his office, which is neither magistracy nor sovereignty. This office, which constitutes the republic, does not enter into its constitution. It is a particular and superior function having nothing in common with the dominion over men. For if he who has command over men must not have command over laws, he who has command over the laws must no longer have any authority over men. Otherwise, his laws, ministers of his passions, would often only serve to perpetuate his injustices, and he could never avoid private opinions altering the sanctity of his work.

When Lycurgus gave laws to his homeland, he began by abdicating the throne. It was the custom of most Greek cities to entrust the establishment of their laws to foreigners. The modern republics of Italy often imitated this custom. The republic of Geneva did the same and things worked out

---

6. A people never becomes famous except when its legislation begins to decline. It is not known for how many centuries the institution established by Lycurgus caused the happiness of the Spartans before the rest of Greece took note of it.

well.[7] In its finest age Rome saw the revival within its midst of all the crimes of tyranny and saw itself on the verge of perishing as a result of having united the legislative authority and the sovereign power in the same hands.

Nevertheless, the decimvirs themselves never claimed the right to have any law passed on their authority alone. *Nothing we propose,* they would tell the people, *can become law without your consent. Romans, be yourselves the authors of the laws that should bring about your happiness.*

He who frames the laws, therefore, does not or should not have any legislative right. And the populace itself cannot, even if it wanted to, deprive itself of this incommunicable right, because, according to the fundamental compact, only the general will obligates private individuals, and there can never be any assurance that a private will is in conformity with the general will until it has been submitted to the free vote of the people. I have already said this, but it is not a waste of time to repeat it.

Thus we find together in the work of legislation two things that seem incompatible: an undertaking that transcends human force, and, to execute it, an authority that is nil.

Another difficulty deserves attention. The wise men who want to speak to the common masses in the former's own language rather than in the common vernacular cannot be understood by the masses. For there are a thousand kinds of ideas that are impossible to translate in the language of the populace. Overly general perspectives and overly distant objects are equally beyond its grasp. Each individual, in having no appreciation for any other plan of government but the one that relates to his own private interest, finds it difficult to realize the advantages he ought to draw from the continual privations that good laws impose. For an emerging people to be capable of appreciating the sound maxims of politics and to follow the fundamental rules of statecraft, the effect would have to become the cause. The social spirit which ought to be the work of that institution, would have to preside over the institution itself. And men would be, prior to the advent of laws, what they ought to become by means of laws. Since, therefore, the legislator is incapable of using either force or reasoning, he must of necessity have recourse to an authority of a different order, which can compel without violence and persuade without convincing.

This is what has always forced the fathers of nations to have recourse to the intervention of heaven and to credit the gods with their own wisdom, so that the peoples, subjected to the laws of the state as to those of nature and recognizing the same power in the formation of man and of the city, might obey with liberty and bear with docility the yoke of public felicity.

---

7. Those who view Calvin simply as a theologian fail to grasp the extent of his genius. The codification of our wise edicts, in which he had a large role, does him as much honor as his *Institutes.* Whatever revolution time may bring out in our cult, so long as the love of homeland and of liberty is not extinguished among us, the memory of this great man will never cease to be held sacred.

It is this sublime reason, which transcends the grasp of ordinary men, whose decisions the legislator puts in the mouth of the immortals in order to compel by divine authority those whom human prudence could not move.[8] But not everybody is capable of making the gods speak or of being believed when he proclaims himself their interpreter. The great soul of the legislator is the true miracle that should prove his mission. Any man can engrave stone tablets, buy an oracle, or feign secret intercourse with some divinity, or train a bird to talk in his ear, or find other crude methods of imposing his beliefs on the people. He who knows no more than this may perchance assemble a troupe of lunatics, but he will never found an empire and his extravagant work will soon die with him. Pointless sleights-of-hand form a fleeting connection; only wisdom can make it lasting. The Judaic Law, which still exists, and that of the child of Ishmael, which has ruled half the world for ten centuries, still proclaim today the great men who enunciated them. And while pride-ridden philosophy or the blind spirit of factionalism sees in them nothing but lucky impostors, the true political theoretician admires in their institutions that great and powerful genius which presides over establishments that endure.

We should not, with Warburton, conclude from this that politics and religion have a common object among us, but that in the beginning stages of nations the one serves as an instrument of the other.

CHAPTER VIII
On the People

Just as an architect, before putting up a large building, surveys and tests the ground to see if it can bear the weight, the wise teacher does not begin by laying down laws that are good in themselves. Rather he first examines whether the people for whom they are destined are fitted to bear them. For this reason, Plato refused to give laws to the Arcadians and to the Cyrenians, knowing that these two peoples were rich and could not abide equality. For this reason, one finds good laws and evil men in Crete, because Minos had disciplined nothing but a vice-ridden people.

A thousand nations have achieved brilliant earthly success that could never have abided good laws; and even those that could have would have been able to have done so for a very short period of their entire existence. Peoples,[9] like men, are docile only in their youth. As they grow older they

8. *And in truth,* says Machiavelli, *there has never been among a people a single legislator who, in proposing extraordinary laws, did not have recourse to God, for otherwise they would not be accepted, since there are many benefits known to a prudent man that do not have in themselves evident reasons enabling him to persuade others. Discourses on Titus Livy, Book I, Ch. XI.* [Rousseau here quotes the Italian.]

9. [*In the 1782 edition, this sentence was revised to read:* "Most people, like men. . . ."]

become incorrigible. Once customs are established and prejudices have become deeply rooted, it is a dangerous and vain undertaking to want to reform them. The people cannot abide having even their evils touched in order to eliminate them, just like those stupid and cowardly patients who quiver at the sight of a physician.

This is not to say that, just as certain maladies unhinge men's minds and remove from them the memory of the past, one does not likewise sometimes find in the period during which states have existed violent epochs when revolutions do to peoples what certain crises do to individuals, when the horror of the past takes the place of forgetfulness, and when the state, set afire by civil wars, is reborn, as it were, from its ashes and takes on again the vigor of youth as it escapes death's embrace. Such was Sparta at the time of Lycurgus; such was Rome after the Tarquins; and such in our time have been Holland and Switzerland after the expulsion of the tyrants.

But these events are rare. They are exceptions whose cause is always to be found in the particular constitution of the states in question. They cannot take place even twice to the same people, for it can make itself free so long as it is merely barbarous; but it can no longer do so when civil strength is exhausted. At that point troubles can destroy it with revolutions being unable to reestablish it. And as soon as its chains are broken, it falls apart and exists no longer. Henceforward a master is needed, not a liberator. Free peoples, remember this axiom: Liberty can be acquired, but it can never be recovered.

For nations, as for men, there is a time of maturity that must be awaited before subjecting them to the laws.[10] But the maturity of a people is not always easily recognized; and if it is foreseen, the work is ruined. One people lends itself to discipline at its inception; another, not even after ten centuries. The Russians will never be truly civilized, since they have been civilized too early. Peter had a genius for imitation. He did not have true genius, the kind that creates and makes everything out of nothing. Some of the things he did were good; most of them were out of place. He saw that his people was barbarous; he did not see that it was not ready for civilization. He wanted to civilize it when all it needed was toughening. First he wanted to make Germans and Englishmen, when he should have made Russians. He prevented his subjects from ever becoming what they could have been by persuading them that they were something they are not. This is exactly how a French tutor trains his pupil to shine for a short time in his childhood, and afterwards never to amount to a thing. The Russian Empire would like to subjugate Europe and will itself be subjugated. The Tartars, its subjects or its neighbors, will become its masters and ours. This revolution appears inevitable to me. All the kings of Europe are working in concert to hasten its occurrence.

10. [*In the 1782 edition, this sentence was revised to read:* "Youth is not childhood. For nations, as for men, maturity must be awaited. . . ."]

CHAPTER IX
The People (continued)

Just as nature has set limits to the status of a well-formed man, beyond which there are but giants or dwarfs, so too, with regard to the best constitution of a state, there are limits to the size it can have, so as not to be too large to be capable of being well governed, nor too small to be capable of preserving itself on its own. In every body politic there is a *maximum* force that it cannot exceed, and which has often fallen short by increasing in size. The more the social bond extends the looser it becomes, and in general a small state is proportionately stronger than a large one.

A thousand reasons prove this maxim. First, administration becomes more difficult over great distances, just as a weight becomes heavier at the end of a longer lever. It also becomes more onerous as the number of administrative levels multiplies, because first each city has its own administration which the populace pays for; each district has its own, again paid for by the people; next each province has one and then the great governments, the satrapies and vice royalties, requiring a greater cost the higher you go, and always at the expense of the unfortunate people. Finally, there is the supreme administration which weights down on everyone. All these surcharges continually exhaust the subjects. Far from being better governed by these different orders, they are worse governed than if there were but one administration over them. Meanwhile, hardly any resources remain for meeting emergencies; and when recourse must be made to them, the state is always on the verge of its ruin.

This is not all. Not only does the government have less vigor and quickness in enforcing the observance of the laws, preventing nuisances, correcting abuses and foreseeing the seditious undertakings that can occur in distant places, but also the populace has less affection for its leaders when it never sees them, for the homeland, which, to its eyes, is like the world, and for its fellow citizens, the majority of whom are foreigners to it. The same laws cannot be suitable to so many diverse provinces which have different customs, live in contrasting climates, and which are incapable of enduring the same form of government. Different laws create only trouble and confusion among the peoples who live under the same rulers and are in continuous communication. They intermingle and intermarry, and, being under the sway of other customs, never know whether their patrimony is actually their own. Talents are hidden; virtues are unknown; vices are unpunished in this multitude of men who are unknown to one another which the seat of supreme administration brings together in one place. The leaders, overwhelmed with work, see nothing for themselves; clerks govern the state. Finally, the measures that need to be taken to maintain the general authority, which so many distant officials want to avoid or harass, absorb all the public attention. Nothing more remains for the people's happiness, and there barely remains enough for its defense in time of need. And thus a body which is too big for its constitution collapses and perishes, crushed by its own weight.

On the other hand, the state ought to provide itself with a firm foundation to give it solidity, to resist the shocks it is bound to experience, as well as the efforts it will have to make to sustain itself. For all the peoples have a kind of centrifugal force, by which they continually act one against the other and tend to expand at the expense of their neighbors, like Descartes' vortices. Thus the weak risk being soon swallowed up; scarcely any people can preserve itself except by putting itself in a kind of equilibrium with all, which nearly equalizes the pressure on all sides.

It is clear from this that there are reasons for expanding and reasons for contracting, and it is not the least of the political theorist's talents to find, between these and other reasons, the proportion most advantageous to the preservation of the state. In general, it can be said that the former reasons, being merely external and relative, should be subordinated to the latter reasons, which are internal and absolute. A strong, healthy constitution is the first thing one needs to look for, and one should count more on the vigor born of a good government than on the resources furnished by a large territory.

Moreover, there have been states so constituted that the necessity for conquests entered into their very constitution, and that, to maintain themselves, they were forced to expand endlessly. Perhaps they congratulated themselves greatly on account of this happy necessity, which nevertheless showed them, together with the limit of their size, the inevitable moment of their fall.

CHAPTER X

The People (continued)

A body politic can be measured in two ways: namely, by the size of its territory and by the number of its people. And between these measurements there is a relationship suitable for giving the state its true greatness. Men are what make up the state and land is what feeds men. This relationship therefore consists in there being enough land for the maintenance of its inhabitants and as many inhabitants as the land can feed. It is in this proportion that the *maximum* force of a given population size is found. For if there is too much land, its defense is onerous, its cultivation inadequate, and its yield surplus. This is the proximate cause of defensive wars. If there is not enough land, the state finds itself at the discretion of its neighbors for what it needs as a supplement. This is the proximate cause of offensive wars. Any people whose position provides it an alternative merely between commerce and war is inherently weak. It depends on its neighbors; it depends on events. It never has anything but an uncertain and brief existence. Either it conquers and changes the situation, or it is conquered and obliterated. It can keep itself free only by means of smallness or greatness.

No one can provide in mathematical terms a fixed relationship between the size of land and the population size which are sufficient for one another, as much because of the differences in the characteristics of the terrain, its degrees of fertility, the nature of its crops, the influence of its climates, as because of the differences to be noted in the temperaments of the men who inhabit them, some of whom consume little in a fertile country, while others consume a great deal on a barren soil. Again, attention must be given to the greater or lesser fertility of women, to what the country can offer that is more or less favorable to the population, to the number of people that the legislator can hope to bring together through his institutions. Thus, the legislator should not base his judgment on what he sees but on what he foresees. And he should dwell less upon the present state of the population as upon the state it should naturally attain. Finally, there are a thousand situations where the idiosyncracies of a place require or permit the assimilation of more land than appears necessary. Thus, there is considerable expansion in mountainous country, where the natural crops—namely, woods and pastures—demand less work; where experience shows that women are more fertile than on the plains; and where a large amount of sloping soil provides only a very small amount of flat land, the only thing that can be counted on for vegetation. On the other hand, people can draw closer to one another at the seashore, even on rocks and nearly barren sand, because fishing can make up to a great degree for the lack of land crops, since men should be more closely gathered together in order to repulse pirates, and since in addition it is easier to unburden the country of surplus inhabitants by means of colonies.

To these conditions for instituting a people must be added one that cannot be a substitute for any other, but without which all the rest are useless: the enjoyment of the fullness of peace. For the time when a state is organized, like the time when a battalion is formed, is the instant when the body is the least capable of resisting and easiest to destroy. There would be better resistance at a time of absolute disorder than at a moment of fermentation, when each man is occupied with his own position rather than with the danger. Were a war, famine, or sedition to arise in this time of crisis the state inevitably is overthrown.

This is not to say that many governments are not established during such storms; but in these instances it is these governments themselves that destroy the state. Usurpers always bring about or choose these times of trouble to use public terror to pass destructive laws that the people never adopt when they have their composure. The choice of the moment of a government's institution is one of the surest signs by which the work of a legislator can be distinguished from that of a tyrant.

What people, therefore, is suited for legislation? One that, finding itself bound by some union of origin, interest or convention, has not yet felt the true yoke of laws. One that has no custom or superstitions that are deeply rooted. One that does not fear being overpowered by sudden invasion. One that can, without entering into the squabbles of its neighbors, resist each of them single-handed or use the help of one to repel another. One where each member can be known to all, and where there is no need to impose a greater burden on a man than a man can bear. One that can get along without peoples and without which every other people can get along.[11] One that is neither rich nor poor and can be sufficient unto itself; finally, one that brings together the stability of an ancient people and the docility of a new people. What makes the work of legislation trying is not so much what must be established or what must be destroyed. And what makes success so rare is the impossibility of finding the simplicity of nature together with the needs of society. All these conditions, it is true, are hard to find in combination. Hence few well constituted states are to be seen.

In Europe there is still one country capable of receiving legislation. It is the island of Corsica. The valor and constancy with which this brave people has regained and defended its liberty would well merit having some wise man teaching them how to preserve it. I have a feeling that some day that little island will astonish Europe.

CHAPTER XI
On the Various Systems of Legislation

If one enquires into precisely wherein the greatest good of all consists, which should be the purpose of every system of legislation, one will find that it boils down to the two principal objects, *liberty* and *equality*. Liberty, because all particular dependence is that much force taken from the body of the state; equality, because liberty cannot subsist without it.

I have already said what civil liberty is. Regarding equality, we need not mean by this word that degrees of power and wealth are to be absolutely the same, but rather that, with regard to power, it should transcend all violence and never be exercised except by virtue of rank and laws; and, with regard to wealth, no citizen should be so rich as to be capable of buying another citizen, and none so poor that he is forced to sell himself. This presupposes moderation in goods and credit on the part of the great, and moderation in avarice and covetousness[12] on the part of the lowly.

---

11. If there were two neighboring peoples, one being unable to get along without the other, it would be a very tough situation for the former and very dangerous for the latter. In such a case, every wise nation will work very quickly to free the other of its dependency. The republic of Thlascala, enclosed within the Mexican empire, preferred to do without salt, rather than buy it from the Mexicans or even take it from them for nothing. The wise Thlascalans saw the trap hidden beneath this generosity. They kept themselves free, and this small state, enclosed within this great empire, was finally the instrument of its ruin.

12. Do you therefore want to give constancy to the State? Bring the extremes as close together as possible. Tolerate neither rich men nor beggars. These two estates, which are naturally inseparable, are equally fatal to the common good. From the one come the fomenters of tyranny, and from the other the tyrants. It is

This equality is said to be a speculative fiction that cannot exist in practice. But if abuse is inevitable, does it follow that it should not at least be regulated? It is precisely because the force of things tends always to destroy equality that the force of legislation should always tend to maintain it.

But these general objects of every good institution should be modified in each country in accordance with the relationships that arise as much from the local situation as from the temperament of the inhabitants. And it is on the basis of these relationships that each people must be assigned a particular institutional system that is the best, not perhaps in itself, but for the state for which it is destined. For example, is the soil barren and unproductive, or the country too confining for its inhabitants? Turn to industry and crafts, whose products you will exchange for the foodstuffs you lack. On the other hand, do you live in rich plains and fertile slopes? Do you lack inhabitants on a good terrain? Put all your effort into agriculture, which increases the number of men, and chase out the crafts that seem only to achieve the depopulation of the country by grouping in a few sectors what few inhabitants there are.[13] Do you occupy long, convenient coastlines? Cover the sea with vessels; cultivate commerce and navigation. You will have a brilliant and brief existence. Does the sea wash against nothing on your coasts but virtually inaccessible rocks? Remain barbarous and fish-eating. You will live in greater tranquillity, better perhaps and certainly happily. In a word, aside from the maxims common to all, each people has within itself some cause that organizes them in a particular way and renders its legislation proper for it alone. Thus it was that long ago the Hebrews and recently the Arabs have had religion as their main object; the Athenians had letters; Carthage and Tyre, commerce; Rhodes, seafaring; Sparta, war; and Rome, virtue. The author of *The Spirit of the Laws* has shown with a large array of examples the art by which the legislator directs the institution toward each of its objects.

What makes the constitution of a state truly solid and lasting is that proprieties are observed with such fidelity that the natural relations and the laws are always in agreement on the same points, and that the latter serve only to assure, accompany and rectify them. But if the legislator is mistaken about his object and takes a principle different from the one arising from the nature of things (whether the one tends toward servitude and the other toward liberty; the one toward riches, the other toward increased population; the one toward peace, the other toward conquests), the laws will weaken imperceptibly, the constitution will be altered, and

---

always between them that public liberty becomes a matter of commerce. The one buys it and the other sells it.

13. Any branch of foreign trade, says the Marquis d'Argenson, creates hardly anything more than a false utility for a kingdom in general. It can enrich some private individuals, even some towns, but the nation as a whole gains nothing and the populace is none the better for it.

the state will not cease being agitated until it is destroyed or changed, and invincible nature has regained her empire.

CHAPTER XII
Classification of the Laws

To set the whole in order or to give the commonwealth the best possible form, there are various relations to consider. First, the action of the entire body acting upon itself, that is, the relationship of the whole to the whole, or of the sovereign to the state, and this relationship, as we will see later, is composed of relationships of intermediate terms.

The laws regulating this relationship bear the name political laws, and are also called fundamental laws, not without reason if these laws are wise. For there is only one way of organizing in each state. The people who have found it should stand by it. But if the established order is evil, why should one accept as fundamental, laws that prevent it from being good? Besides, a people is in any case always in a position to change its laws, even the best laws. For if it wishes to do itself harm, who has the right to prevent it from doing so?

The second relation is that of the members to each other or to the entire body. And this relationship should be as small as possible in regard to the former and as large as possible in regard to the latter, so that each citizen would be perfectly independent of all the others and excessively dependent upon the city. This always takes place by the same means, for only the force of the state brings about the liberty of its members. It is from this second relationship that civil laws arise.

We may consider a third sort of relation between man and law, namely that of disobedience and penalty. And this gives rise to the establishment of criminal laws, which basically are not so much a particular kind of law as the sanction for all the others.

To these three sorts of law is added a fourth, the most important of all. It is not engraved on marble or bronze, but in the hearts of citizens. It is the true constitution of the state. Everyday it takes on new forces. When other laws grow old and die away, it revives and replaces them, preserves a people in the spirit of its institution and imperceptibly substitutes the force of habit for that of authority. I am speaking of mores, customs, and especially of opinion, a part of the law unknown to our political theorists but one on which depends the success of all the others; a part with which the great legislator secretly occupies himself, though he seems to confine himself to the particular regulations that are merely the arching of the vault, whereas mores, slower to arise, form in the end its immovable keystone.

Among these various classes, only political laws, which constitute the form of government, are relevant to my subject.

END OF THE SECOND BOOK

BOOK III

Before speaking of the various forms of government, let us try to determine the precise meaning of this word, which has not as yet been explained very well.

CHAPTER I
On Government in General

I am warning the reader that this chapter should be read carefully and that I do not know the art of being clear to those who do not want to be attentive.

Every free action has two causes that come together to produce it. The one is moral, namely the will that determines the act; the other is physical, namely the power that executes it. When I walk toward an object, I must first want to go there. Second, my feet must take me there. A paralyzed man who wants to walk or an agile man who does not want to walk will both remain where they are. The body politic has the same moving causes. The same distinction can be made between force and the will; the one under the name *legislative power* and the other under the name *executive power*. Nothing is done and ought to be done without their concurrence.

We have seen that legislative power belongs to the people and can belong to it alone. On the contrary, it is easy to see, by the principles established above, that executive power cannot belong to the people at large in its role as legislator or sovereign, since this power consists solely of particular acts that are not within the province of the law, nor consequently of the sovereign, none of whose acts can avoid being laws.

Therefore the public force must have an agent of its own that unifies it and gets it working in accordance with the directions of the general will, that serves as a means of communication between the state and the sovereign, and that accomplishes in the public person just about what the union of soul and body accomplishes in man. This is the reason for having government in the state, something often badly confused with the sovereign, of which it is merely the minister.

What then is the government? An intermediate body established between the subjects and the sovereign for their mutual communication, and charged with the execution of the laws and the preservation of liberty, both civil and political.

The members of this body are called magistrates or *kings,* that is to say, *governors,* and the entire body bears the name *prince.*[1] Therefore those who claim that the act by which a people submits itself to leaders is not a contract are quite correct. It is absolutely nothing but a commission, an employment in which the leaders, as simple officials of the

---

1. Thus in Venice the College is given the name *Most Serene Prince* even when the Doge is not present.

sovereign, exercise in its own name the power with which it has entrusted them. The sovereign can limit, modify, or appropriate this power as it pleases, since the alienation of such a right is incompatible with the nature of the social body and contrary to the purpose of the association.

Therefore, I call *government* or supreme administration the legitimate exercise of executive power; I call prince or magistrate the man or the body charged with that administration.

In government one finds the intermediate forces whose relationships make up that of the whole to the whole or of the sovereign to the state. This last relationship can be represented as one between the extremes of a continuous proportion, whose proportional mean is the government. The government receives from the sovereign the orders it gives the people, and, for the state to be in good equilibrium, there must, all things considered, be an equality between the output or the power of the government, taken by itself, and the output or power of the citizens, who are sovereigns on the one hand and subjects on the other.

Moreover, none of these three terms could be altered without the simultaneous destruction of the proportion. If the sovereign wishes to govern, or if the magistrate wishes to give laws, or if the subjects refuse to obey, disorder replaces rule, force and will no longer act in concert, and thus the state dissolves and falls into despotism or anarchy. Finally, since there is only one proportional mean between each relationship, there is only one good government possible for a state. But since a thousand events can change the relationships of a people, not only can different governments be good for different peoples, but also for the same people at different times.

In trying to provide an idea of the various relationships that can obtain between these two extremes, I will take as an example the number of people, since it is a more easily expressed relationship.

Suppose the state is composed of ten thousand citizens. The sovereign can only be considered collectively and as a body. But each private individual in his position as a subject is regarded as an individual. Thus the sovereign is to the subject as ten thousand is to one. In other words, each member of the state has as his share only one ten-thousandth of the sovereign authority, even though he is totally in subjection to it. If the populace is made up of a hundred thousand men, the condition of the subjects does not change, and each bears equally the entire dominion of the laws, while his vote, reduced to one hundred-thousandth, has ten times less influence in the drafting of them. In that case, since the subject always remains one, the ratio of the sovereign to the subject increases in proportion to the number of citizens. Whence it follows that the larger the state becomes, the less liberty there is.

When I say that the ratio increases, I mean that it places a distance between itself and equality. Thus the greater the ratio is in the sense employed by geometricians, the less relationship there is in the everyday sense of the word. In the former sense, the ratio, seen in terms of quantity, is measured by the quotient; in the latter sense, ratio, seen in terms of identity, is reckoned by similarity.

Now the less relationship there is between private wills and the general will, that is, between mores and the laws, the more repressive force ought to increase. Therefore, in order to be good, the government must be relatively stronger in proportion as the populace is more numerous.

On the other hand, as the growth of the state gives the trustees of the public authority more temptations and the means of abusing their power, the more the force the government must have in order to contain the people, the more the force the sovereign must have in order to contain the government. I am speaking here not of an absolute force but of the relative force of the various parts of the state.

It follows from this twofold relationship that the continuous proportion between the sovereign, the prince and the people, is in no way an arbitrary idea, but a necessary consequence of the nature of the body politic. It also follows that since one of the extremes, namely the people as subject, is fixed and represented by unity, whenever the doubled ratio increases or decreases, the simple ratio increases or decreases in like fashion, and that as a consequence the middle term is changed. This makes it clear that there is no unique and absolute constitution of government, but that there can be as many governments of differing natures as there are states of differing sizes.

If, in ridiculing this system, someone were to say that in order to find this proportional mean and to form the body of the government, it is necessary merely, in my opinion, to derive the square root of the number of people, I would reply that here I am taking this number only as an example; that the relationships I am speaking of are not measured solely by the number of men, but in general by the quantity of action, which is the combination of a multitude of causes; and that, in addition, if to express myself in fewer words I borrow for the moment the terminology of geometry, I nevertheless am not unaware of the fact that geometrical precision has no place in moral quantities.

The government is on a small scale what the body politic which contains it is on a large scale. It is a moral person endowed with certain faculties, active like the sovereign and passive like the state, and capable of being broken down into other similar relationships whence there arises as a consequence a new proportion and yet again another within this one according to the order of tribunals, until an indivisible middle term is reached; that is, a single leader or supreme magistrate, who can be represented in the midst of this progression as the unity between the series of fractions and that of whole numbers.

Without involving ourselves in this multiplication of terms, let us content ourselves with considering the government as a new body in the state, distinct from the people and sovereign, and intermediate between them.

The essential difference between these two bodies is that the state exists by itself, while the government exists only through the sovereign. Thus the dominant will of the prince is not and should not be anything other than the general will or the law. His force is merely the public force concentrated in him. As soon as he wants to derive from himself some absolute and independent act, the bond that links everything together begins to come loose. If it should finally happen that the prince had a private will more active than that of the sovereign, and that he had made use of some of the public force that is available to him in order to obey this private will, so that there would be, so to speak, two sovereigns—one de jure and the other de facto, at that moment the social union would vanish and the body politic would be dissolved.

However, for the body of the government to have an existence, a real life that distinguishes it from the body of the state, and for all its members to be able to act in concert and to fulfill the purpose for which it is instituted, there must be a particular *self,* a sensibility common to all its members, a force or will of its own that tends toward its preservation. This particular existence presupposes assemblies, councils, a power to deliberate and decide, rights, titles and privileges that belong exclusively to the prince and that render the condition of the magistrate more honorable in proportion as it is more onerous. The difficulties lie in the manner in which this subordinate whole is so organized within the whole, that it in no way alters the general constitution by strengthening its own, that it always distinguishes its particular force, which is intended for its own preservation, from the public force intended for the preservation of the state, and that, in a word, it is always ready to sacrifice the government to the people and not the people to the government.

In addition, although the artificial body of the government is the work of another artificial body and has, in a sense, only a borrowed and subordinate life, this does not prevent it from being capable of acting with more or less vigor or speed, or from enjoying, so to speak, more or less robust health. Finally, without departing directly from the purpose of its institution, it can deviate more or less from it, according to the manner in which it is constituted.

From all these differences arise the diverse relationships that the government should have with the body of the state, according to the accidental and particular relationships by which the state itself is modified. For often the government that is best in itself will become the most vicious, if its relationships are not altered according to the defects of the body politic to which it belongs.

CHAPTER II
On the Principle that Constitutes
the Various Forms of Government

In order to lay out the general cause of these differences, a distinction must be made here between the prince and the government, as I had done before between the state and the sovereign.

The body of the magistrates can be made up of a larger or smaller number of members. We have said that the ratio of the sovereign to the subjects was greater in proportion as the populace was more numerous, and by a manifest analogy we can say the same thing about the government in relation to the magistrates.

Since the total force of the government is always that of the state, it does not vary. Whence it follows that the more of this force it uses on its own members, the less that is left to it for acting on the whole populace.

Therefore, the more numerous the magistrates, the weaker the government. Since this maxim is fundamental, let us attempt to explain it more clearly.

We can distinguish in the person of the magistrate three essentially different wills. First, the individual's own will, which tends only to its own advantage. Second, the common will of the magistrates which is uniquely related to the advantage of the prince. This latter can be called the corporate will, and is general in relation to the government, and particular in relation to the state, of which the government forms a part. Third, the will of the people or the sovereign will, which is general both in relation to the state considered as the whole and in relation to the government considered as a part of the whole.

In a perfect act of legislation, the private or individual will should be nonexistent; the corporate will proper to the government should be very subordinate; and consequently the general or sovereign will should always be dominant and the unique rule of all the others.

According to the natural order, on the contrary, these various wills become more active in proportion as they are the more concentrated. Thus the general will is always the weakest, the corporate will has second place, and the private will is first of all, so that in the government each member is first himself, then a magistrate, and then a citizen—a gradation directly opposite to the one required by the social order.

Granting this, let us suppose the entire government is in the hands of one single man. In that case the private will and the corporate will are perfectly united, and consequently the latter is at the highest degree of intensity it can reach. But since the use of force is dependent upon the degree of will, and since the absolute force of the government does not vary one bit, it follows that the most active of governments is that of one single man.

On the other hand, let us suppose we are uniting the government to the legislative authority. Let us make the sovereign the prince and all the citizens that many magistrates. Then the corporate will, confused with the general will, will have no more activity than the latter, and will leave the private will all its force. Thus the government, always with the same absolute force, will have its *minimum* relative force or activity.

These relationships are incontestable, and there are still other considerations that serve to confirm them. We see, for example, that each magistrate is more active in his body than each citizen is in his, and consequently that the private will has much more influence on the acts of the government than on those of the sovereign. For each magistrate is nearly always charged with the responsibility for some function of government, whereas each citizen, taken by himself, exercises no function of sovereignty. Moreover, the more the state is extended, the more its real force increases, although it does not increase not in proportion to its size. But if the state remains the same, the magistrates may well be multiplied without the government acquiring any greater real force, since this force is that of the state, whose size is always equal. Thus the relative force or activity of the government diminishes without its absolute or real force being able to increase.

It is also certain that the execution of public business becomes slower in proportion as more people are charged with the responsibility for it; that in attaching too much importance to prudence, too little importance is attached to fortune, opportunities are missed, and the fruits of deliberation are often lost by dint of deliberation.

I have just proved that the government becomes slack in proportion as the magistrates are multiplied; and I have previously proved that the more numerous the people, the greater should be the increase of repressive force. Whence it follows that the ratio of the magistrate to the government should be the inverse of the ratio of the subjects to the sovereign; that is to say, the more the state increases in size, the more the government should shrink, so that the number of leaders decreases in proportion to the increase in the number of people.

I should add that I am speaking here only about the relative force of the government and not about its rectitude. For, on the contrary, the more numerous the magistrates, the more closely the corporate will approaches the general will, whereas under a single magistrate, the same corporate will is, as I have said, merely a particular will. Thus what can be gained on the one hand is lost on the other, and the art of the legislator is to know how to determine the point at which the government's will and force, always in a reciprocal proportion, are combined in the relationship that is most advantageous to the state.

CHAPTER III

Classification of Governments

We have seen in the previous chapter why the various kinds or forms of government are distinguished by the number of members that compose them. It remains to be seen in this chapter how this classification is made.

In the first place, the sovereign can entrust the government to the entire people or to the majority of the people, so that there are more citizens who are magistrates than who are ordinary private citizens. This form of government is given the name *democracy*.

Or else it can restrict the government to the hands of a small number, so that there are more ordinary citizens than magistrates; and this form is called *aristocracy*.

Finally, it can concentrate the entire government in the hands of a single magistrate from whom all the others derive their power. This third form is the most common and is called *monarchy* or royal government.

It should be noted that all these forms, or at least the first two, can be had in greater or lesser degrees, and even have a rather wide range. For democracy can include the entire populace or be restricted to half. Aristocracy, for its part, can be indeterminately restricted from half the people down to the smallest number. Even royalty can be had in varying levels of distribution. Sparta always had two kings, as required by its constitution; and the Roman Empire is known to have had up to eight emperors at a time, without it being possible to say that the empire was divided. Thus there is a point at which each form of government is indistinguishable from the next, and it is apparent that, under just three names, government can take on as many diverse forms as the state has citizens.

Moreover, since this same government can, in certain respects, be subdivided into other parts, one administered in one way, another in another, there can result from the combination of these three forms a multitude of mixed forms, each of which can be multiplied by all the simple forms.

There has always been a great deal of argument over the best form of government, without considering that each one of them is best in certain cases and the worst in others.

If the number of supreme magistrates in the different states ought to be in inverse ratio to that of the citizens, it follows that in general democratic government is suited to small states, aristocratic government to states of intermediate size, and monarchical government to large ones. This rule is derived immediately from the principle; but how is one to count the multitude of circumstances that can furnish exceptions?

CHAPTER IV
On Democracy

He who makes the law knows better than anyone else how it should be executed and interpreted. It seems therefore to be impossible to have a better constitution than one in which the executive power is united to the legislative power. But this is precisely what renders such a government inadequate in certain respects, since things that should be distinguished are not, and the prince and sovereign, being merely the same person, form, as it were, only a government without a government.

It is not good for the one who makes the laws to execute them, nor for the body of the people to turn its attention away from general perspectives in order to give it particular objects. Nothing is more dangerous than the influence of private interests on public affairs; and the abuse of the laws by the government is a lesser evil than the corruption of the legislator, which is the inevitable outcome of particular perspectives. In such a situation, since the state is being substantially altered, all reform becomes impossible. A people that would never misuse the government would never misuse independence. A people that would always govern well would not need to be governed.

Taking the term in the strict sense, a true democracy has never existed and never will. It is contrary to the natural order that the majority govern and the minority is governed. It is unimaginable that the people would remain constantly assembled to handle public affairs; and it is readily apparent that it could not establish commissions for this purpose without changing the form of administration.

In fact, I believe I can lay down as a principle that when the functions of the government are shared among several tribunals, those with the fewest members sooner or later acquire the greatest authority, if only because of the facility in expediting public business which brings this about naturally.

Besides, how many things that are difficult to unite are presupposed by this government? First, a very small state where it is easy for the people to gather together and where each citizen can easily know all the others. Second, a great simplicity of mores, which prevents the multitude of public business and thorny discussions. Next, a high degree of equality in ranks and fortunes, without which equality in rights and authority cannot subsist for long. Finally, little or no luxury, for luxury either is the effect of wealth or it makes wealth necessary. It simultaneously corrupts both the rich and the poor, the one by possession, the other by covetousness. It sells the homeland to softness and vanity. It takes all its citizens from the state in order to make them slaves to one another, and all of them to opinion.

This is why a famous author has made virtue the principle of the republic. For all these conditions could not subsist without virtue. But owing to his failure to have made the necessary distinctions, this great genius often lacked precision and sometimes clarity. And he did not realize that since the sovereign authority is everywhere the same, the same principle should have a place in every well constituted state, though in a greater or lesser degree, it is true, according to the form of government.

Let us add that no government is so subject to civil wars and internal agitations as a democratic or popular one, since there is none that tends so forcefully and continuously to change its form, or that demands greater vigilance and courage to be maintained in its own form. Above all, it is under this constitution that the citizen ought to arm himself with force and constancy, and to say each day of his life from the bottom of his heart what a virtuous Palatine[2] said in the Diet of Poland: *Better to have liberty fraught with danger than servitude in peace.*

Were there a people of gods, it would govern itself democratically. So perfect a government is not suited to men.

---

2. The Palatine of Posen, father of the King of Poland, Duke of Lorraine. [Rousseau quotes in Latin the maxim which follows.]

CHAPTER V
On Aristocracy

We have here two very distinct moral persons, namely the government and the sovereign, and consequently two general wills, one in relation to all the citizens, the other only for the members of the administration. Thus, although the government can regulate its internal administration as it chooses, it can never speak to the people except in the name of the sovereign, that is to say, in the name of the populace itself. This is something not to be forgotten.

The first societies governed themselves aristocratically. The leaders of families deliberated among themselves about public affairs. Young people deferred without difficulty to the authority of experience. This is the origin of the words *priests, ancients, senate* and *elders*. The savages of North America still govern themselves that way to this day, and are very well governed.

But to the extent that inequality occasioned by social institutions came to prevail over natural inequality, wealth or power[3] was preferred to age, and aristocracy became elective. Finally, the transmission of the father's power, together with his goods, to his children created patrician families; the government was made hereditary, and we know of senators who were only twenty years old.

There are therefore three sorts of aristocracy: natural, elective and hereditary. The first is suited only to simple people; the third is the worst of any government. The second is the best; it is aristocracy properly so-called.

In addition to the advantage of the distinction between the two powers, aristocracy has that of the choice of its members. For in popular government all the citizens are born magistrates; however, this type of government limits them to a small number, and they become magistrates only through election,[4] a means by which probity, enlightenment, experience, and all the other reasons for public preference and esteem are so many new guarantees of being well governed.

Furthermore, assemblies are more conveniently held, public business better discussed and carried out with more orderliness and diligence, the reputation of the state is better sustained abroad by venerable senators than by a multitude that is unknown or despised.

---

3. It is clear that among the ancients the word *optimates* does not mean the best, but the most powerful.

4. It is of great importance that laws should regulate the form of the election of magistrates, for if it is left to the will of the prince, it is impossible to avoid falling into a hereditary aristocracy, as has taken place in the Republics of *Venice* and *Berne*. Thus the former has long been a state in dissolution, while the latter maintains itself through the extreme wisdom of its senate. It is a very honorable and very dangerous exception.

In a word, it is the best and most natural order for the wisest to govern the multitude, when it is certain that they will govern for its profit and not for their own. There is no need for multiplying devices uselessly or for doing with twenty thousand men what one hundred hand-picked men can do even better. But it must be noted here that the corporate interest begins to direct the public force in less strict a conformity with the rule of the general will, and that another inevitable tendency removes from the laws a part of the executive power.

With regard to the circumstances that are specifically suitable, a state must not be so small, nor its people so simple and upright that the execution of the laws follows immediately from the public will, as is the case in a good democracy. Nor must a nation be so large that the leaders, scattered about in order to govern it, can each play the sovereign in his own department, and begin by making themselves independent in order finally to become the masters.

But if aristocracy requires somewhat fewer virtues than popular government, it also demands others that are proper to it, such as moderation among the wealthy and contentment among the poor. For it appears that rigorous equality would be out of place here. It was not observed even in Sparta.

Moreover, if this form of government carries with it a certain inequality of fortune, this is simply in order that in general the administration of public business may be entrusted to those who are best able to give all their time to it, but not, as Aristotle claims, in order that the rich may always be given preference. On the contrary, it is important that an opposite choice should occasionally teach the people that more important reasons for preference are to be found in a man's merit than in his wealth.

CHAPTER VI
On Monarchy

So far, we have considered the prince as a moral and collective person, united by the force of laws, and as the trustee of the executive power in the state. We have now to consider this power when it is joined together in the hands of a natural person, of a real man, who alone has the right to dispose of it in accordance with the laws. Such a person is called a monarch or a king.

In utter contrast with the other forms of administration where a collective entity represents an individual, in this form of administration an individual represents a collective entity; so that the moral unity constituting the prince is at the same time a physical unity, in which all the faculties which are combined by the law in the other forms of administration with such difficulty are found naturally combined.

Thus the will of the people, the will of the prince, the public force of the state, and the particular force of the government, all respond to the same moving agent; all the springs of the machine are in the same hand; everything moves toward the same end; there are no opposing movements which are at cross purposes with one another; and no constitution is imaginable in which a lesser effort produces a more considerable action. Archimedes sitting serenely on the shore and effortlessly launching a huge vessel is what comes to mind when I think of a capable monarch governing his vast states from his private study, and making everything move while appearing himself to be immovable.

But if there is no government that has more vigor, there is none where the private will has greater sway and more easily dominates the others. Everything moves toward the same end, it is true; but this end is not that of public felicity, and the very force of the administration unceasingly operates to the detriment of the state.

Kings want to be absolute, and from a distance one cries out to them that the best way to be so is to make themselves loved by their peoples. This maxim is very noble and even very true in certain respects. Unfortunately it will always be an object of derision in courts. The power that comes from the peoples' love is undoubtedly the greatest, but it is precarious and conditional. Princes will never be satisfied with it. The best kings want to be able to be wicked if it pleases them, without ceasing to be the masters. A political sermonizer might well say to them that since the people's force is their force, their greatest interest is that the people should be flourishing, numerous and formidable. They know perfectly well that this is not true. Their personal interest is first of all that the people should be weak and miserable and incapable of ever resisting them. I admit that, assuming the subjects were always in perfect submission, the interest of the prince would then be for the people to be powerful, so that this power, being his own, would render him formidable in the eyes of his neighbors. But since this interest is merely secondary and subordinate, and since the two suppositions are incompatible, it is natural that the princes should always give preference to the maxim that is the most immediately useful to them. This is the point that Samuel made so forcefully to the Hebrews, and that Machiavelli has made apparent. Under the pretext of teaching kings, he has taught important lessons to the peoples. Machiavelli's *The Prince* is the book of republicans.[5]

We have found, through general relationships, that the monarchy is suited only to large states, and we find this again in examining the monarchy itself. The more numerous the public administration, the more the ratio of the prince to subject diminishes and approaches equality, so that

---

5. [The following was inserted in the 1782 edition: "Machiavelli was a decent man and a good citizen. But since he was attached to the house of Medici, he was forced during the oppression of his homeland to disguise his love of liberty. The very choice of his execrable hero makes clear enough his hidden intention. And the contrast between the maxims of his book *The Prince* and those of his *Discourses on Titus Livy* and of his *History of Florence* shows that this profound political theorist has until now had only superficial or corrupt readers. The court of Rome has sternly prohibited his book. I can well believe it; it is the court he most clearly depicts."]

this ratio increases in proportion as the government is restricted, and is at its *maximum* when the government is in the hands of a single man. Then there is too great a distance between the prince and the people, and the state lacks cohesiveness. In order to bring about this cohesiveness, there must therefore be intermediate orders; there must be princes, grandees, and a nobility to fill them. Now none of this is suited to a small state, which is ruined by all these social levels.

But if it is difficult for a large state to be well governed, it is much harder still for it to be well governed by just one man, and everyone knows what happens when the king appoints substitutes.

An essential and inevitable defect, which will always place the monarchical form of government below the republican form, is that in the latter form the public voice hardly ever raises to the highest positions men who are not enlightened and capable and who would not fill their positions with honor. On the other hand, those who attain these positions in monarchies are most often petty bunglers, petty swindlers, petty intriguers, whose petty talents, which cause them to attain high positions at court, serve only to display their incompetence to the public as soon as they reach these positions. The populace is much less often in error in its choice than the prince, and a man of real merit in the ministry is almost as rare as a fool at the head of a republican government. Thus, when by some happy chance one of these men who are born to govern takes the helm of public business in a monarchy that has nearly been sunk by this crowd of fine managers, there is utter amazement at the resources he finds, and his arrival marks an era in the history of the country.

For a monarchical state to be capable of being well governed, its size or extent must be proportionate to the faculties of the one who governs. It is easier to conquer than to rule. With a long enough lever it is possible for a single finger to make the world shake; but holding it in place requires the shoulders of Hercules. However small a state may be, the prince is nearly always too small for it. When, on the contrary, it happens that the state is too small for its leader, which is quite rare, it is still poorly governed, since the leader, always pursuing his grand schemes, forgets the interests of the peoples, making them no less wretched through the abuse of talents he has too much of than does a leader who is limited for want of what he lacks. A kingdom must, so to speak, expand or contract with each reign, depending on the ability of the prince. On the other hand, since the talents of a senate have a greater degree of stability, the state can have permanent boundaries without the administration working any less well.

The most obvious disadvantage of the government of just one man is the lack of that continuous line of succession which forms an unbroken bond of unity in the other two forms of government. When one king dies, another is needed. Elections leave dangerous intervals and are stormy. And unless the citizens have a disinterestedness and integrity that seldom accompanies this form of government, intrigue and corruption enter the picture. It is difficult for one to whom the state has sold itself not to sell it in turn, and reimburse himself at the expense of the weak for the money extorted from him by the powerful. Sooner or later everything becomes venal under such an administration, and in these circumstances, the peace enjoyed under kings is worse than the disorders of the interregna.

What has been done to prevent these ills? In certain families, crowns have been made hereditary, and an order of succession has been established which prevents all dispute when kings die. That is to say, by substituting the disadvantage of regencies for that of elections, an apparent tranquillity has been preferred to a wise administration, the risk of having children, monsters, or imbeciles for leaders has been preferred to having to argue over the choice of good kings. No consideration has been given to the fact that in being thus exposed to the risk of the alternative, nearly all the odds are against them. There was a lot of sense in what Dionysius the Younger said in reply to his father, who, while reproaching his son for some shameful action, said "Have I given you such an example?" "Ah," replied the son, "but your father was not king."

When a man has been elevated to command others, everything conspires to deprive him of justice and reason. A great deal of effort is made, it is said, to teach young princes the art of ruling. It does not appear that this education does them any good. It would be better to begin by teaching them the art of obeying. The greatest kings whom history celebrates were not brought up to reign. It is a science one is never less in possession of than after one has learned too much, and that one acquires it better in obeying than in commanding. *For the most useful as well as the shortest method of finding out what is good and what is bad is to consider what you would have wished or not wished to have happened under another prince.*[6]

One result of this lack of coherence is the instability of the royal form of government, which, now regulated by one plan now by another according to the character of the ruling prince or of those who rule for him, cannot have a fixed object for very long or a consistent policy. This variation always causes the state to drift from maxim to maxim, from project to project, and does not take place in the other forms of government, where the prince is always the same. It is also apparent that in general, if there is more cunning in a royal court, there is more wisdom in a senate; and that republics proceed toward their objectives by means of policies that are more consistent and better followed. On the other hand, each revolution in the ministry produces a revolution in the state, since the maxim common to all ministers and nearly all kings is to do the reverse of their predecessor in everything.

From this same incoherence we derive the solution to a sophism that is very familiar to royalist political theorists. Not only is civil government compared to domestic government and the prince to the father of the family (an error already refuted), but this magistrate is also liberally

6. Tacitus, *Histories,* Book I. [Rousseau here quotes the Latin.]

given all the virtues he might need, and it is always presupposed that the prince is what he ought to be. With the help of this presupposition, the royal form of government is obviously preferable to any other, since it is unquestionably the strongest; and it lacks only a corporate will that is more in conformity with the general will in order to be the best as well.

But if according to Plato,[7] a king by nature is such a rare person, how many times will nature and fortune converge to crown him; and if a royal education necessarily corrupts those who receive it, what is to be hoped from a series of men who have been brought up to reign? Surely then it is deliberate self-deception to confuse the royal form of government with that of a good king. To see what this form of government is in itself, we need to consider it under princes who are incompetent or wicked, for either they come to the throne wicked or incompetent, or else the throne makes them so.

These difficulties have not escaped the attention of our authors, but they have not been troubled by them. The remedy, they say, is to obey without a murmur. God in his anger gives us bad kings, and they must be endured as punishments from heaven. No doubt this sort of talk is edifying, however I do not know but that it belongs more in a pulpit than in a book on political theory. What is to be said of a physician who promises miracles, and whose art consists entirely of exhorting his sick patient to practice patience? It is quite obvious that we must put up with a bad government when that is what we have. The question would be how to find a good one.

CHAPTER VII
On Mixed Government

Strictly speaking, there is no such thing as a simple form of government. A single leader must have subordinate magistrates; a popular government must have a leader. Thus in the distribution of the executive power there is always a gradation from the greater to the lesser number, with the difference that sometimes the greater number depends on the few, and sometimes the few depend on the greater number.

At times the distribution is equal, either when the constitutive parts are in a state of mutual dependence, as in the government of England; or when the authority of each part is independent but imperfect, as in Poland. This latter form is bad, since there is no unity in the government and the state lacks a bond of unity.

Which one is better, a simple or a mixed form of government? A question much debated among political theorists, to which the same reply must be given that I gave above regarding every form of government.

In itself the simple form of government is the best, precisely because it is simple. But when the executive power is not sufficiently dependent upon the legislative power, that is to say, when there is more of a ratio

7. *The Statesman.*

between the prince and the sovereign than between the people and the prince, this defect in the proportion must be remedied by dividing the government; for then all of its parts have no less authority over the subjects, and their division makes all of them together less forceful against the sovereign.

The same disadvantage can also be prevented through the establishment of intermediate magistrates, who, by being utterly separate from the government, serve merely to balance the two powers and to maintain their respective rights. In that case, the government is not mixed; it is tempered.

The opposite difficulty can be remedied by similar means. And when the government is too slack, tribunals can be set up to give it a concentrated focus. This is done in all democracies. In the first case the government is divided in order to weaken it, and in the second to strengthen it. For the *maximum* of force and weakness are found equally in the simple forms of government, while the mixed forms of government provide an intermediate amount of strength.

CHAPTER VIII
That Not All Forms of Government
Are Suited to All Countries

Since liberty is not a fruit of every climate, it is not within the reach of all peoples. The more one meditates on this principle established by Montesquieu, the more one is aware of its truth. The more one contests it, the more occasions there are for establishing it by means of new proofs.

In all the governments in the world, the public person consumes, but produces nothing. Whence therefore does it get the substance it consumes? It is from the labor of its members. It is the surplus of private individuals that produces what is needed by the public. Whence it follows that the civil state can subsist only so long as men's labor produces more than they need.

Now this surplus is not the same in every country in the world. In many countries it is considerable; in others it is moderate; in others it is nil; in still others it is negative.

This ratio depends on the fertility of the climate, the sort of labor the land requires, the nature of its products, the force of its inhabitants, the greater or lesser consumption they need, and many other similar ratios of which it is composed.

On the other hand, not all governments are of the same nature. They are more or less voracious; and the differences are founded on this added principle that the greater the distance the public contributions are from their source, the more onerous they are. It is not on the basis of the amount of the taxes that this burden is to be measured, but on the basis of the path they have to travel in order to return to the hands from which they came. When this circulation is prompt and well established, it is unimportant whether one pays little or a great deal. The populace is always rich and the finances are always in good shape. On the contrary, however little the populace gives, when this small amount does not return, it is soon wiped out by continual giving. The state is never rich and the populace is always destitute.

It follows from this that the greater the distance between the people and the government, the more onerous the taxes become. Thus in a democracy the populace is the least burdened; in an aristocracy it is more so; in a monarchy it bears the heaviest weight. Monarchy, therefore, is suited only to wealthy nations; aristocracy to states of moderate wealth and size; democracy to states that are small and poor.

In fact, the more one reflects on it, the more one finds in it the difference between free and monarchical states. In the former, everything is used for the common utility. In the latter, the public and private forces are reciprocal, the one being augmented by the weakening of the other. Finally, instead of governing subjects in order to make them happy, despotism makes them miserable in order to govern them.

Thus in each climate there are natural causes on the basis of which one can assign the form of government that the force of the climate requires, and can even say what kind of inhabitants it should have. Barren and unproductive lands, where the product is not worth the labor, ought to remain uncultivated and deserted, or peopled only by savages. Places where men's labor yields only what is necessary ought to be inhabited by barbarous peoples; in places such as these all polity would be impossible. Places where the surplus of products over labor is moderate are suited to free peoples. Those where an abundant and fertile soil produces a great deal in return for a small amount of labor require a monarchical form of government, in order that the subject's excess of surplus may be consumed by the prince's luxurious living. For it is better for this excess to be absorbed by the government than dissipated by private individuals. I realize that there are exceptions; but these exceptions themselves prove the rule, in that sooner or later they produce revolutions that restore things to the order of nature.

General laws should always be distinguished from the particular causes that can modify their effect. Even if the entire south were covered with republics and the entire north with despotic states, it would still be no less true that the effect of climate makes despotism suited to hot countries, barbarism to cold countries, and good polity to intermediate regions. I also realize that, while granting the principle, disputes may arise over its application. It could be said that there are cold countries that are very fertile and southern ones that are quite barren. But this poses a difficulty only for those who have not examined the thing in all its relationships. As I have said, it is necessary to take into account those of labor, force, consumption, and so on.

Let us suppose that there are two parcels of land of equal size, one of which yields five units and the other yields ten. If the inhabitants of the first parcel consume four units and the inhabitants of the second consume nine, the excess of the first will be one-fifth and that of the other will be one-tenth. Since the ratio of these two excesses is therefore the inverse of that of the products, the parcel of land that produces only five units will yield a surplus that is double that of the parcel of land that produces ten.

But it is not a question of a double product, and I do not believe that anyone dares, as a general rule, to place the fertility of a cold country even on an equal footing with that of hot countries. Nevertheless, let us assume that this equality does obtain. Let us, if you will, reckon England to be the equal of Sicily, and Poland the equal of Egypt. Further south we have Africa and the Indies; further north we have nothing at all. To achieve this equality of product, what difference must there be in agricultural techniques? In Sicily one needs merely to scratch the soil; in England what efforts it demands to work it! Now where more hands are needed to obtain the same product, the surplus ought necessarily to be less.

Consider too that the same number of men consumes much less in hot countries. The climate demands that a person keep sober in order to be in good health. Europeans wanting to live there just as they do at home would all die of dysentery and indigestion. *We are,* says Chardin, *carnivorous beasts, wolves, in comparison with the Asians. Some attribute the sobriety of the Persians to the fact that their land is less cultivated. On the contrary, I believe that this country is less abundant in commodities because the inhabitants need less. If their frugality,* he continues, *were an effect of the country's scarcity, only the poor would eat little; however, it is generally the case that everyone does so. And more or less would be eaten in each province according to the fertility of the country; however, the same sobriety is found throughout the kingdom. They take great pride in their lifestyle, saying that one has only to look at their complexions to recognize how far it excels that of the Christians. In fact, the complexion of the Persians is clear. They have fair skin, fine and polished, whereas the complexion of their Armenian subjects, who live in the European style, is coarse and blotchy, and their bodies are fat and heavy.*

The closer you come to the equator, the less people live on. They rarely eat meat; rice, maize, couscous, millet and cassava are their usual diet. In the Indies there are millions of men whose sustenance costs less than a penny a day. In Europe itself we see noticeable differences in appetite between the peoples of the north and the south. A Spaniard will live for eight days on a German's dinner. In countries where men are the most voracious, luxury too turns toward things edible. In England, luxury is shown in a table loaded with meats; in Italy you are regaled on sugar and flowers.

Luxury in clothing also offers similar differences. In the climate where the seasonal changes are sudden and violent, people have better and simpler clothing. In climates where people clothe themselves merely for ornamental purposes, flashiness is more sought after than utility. The clothes themselves are a luxury there. In Naples you see men strolling everyday along the Posilippo decked out in gold-embroidered coats and bare legged. It is the same with buildings; magnificence is the sole consideration when there is nothing to fear from the weather. In Paris or

London, people want to be housed warmly and comfortably. In Madrid, there are superb salons, but no windows that close, and people sleep in rat holes.

In hot countries foodstuffs are considerably more substantial and succulent. This is a third difference which cannot help but influence the second. Why do people eat so many vegetables in Italy? Because there they are good, nourishing, and have an excellent flavor. In France, where they are fed nothing but water, they are not nourishing at all, and are nearly counted for nothing at table. Be that as it may, they occupy no less land and cost at least as much effort to cultivate. It is a known fact that the wheats of Barbary, in other respects inferior to those of France, yield far more flour, and that those of France, for their part, yield more wheats than those of the north. It can be inferred from this that a similar gradation in the same direction is generally observed from the equator to the pole. Now is it not a distinct disadvantage to have a smaller quantity of food in an equal amount of produce?

To all these different considerations, I can add one which depends on and strengthens them. It is that hot countries have less of a need for inhabitants than do cold countries, and yet could feed more of them. This produces a double surplus, always to the advantage of despotism. The greater the area occupied by the same number of inhabitants, the more difficult it becomes to revolt, since concerted action cannot be taken promptly and secretly; and it is always easy for the government to discover plots and cut off communications. But the closer together a numerous people is drawn, the less the government can usurp from the sovereign. The leaders deliberate as safely in their rooms as the prince does in his council; and the crowd assembles as quickly in public squares as do troops in their quarters. In this regard, the advantage of a tyrannical government, therefore, is that of acting over great distances. With the help of the points of support it establishes, its force increases with distance like that of levers.[8] On the other hand, the strength of the people acts only when concentrated; it evaporates and is lost as it spreads, like the effect of gunpowder scattered on the ground, which catches fire only one grain at a time. The least populated countries are thus the best suited for tyranny. Ferocious animals reign only in deserts.

CHAPTER IX

On the Signs of a Good Government

When the question arises which one is absolutely the best government, an insoluble question is being raised because it is indeterminate. Or, if you wish, it has as many good answers as there are possible combinations in the absolute and relative positions of peoples.

8. This does not contradict what I said earlier in Book II, Chapter IX, regarding the disadvantages of large states, for there it was a question of the authority of the government over its members, and here it is a question of its force against the subjects. Its scattered members serve it as points of support for acting from a distance

But if it is asked by what sign it is possible to know that a given people is well or poorly governed, this is another matter, and the question of fact could be resolved.

However, nothing is answered, since each wants to answer it in his own way. The subjects praise public tranquillity; the citizens praise the liberty of private individuals. The former prefers the security of possessions; the latter that of persons. The former has it that the best government is the one that is most severe; the latter maintains that the best government is the one that is mildest. This one wants crimes to be punished, and that one wants them prevented. The former think it a good thing to be feared by their neighbors; the latter prefer to be ignored by them. The one is content so long as money circulates; the other demands that the people have bread. Even if agreement were had on these and similar points, would we be any closer to an answer? Since moral quantities do not allow of precise measurement, even if there were agreement regarding the sign, how could there be agreement regarding the evaluation.

For my part, I am always astonished that such a simple sign is overlooked or that people are of such bad faith as not to agree on it. What is the goal of the political association? It is the preservation and prosperity of its members. And what is the surest sign that they are preserved and prospering? It is their number and their population. Therefore do not go looking elsewhere for this much disputed sign. All other things being equal, the government under which, without external means, without naturalizations, without colonies, the citizens become populous and multiply the most, is infallibly the best government. That government under which a populace diminishes and dies out is the worst. Calculators, it is now up to you. Count, measure, compare.[9]

---

upon the people, but it has no support for acting directly on these members themselves. Thus in the one case the length of the lever causes its weakness, and in the other case its force.

9. We should judge on this same principle the centuries that merit preference with respect to the prosperity of the human race. Those in which letters and arts are known to have flourished have been admired too much, without penetrating the secret object of their cultivation, and without considering its devastating effect, *and this was called humanity by the inexperienced, when it was a part of servitude.* [Rousseau here quotes Tacitus, *Agricola,* 21, in Latin.] Will we never see in the maxims of books the crude interest that causes the authors to speak? No. Whatever they may say, when a country is depopulated, it is not true, despite its brilliance, that all goes well; and the fact that a poet has an income of hundred thousand livres is not sufficient to make his century the best of all. The apparent calm and tranquillity of the leader ought to be less of an object of consideration than the well-being of whole nations and especially of the most populous states. A hailstorm may devastate a few cantons, but it rarely causes famine. Riots and civil wars may greatly disturb the leaders, but they are not the true misfortunes of the people, who may even have a reprieve while people argue over who will tyrannize them. It is their permanent condition that causes real periods of prosperity or calamity. It is when everything remains crushed under the yoke that everything decays. It is then that the leaders destroy them at will, *where they bring about solitude they call it peace.*

CHAPTER X
On the Abuse of Government and
Its Tendency to Degenerate

Just as the private will acts constantly against the general will, so the government makes a continual effort against sovereignty. The more this effort increases, the more the constitution is altered. And since there is here no other corporate will which, by resisting the will of the prince, would create an equilibrium with it, sooner or later the prince must finally oppress the sovereign and break the social treaty. That is the inherent and inevitable vice which, from the birth of the body politic, tends unceasingly to destroy it, just as old age and death destroy the human body.

There are two general ways in which a government degenerates, namely, when it shrinks, or when the state dissolves.

The government shrinks when it passes from a large to a small number, that is to say, from democracy to aristocracy, and from aristocracy to royalty. That is its natural inclination.[10] If it were to go backward from a small number to a large number, it could be said to slacken, but this reverse progression is impossible.

[Rousseau here quotes Tacitus, *Agricola,* 31, in Latin.] When the quarrels of the great disturbed the kingdom of France, and the Coadjutor of Paris brought with him to the Parliament a knife in his pocket, this did not keep the French people from living happily and in great numbers in a free and decent ease. Long ago, Greece flourished in the midst of the cruelest wars. Blood flowed in waves, and the whole country was covered with men. It seemed, says Machiavelli, that in the midst of murders, proscriptions, and civil wars, our republic became more powerful; the virtue of its citizens, their mores, and their independence did more to reinforce it than all its dissensions did to weaken it. A little agitation gives strength to souls, and what truly brings about prosperity for the species is not so much peace as liberty.

10. The slow formation and the progress of the Republic of Venice in its lagoons offers a notable example of this succession. And it is rather astonishing that after more than twelve hundred years the Venetians seem to be no further than the second stage, which began with *Serrar di Consiglio* in 1198. As for the ancient dukes, for whom the Venetians are reproached, whatever the *squitinio della libertà veneta* may say about them, it has been proved that they were not their sovereigns.

The Roman Republic does not fail to be brought forward as an objection against me, which, it will be said, followed a completely opposite course, passing from monarchy to aristocracy to democracy. I am quite far from thinking of it in this way.

The first establishment of Romulus was a mixed government that promptly degenerated into despotism. For some particular reasons, the state perished before its time, just as one sees a newborn die before reaching manhood. The expulsion of the Tarquins was the true epoch of the birth of the republic. But it did not at first take on a constant form, because in failing to abolish the patriciate, only half the work was completed. For in this way, since hereditary aristocracy, which is the worst of all forms of legitimate administration, remained in conflict with democracy, a form of government that is always uncertain and adrift, it was not determined, as Machiavelli has proved, until the establishment of the tribunes. It was only then that there was a true government and a veritable democracy. In fact, the populace then was not

In fact, the government never changes its form except when its exhausted energy leaves it too enfeebled to be capable of preserving what belongs to it. Now if it were to become still more slack while it expanded, its force would become entirely nil; it would be still less likely to subsist. It must therefore wind up and tighten its force in proportion as it gives way; otherwise the state it sustains would fall into ruin.

The dissolution of the state can come about in two ways.

First, when the prince no longer administers the state in accordance with the laws and usurps the sovereign power. In that case a remarkable change takes place, namely that it is not the government but the state that shrinks. I mean that the state as a whole is dissolved, and another is formed inside it, composed exclusively of the members of the government, and which is no longer anything for the rest of the populace but its master and tyrant. So that the instant that the government usurps sovereignty, the social compact is broken, and all ordinary citizens, on recovering by right their natural liberty, are forced but not obliged to obey.

The same thing happens also when the members of the government separately usurp the power they should only exercise as a body. This is no less an infraction of the laws, and produces even greater disorder. Under these circumstances, there are, so to speak, as many princes as magistrates, and the state, no less divided than the government, perishes or changes its form.

When the state dissolves, the abuse of government, whatever it is, takes the common name *anarchy*. To distinguish, democracy degenerates into *ochlocracy,* aristocracy into *oligarchy*. I would add that royalty degenerates into *tyranny,* however this latter term is equivocal and requires an explanation.

In the ordinary sense a tyrant is a king who governs with violence and without regard for justice and the laws. In the strict sense, a tyrant is a private individual who arrogates to himself royal authority without having any right to it. This is how the Greeks understood the word tyrant. They gave the name indifferently to good and bad princes whose authority

---

merely sovereign but also magistrate and judge. The senate was merely a subordinate tribunal whose purpose was to temper and concentrate the government; and the consuls themselves, though they were patricians, magistrates, and absolute generals in war, in Rome were merely presidents of the people.

From that point on, the government was also seen to follow its natural inclination and to tend strongly toward aristocracy. With the patriciate having abolished itself, as it were, the aristocracy was no longer in the body of patricians, as it was in Venice and Genoa, but in the body of the senate which was composed of patricians and plebeians, and even in the body of the tribunes when they began to usurp an active power. For words do not affect things, and when the populace has leaders who govern for it, it is always an aristocracy, regardless of the name these leaders bear.

The abuse of aristocracy gave birth to civil wars and the triumvirate. Sulla, Julius Caesar, and Augustus became in fact veritable monarchs, and finally, under the despotism of Tiberius, the state was dissolved. Roman history therefore does not invalidate my principle; it confirms it.

was not legitimate.[11] Thus *tyrant* and *usurper* are two perfectly synonymous words.

To give different names to different things, I call the usurper of royal authority a *tyrant,* and the usurper of sovereign power a *despot.* The tyrant is someone who intrudes himself, contrary to the laws, in order to govern according to the laws. The despot is someone who places himself above the laws themselves. Thus the tyrant cannot be a despot, but the despot is always a tyrant.

CHAPTER XI
On the Death of the Body Politic

Such is the natural and inevitable tendency of the best constituted governments. If Sparta and Rome perished, what state can hope to last forever? If we wish to form a durable establishment, let us then not dream of making it eternal. To succeed, one must not attempt the impossible or flatter oneself with giving to the work of men a solidity that things human do not allow.

The body politic, like the human body, begins to die from the very moment of its birth, and carries within itself the causes of its destruction. But both can have a constitution that is more or less robust and suited to preserve them for a longer or shorter time. The constitution of man is the work of nature; the constitution of the state is the work of art. It is not within men's power to prolong their lives; it is within their power to prolong the life of the state as far as possible, by giving it the best constitution it can have. The best constituted state will come to an end, but later than another, if no unforeseen accident brings about its premature fall.

The principle of political life is in the sovereign authority. Legislative power is the heart of the state; the executive power is the brain, which gives movement to all the parts. The brain can fall into paralysis and yet the individual may still live. A man may remain an imbecile and live. But once the heart has ceased its functions, the animal is dead.

It is not through laws that the state subsists; it is through legislative power. Yesterday's law does not obligate today, but tacit consent is presumed from silence, and the sovereign is taken to be giving incessant confirmation to the laws it does not abrogate while having the power to do so. Whatever it has once declared it wants, it always wants, unless it revokes its declaration.

---

11. *For all are considered and are called tyrants who use perpetual power in a city accustomed to liberty.* [Rousseau here quotes the Latin.] Cornelius Nepos, *Life of Miltiades.* It is true that Aristotle, *Nicomachean Ethics,* Book XVIII, Chapter 10, distinguishes between a tyrant and a king, in that the former governs for his own utility and the latter governs only for the utility of his subjects. But besides the fact that generally all the Greek authors used the word tyrant in another sense, as appears most clearly in Xenophon's *Hiero,* it would follow from Aristotle's distinction that there has not yet been a single king since the beginning of the world.

Why then is so much respect paid to ancient laws? For just this very reason. We must believe that nothing but the excellence of the ancient wills that could have preserved them for so long. If the sovereign had not constantly recognized them to be salutary, it would have revoked them a thousand times. This is why, far from growing weak, the laws continually acquire new force in every well constituted state. The prejudice in favor of antiquity each day renders them more venerable. On the other hand, wherever the laws weaken as they grow old, this proves that there is no longer a legislative power, and that the state is no longer alive.

CHAPTER XII
How the Sovereign Authority Is Maintained

The sovereign, having no other force than legislative power, acts only through the laws. And since the laws are only authentic acts of the general will, the sovereign can act only when the populace is assembled. With the populace assembled, it will be said: what a chimera! It is a chimera today, but two thousand years ago it was not. Have men changed their nature?

The boundaries of what is possible in moral matters are less narrow than we think. It is our weaknesses, our vices and our prejudices that shrink them. Base souls do not believe in great men; vile slaves smile with an air of mockery at the word liberty.

Let us consider what can be done in the light of what has been done. I will not speak of the ancient republics of Greece; however, the Roman Republic was, to my mind, a great state, and the town of Rome was a great town. The last census in Rome gave four thousand citizens bearing arms, and the last census count of the empire gave four million citizens, not counting subjects, foreigners, women, children, and slaves.

What difficulty might not be imagined in frequently calling assemblies of the immense populace of that capital and its environs. Nevertheless, few weeks passed by without the Roman people being assembled, and even several times in one week. It exercised not only the rights of sovereignty but also a part of those of the government. It took care of certain matters of public business; it tried certain cases; and this entire populace was in the public meeting place hardly less often as magistrate than as citizen.

In looking back to the earliest history of nations, one would find that most of the ancient governments, even the monarchical ones such as those of the Macedonians and the Franks, had similar councils. Be that as it may, this lone contestable fact answers every difficulty: arguing from the actual to the possible seems like good logic to me.

CHAPTER XIII
Continuation

It is not enough for an assembled people to have once determined the constitution of the state by sanctioning a body of laws. It is not enough for it to have established a perpetual government or to have provided once and for all for the election of magistrates. In addition to the extraordinary assemblies that unforeseen situations can necessitate, there must be some fixed, periodic assemblies that nothing can abolish or prorogue, so that on a specified day the populace is rightfully convened by law, without the need for any other formal convocation.

But apart from these assemblies which are lawful by their date alone, any assembly of the people that has not been convened by the magistrates appointed for that task and in accordance with the prescribed forms should be regarded as illegitimate, and all that takes place there should be regarded as null, since the order itself to assemble ought to emanate from the law.

As to the question of the greater or lesser frequency of legitimate assemblies, this depends on so many considerations that no precise rules can be given about it. All that can be said is that in general the more force a government has, the more frequently the sovereign ought to show itself.

I will be told that this may be fine for a single town, but what is to be done when the state includes several? Will the sovereign authority be divided, or will it be concentrated in a single town with all the rest made subject to it?

I answer that neither should be done. In the first place, the sovereign authority is simple and one; it cannot be divided without being destroyed. In the second place, a town cannot legitimately be in subjection to another town, any more than a nation can be in subjection to another nation, since the essence of the body politic consists in the harmony of obedience and liberty; and the words *subject* and *sovereign* are identical correlatives, whose meaning is combined in the single word "citizen."

I answer further that it is always an evil to unite several towns in a single city, and that anyone wanting to bring about this union should not expect to avoid its natural disadvantages. The abuses of large states should not be raised as an objection against someone who wants only small ones. But how are small states to be given enough force to resist the large ones, just as the Greek cities long ago resisted a great king, and more recently Holland and Switzerland have resisted the house of Austria?

Nevertheless, if the state cannot be reduced to appropriate boundaries, one expedient still remains: not to allow a fixed capital, to make the seat of government move from one town to another, and to assemble the estates of the country in each of them in their turn.

Populate the territory uniformly, extend the same rights everywhere, spread abundance and life all over. In this way the state will become simultaneously as strong and as well governed as possible. Recall that town walls are made from the mere debris of rural houses. With each palace I see being erected in the capital, I believe I see an entire countryside turned into hovels.

CHAPTER XIV
Continuation

Once the populace is legitimately assembled as a sovereign body, all jurisdiction of the government ceases; the executive power is suspended, and the person of the humblest citizen is as sacred and inviolable as that of the first magistrate, for where those who are represented are found, there is no longer any representative. Most of the tumults that arose in the comitia in Rome were due to ignorance or neglect of this rule. On such occasions the consuls were merely the presidents of the people; the tribunes, ordinary speakers;[12] the senate, nothing at all.

These intervals of suspension, during which the prince recognizes or ought to recognize an actual superior, have always been disturbing to him. And these assemblies of the people, which are the aegis of the body politic and the curb on the government, have at all times been the horror of leaders. Thus they never spare efforts, objections, difficulties, or promises to keep the citizens from having them. When the citizens were greedy, cowardly, and pusillanimous, more enamored of repose than with liberty, they do not hold out very long against the redoubled efforts of the government. Thus it is that, as the resisting force constantly grows, the sovereign authority finally vanishes, and the majority of the cities fall and perish prematurely.

But between the sovereign authority and arbitrary government, there sometimes is introduced an intermediate power about which we must speak.

CHAPTER XV
On Deputies or Representatives

Once public service ceases to be the chief business of the citizens, and they prefer to serve with their wallet rather than with their person, the state is already near its ruin. Is it necessary to march off to battle? They pay mercenary troops and stay at home. Is it necessary to go to the council? They name deputies and stay at home. By dint of laziness and money, they finally have soldiers to enslave the country and representatives to sell it.

The hustle and bustle of commerce and the arts, the avid interest in profits, softness and the love of amenities: these are what change personal services into money. A person gives up part of his profit in order to increase it at leisure. Give money and soon you will be in chains. The

---

12. In nearly the same sense as is given this word in English Parliament. The similarity between these activities would have put the consuls and the tribunes in conflict, even if all jurisdiction had been suspended.

word *finance* is a slave's word. It is unknown in the city. In a truly free state the citizens do everything with their own hands and nothing with money. Far from paying to be exempted from their duties, they would pay to fulfill them themselves. Far be it from me to be sharing commonly held ideas. I believe that forced labor is less opposed to liberty than are taxes.

The better a state is constituted, the more public business takes precedence over private business in the minds of the citizens. There even is far less private business, since, with the sum of common happiness providing a more considerable portion of each individual's happiness, less remains for him to look for through private efforts. In a well run city everyone flies to the assemblies; under a bad government no one wants to take a step to get to them, since no one takes an interest in what happens there, for it is predictable that the general will will not predominate, and that in the end domestic concerns absorb everything. Good laws lead to making better laws; bad laws bring about worse ones. Once someone says *what do I care?* about the affairs of state, the state should be considered lost.

The cooling off of patriotism, the activity of private interest, the largeness of states, conquests, the abuse of government: these have suggested the route of using deputies or representatives of the people in the nation's assemblies. It is what in certain countries is called the third estate. Thus the private interest of two orders is given first and second place; the public interest is given merely third place.

Sovereignty cannot be represented for the same reason that it cannot be alienated. It consists essentially in the general will, and the will does not allow of being represented. It is either itself or something else; there is nothing in between. The deputies of the people, therefore, neither are nor can be its representatives; they are merely its agents. They cannot conclude anything definitively. Any law that the populace has not ratified in person is null; it is not a law at all. The English people believes itself to be free. It is greatly mistaken; it is free only during the election of the members of Parliament. Once they are elected, the populace is enslaved; it is nothing. The use the English people makes of that freedom in the brief moments of its liberty certainly warrants their losing it.

The idea of representatives is modern. It comes to us from feudal government, that iniquitous and absurd government in which the human race is degraded and the name of man is in dishonor. In the ancient republics and even in monarchies, the people never had representatives. The word itself was unknown. It is quite remarkable that in Rome where the tribunes were so sacred, no one even imagined that they could usurp the functions of the people, and that in the midst of such a great multitude, they never tried to pass a single plebiscite on their own authority. However, we can size up the difficulties that were sometimes caused by the crowd by what took place in the time of the Gracchi, when part of the citizenry voted from the rooftops.

Where right and liberty are everything, inconveniences are nothing. In the care of this wise people, everything was handled correctly. It allowed its lictors to do what its tribunes would not have dared to do. It had no fear that its lictors would want to represent it.

However, to explain how the tribunes sometimes represented it, it is enough to conceive how the government represents the sovereign. Since the law is merely the declaration of the general will, it is clear that the people cannot be represented in the legislative power. But it can and should be represented in the executive power, which is merely force applied to the law. This demonstrates that, on close examination, very few nations would be found to have laws. Be that as it may, it is certain that, since they have no share in the executive power, the tribunes could never represent the Roman people by the rights of their office, but only by usurping those of the senate.

Among the Greeks, whatever the populace had to do, it did by itself. It was constantly assembled at the public square. It inhabited a mild climate; it was not greedy; its slaves did the work; its chief item of business was its liberty. No longer having the same advantages, how are the same rights to be preserved? Your harsher climates cause you to have more needs;[13] six months out of the year the public square is uninhabitable; your muted tongues cannot make themselves understood in the open air; you pay more attention to your profits than to your liberty; and you are less fearful of slavery than you are of misery.

What! Can liberty be maintained only with the support of servitude? Perhaps. The two extremes meet. Everything that is not in nature has its drawbacks, and civil society more so than all the rest. There are some unfortunate circumstances where one's liberty can be preserved only at the expense of someone else's, and where the citizen can be perfectly free only if the slave is completely enslaved. Such was the situation in Sparta. As for you, modern peoples, you do not have slaves, but you yourselves are slaves. You pay for their liberty with your own. It is in vain that you crow about that preference. I find more cowardice in it than humanity.

I do not mean by all this that having slaves is necessary, nor that the right of slavery is legitimate, for I have proved the contrary. I am merely stating the reasons why modern peoples who believe themselves free have representatives, and why ancient peoples did not have them. Be that as it may, the moment a people gives itself representatives, it is no longer free; it no longer exists.

All things considered, I do not see that it is possible henceforth for the sovereign to preserve among us the exercise of its rights, unless the city is very small. But if it is very small, will it be subjugated? No. I will show

13. To adopt in cold countries the luxury and softness of the orientals is to desire to be given their chains; it is submitting to these with even greater necessity than they did.

later[14] how the external power of a great people can be combined with the ease of administration and the good order of a small state.

CHAPTER XVI

That the Institution of Government Is Not a Contract

Once the legislative power has been well established, it is a matter of establishing the executive power in the same way. For this latter, which functions only by means of particular acts, not being of the essence of the former, is naturally separate from it. Were it possible for the sovereign, considered as such, to have the executive power, right and fact would be so completely confounded that we would no longer know what is law and what is not. And the body politic, thus denatured, would soon fall prey to the violence against which it was instituted.

Since the citizens are all equal by the social contract, what everyone should do can be prescribed by everyone. On the other hand, no one has the right to demand that someone else do what he does not do for himself. Now it is precisely this right, indispensable for making the body politic live and move, that the sovereign gives the prince in instituting the government.

Several people have claimed that this act of establishment was a contract between the populace and the leaders it gives itself, a contract by which are stipulated between the two parties the conditions under which the one obliges itself to command and the other to obey. It will be granted, I am sure, that this is a strange way of entering into a social contract! But let us see if this opinion is tenable.

First, the supreme authority cannot be modified any more than it can be alienated; to limit it is to destroy it. It is absurd and contradictory for the sovereign to acquire a superior. To obligate oneself to obey a master is to return to full liberty.

Moreover, it is evident that this contract between the people and some or other persons would be a particular act. Whence it follows that this contract could be neither a law nor an act of sovereignty, and that consequently it would be illegitimate.

It is also clear that the contracting parties would, in relation to one another, be under only the law of nature and without any guarantee of their reciprocal commitments, which is contrary in every way to the civil state. Since the one who has force at his disposal is always in control of its employment, it would come to the same thing if we were to give the name contract to the act of a man who would say to another, "I am giving you all my goods, on the condition that you give me back whatever you wish." There is only one contract in the state, that of the association, and

---

14. This is what I intended to do in the rest of this work, when in treating external relations I would have come to confederations. An entirely new subject, and its principles have yet to be established.

that alone excludes any other. It is impossible to imagine any public contract that was not a violation of the first contract.

CHAPTER XVII
On the Institution of the Government

What should be the terms under which we should conceive the act by which the government is instituted? I will begin by saying that this act is complex or composed of two others, namely the establishment of the law and the execution of the law.

By the first, the sovereign decrees that there will be a governing body established under some or other form. And it is clear that this act is a law.

By the second, the people names the leaders who will be placed in charge of the established government. And since this nomination is a particular act, it is not a second law, but merely a consequence of the first and a function of the government.

The problem is to understand how there can be an act of government before a government exists, and how the people, which is only sovereign or subject, can in certain circumstances become prince or magistrate.

Moreover, it is here that we discover one of those remarkable properties of the body politic, by which it reconciles seemingly contradictory operations. For this takes place by a sudden conversion of sovereignty into democracy, so that, without any noticeable change, and solely by a new relation of all to all, the citizens, having become magistrates, pass from general to particular acts, and from the law to its execution.

This change of relation is not a speculative subtlety without exemplification in practice. It takes place everyday in the English Parliament, where the lower chamber on certain occasions turns itself into a committee of the whole in order to discuss better the business of the sovereign court, thus becoming the simple commission of the sovereign court (the latter being what it was the moment before), so that it later reports to itself, as the House of Commons, the result of what it has just settled in the committee of the whole, and deliberates all over again under one title about what it had already settled under another.

The peculiar advantage to democratic government is that it can be established in actual fact by a simple act of the general will. After this, the provisional government remains in power, if this is the form adopted, or establishes in the name of the sovereign the government prescribed by the law; and thus everything is in accordance with the rule. It is not possible to institute the government in any other legitimate way without renouncing the principles established above.

CHAPTER XVIII

The Means of Preventing
Usurpations of the Government

From these clarifications, it follows, in confirmation of Chapter XVI, that the act that institutes the government is not a contract but a law; that the trustees of the executive power are not the masters of the populace but its officers; that it can establish and remove them when it pleases; that for them there is no question of contracting, but of obeying; and that in taking on the functions the state imposes on them, they merely fulfill their duty as citizens, without in any way having the right to dispute over the conditions.

Thus, when it happens that the populace institutes a hereditary government, whether it is monarchical within a single family or aristocratic within a class of citizens, this is not a commitment it is entering. It is a provisional form that it gives the administration, until the populace is pleased to order it otherwise.

It is true that these changes are always dangerous, and that the established government should never be touched except when it becomes incompatible with the public good. But this circumspection is a maxim of politics and not a rule of law [droit], and the state is no more bound to leave civil authority to its leaders than it is to leave military authority to its generals.

Again, it is true that in such cases it is impossible to be too careful about observing all the formalities required in order to distinguish a regular and legitimate act from a seditious tumult, and the will of an entire people from the clamor of a faction. And it is here above all that one must not grant anything to odious cases except what cannot be refused according to the full rigor of the law [droit]. And it is also from this obligation that the prince derives a great advantage in preserving his power in spite of the people, without anyone being able to say that he has usurped it. For in appearing to use only his rights, it is quite easy for him to extend them, and under the pretext of public peace, to prevent assemblies destined to reestablish good order. Thus he avails himself of a silence he keeps from being broken, or of irregularities he causes to be committed, to assume that the opinion of those who are silenced by fear is supportive of him, and to punish those who dare to speak. This is how the decemvirs, having been first elected for one year and then continued for another year, tried to retain their power in perpetuity by no longer permitting the comitia to assemble. And it is by this simple means that all the governments of the world, once armed with the public force, sooner or later usurp the public authority.

The periodic assemblies I have spoken of earlier are suited to the prevention or postponement of this misfortune, especially when they have no need for a formal convocation. For then the prince could not prevent them without openly declaring himself a violator of the laws and an enemy of the state.

The opening of these assemblies, which have as their sole object the preservation of the social treaty, should always take place through two propositions which can never be suppressed, and which are voted on separately:

The first: *Does it please the sovereign to preserve the present form of government?*

The second: *Does it please the people to leave its administration to those who are now in charge of it?*

I am presupposing here what I believe I have demonstrated, namely that in the state there is no fundamental law that cannot be revoked, not even the social compact. For if all the citizens were to assemble in order to break this compact by common agreement, no one could doubt that it was legitimately broken. Grotius even thinks that each person can renounce the state of which he is a member and recover his natural liberty and his goods by leaving the country.[15] But it would be absurd that all the citizens together could not do what each of them can do separately.

END OF THE THIRD BOOK

BOOK IV

CHAPTER I
That the General Will Is Indestructible

So long as several men together consider themselves to be a single body, they have but a single will, which is concerned with their common preservation and the general well-being. Then all the energies of the state are vigorous and simple; its maxims are clear and luminous; there are no entangled, contradictory interests; the common good is clearly apparent everywhere, demanding only good sense in order to be perceived. Peace, union, equality are enemies of political subtleties. Upright and simple men are difficult to deceive on account of their simplicity. Traps and clever pretexts do not fool them. They are not even clever enough to be duped. When, among the happiest people in the world, bands of peasants are seen regulating their affairs of state under an oak tree, and always acting wisely, can one help scorning the refinements of other nations, which make themselves illustrious and miserable with so much art and mystery?

A state thus governed needs very few laws; and in proportion as it becomes necessary to promulgate new ones, this necessity is universally

15. On the understanding that one does not leave in order to evade one's duty and to be exempt from serving the homeland the moment it needs us. In such circumstances, taking flight would be criminal and punishable; it would no longer be withdrawal, but desertion.

understood. The first to propose them merely says what everybody has already felt; and there is no question of either intrigues or eloquence to secure the passage into law of what each has already resolved to do, once he is sure the others will do likewise.

What misleads argumentative types is the fact that, since they take into account only the states that were badly constituted from the beginning, they are struck by the impossibility of maintaining such an administration. They laugh when they imagine all the foolishness a clever knave or a sly orator could get the people of Paris or London to believe. They do not know that Cromwell would have been sentenced to hard labor by the people of Berne, and the Duc de Beaufort imprisoned by the Genevans.

But when the social bond begins to relax and the state to grow weak, when private interests begin to make themselves felt and small societies begin to influence the large one, the common interest changes and finds opponents. Unanimity no longer reigns in the votes; the general will is no longer the will of all. Contradictions and debates arise, and the best advice does not pass without disputes.

Finally, when the state, on the verge of ruin, subsists only in an illusory and vain form, when the social bond of unity is broken in all hearts, when the meanest interest brazenly appropriates the sacred name of the public good, then the general will becomes mute. Everyone, guided by secret motives, no more express their opinions as citizens than if the state had never existed; and iniquitous decrees having as their sole purpose the private interest are falsely passed under the name of laws.

Does it follow from this that the general will is annihilated or corrupted? No, it is always constant, unalterable and pure; but it is subordinate to other wills that prevail over it. Each man, in detaching his interest from the common interest, clearly sees that he cannot totally separate himself from it; but his share of the public misfortune seems insignificant to him compared to the exclusive good he intends to make his own. Apart from this private good, he wants the general good in his own interest, just as strongly as anyone else. Even in selling his vote for money he does not extinguish the general will in himself; he evades it. The error he commits is that of changing the thrust of the question and answering a different question from the one he was asked. Thus, instead of saying through his vote *it is advantageous to the state,* he says *it is advantageous to this man or that party that this or that view should pass.* Thus the law of the public order in the assemblies is not so much to maintain the general will, as to bring it about that it is always questioned and that it always answers.

I could present here a number of reflections about the simple right to vote in every act of sovereignty, a right that nothing can take away from the citizens; and on the right to state an opinion, to offer proposals, to divide, to discuss, which the government always takes great care to allow only to its members. But this important subject would require a separate treatise, and I cannot say everything in this one.

CHAPTER II
On Voting

It is clear from the preceding chapter that the manner in which general business is taken care of can provide a rather accurate indication of the present state of mores and of the health of the body politic. The more harmony reigns in the assemblies, that is to say, the closer opinions come to unanimity, the more dominant too is the general will. But long debates, dissensions, and tumult betoken the ascendance of private interests and the decline of the state.

This seems less evident when two or more orders enter into its constitution, as had been done in Rome by the patricians and the plebeians, whose quarrels often disturbed the comitia, even in the best of times in the Republic. But this exception is more apparent than real. For then, by the vice inherent in the body politic, there are, as it were, two states in one. What is not true of the two together is true of each of them separately. And indeed even in the most tumultuous times, the plebiscites of the people, when the senate did not interfere with them, always passed quietly and by a large majority of votes. Since the citizens have but one interest, the people had but one will.

At the other extreme of the circle, unanimity returns. It is when the citizens, having fallen into servitude, no longer have either liberty or will. Then fear and flattery turn voting into acclamations. People no longer deliberate; either they adore or they curse. Such was the vile manner in which the senate expressed its opinions under the emperors; sometimes it did so with ridiculous precautions. Tacitus observes that under Otho, the senators, while heaping curses upon Vitellius, contrived at the same time to make a frightening noise, so that, if by chance he became master, he would be unable to know what each of them had said.

From these various considerations there arise the maxims by which the manner of counting votes and comparing opinions should be regulated, depending on whether the general will is more or less easy to know and the state more or less in decline.

There is but one law that by its nature requires unanimous consent. This is the social compact. For civil association is the most voluntary act in the world. Since every man is born free and master of himself, no one can, under any pretext whatever, place another under subjection without his consent. To decide that the son of a slave is born a slave is to decide that he was not a man.

If, therefore, at the time of the social compact, there are opponents to it, their opposition does not invalidate the contract; it merely prevents them from being included in it. They are foreigners among citizens. Once the state is instituted, residency implies consent. To inhabit the territory is to submit to sovereignty.[1]

1. This should always be understood in connection with a free state, for otherwise the family, goods, the lack of shelter, necessity, or violence can keep an inhabitant

Aside from this primitive contract, the vote of the majority always obligates all the others. This is a consequence of the contract itself. But it is asked how a man can be both free and forced to conform to wills that are not his own. How can the opponents be both free and be placed in subjection to laws to which they have not consented?

I answer that the question is not put properly. The citizen consents to all the laws, even to those that pass in spite of his opposition, and even to those that punish him when he dares to violate any of them. The constant will of all the members of the state is the general will; through it they are citizens and free.[2] When a law is proposed in the people's assembly, what is asked of them is not precisely whether they approve or reject, but whether or not it conforms to the general will that is theirs. Each man, in giving his vote, states his opinion on this matter, and the declaration of the general will is drawn from the counting of votes. When, therefore, the opinion contrary to mine prevails, this proves merely that I was in error, and that what I took to be the general will was not so. If my private opinion had prevailed, I would have done something other than what I had wanted. In that case I would not have been free.

This presupposes, it is true, that all the characteristics of the general will are still in the majority. When they cease to be free, there is no longer any liberty regardless of the side one takes.

In showing earlier how private wills were substituted for the general will in public deliberations, I have given an adequate indication of the possible ways of preventing this abuse. I will discuss this again at a later time. With respect to the proportional number of votes needed to declare this will, I have also given the principles on the basis of which it can be determined. The differences of a single vote breaks a tie vote; a single opponent destroys a unanimous vote. But between a unanimous and a tie vote there are several unequal divisions, at any of which this proportionate number can be fixed in accordance with the condition and needs of the body politic.

Two general maxims can serve to regulate these ratios. One, that the more important and serious the deliberations are, the closer the prevailing opinion should be to unanimity. The other, that the more the matter at hand calls for alacrity, the smaller the prescribed difference in the division of opinion should be. In decisions that must be reached immediately, a majority of a single vote should suffice. The first of these maxims seems more suited to the laws, and the second to public business. Be that as it

---

in a country in spite of himself; and then his sojourn alone no longer presupposes his consent to the contract or to the violation of the contract.

2. In Genoa, the word *libertas* [liberty] can be read on the front of prisons and on the chains of galley-slaves. This application of the motto is fine and just. Indeed it is only malefactors of all social classes who prevent the citizen from being free. In a country where all such people were in the galleys, the most perfect liberty would be enjoyed.

may, it is the combination of the two that establishes the ratios that best help the majority to render its decision.

CHAPTER III
On Elections

With regard to the elections of the prince and the magistrates, which are, as I have said, complex acts, there are two ways to proceed, namely by choice or by lots. Both of these have been used in various republics, and at present we still see a very complicated mixture of the two in the election of the Doge of Venice.

Voting by lot, says Montesquieu, *is of the essence of democracy.* I agree, but why is this the case? *Drawing lots,* he continues, *is a way of electing that harms no one; it leaves each citizen a reasonable hope of serving the homeland.* These are not reasons.

If we keep in mind that the election of leaders is a function of government and not of the sovereignty, we will see why the method of drawing lots is more in the nature of democracy, where the administration is better in proportion as its acts are less numerous.

In every true democracy the magistrature is not an advantage but a heavy responsibility that cannot justly be imposed on one private individual rather than another. The law alone can impose this responsibility on the one to whom it falls by lot. For in that case, with the condition being equal for all and the choice not depending on any human will, there is no particular application that alters the universality of the law.

In any aristocracy, the prince chooses the prince; the government is preserved by itself, and it is there that voting is appropriate.

The example of the election of the Doge of Venice, far from destroying this distinction, confirms it. This mixed form suits a mixed government. For it is an error to regard the government of Venice as a true aristocracy. For although the populace there has no part in the government, the nobility is itself the people. A multitude of poor Barnabites never came near any magistrature, have nothing to show for their nobility but the vain title of excellency and the right to be present at the grand council. Since this grand council is as numerous as our general council in Geneva, its illustrious members have no more privileges than our single citizens. It is certain that, aside from the extreme disparity between the two republics, the bourgeoisie of Geneva exactly corresponds to the Venetian patriciate. Our natives and inhabitants correspond to the townsmen and people of Venice. Our peasants correspond to the subjects on the mainland. Finally, whatever way one considers this Republic, apart from its size, its government is no more aristocratic than ours. The whole difference lies in the fact that, since we do not have leaders who serve for life, we do not have the same need to draw lots.

Elections by lot would have few disadvantages in a true democracy where, all things being equal both in mores and talents as well as in maxims and fortunes, the choice would become almost indifferent. But I have already said there is no such thing as a true democracy.

When choice and lots are mixed, the former should fill the position requiring special talents, such as military posts. The latter is suited to those positions, such as the responsibilities of judicature, where good sense, justice, and integrity are enough, because in a well constituted state these qualities are common to all the citizens.

Neither the drawing of lots nor voting have any place in a monarchical government. Since the monarch is by right the only prince and sole magistrate, the choice of his lieutenants belongs to him alone. When the Abbé de St. Pierre proposed multiplying the Councils of the King of France and electing the members by ballot, he did not realize that he was proposing to change the form of government.

It remains for me to speak of the manner in which the votes are cast and gathered in the people's assembly. But perhaps in this regard the history of the Roman system of administration will explain more clearly all the maxims I could establish. It is not beneath the dignity of a judicious reader to consider in some detail how public and private business was conducted in a council made of two hundred thousand men.

CHAPTER IV

On the Roman Comitia

We have no especially reliable records of the earliest period of Rome's history. It even appears quite likely that most of the things reported about it are fables.[3] And in general the most instructive part of the annals of peoples, which is the history of their founding, is the part we most lack. Experience teaches us every day the causes that lead to the revolutions of empires. But since peoples are no longer being formed, we have almost nothing but conjecture to explain how they were formed.

The customs we find established attest at the very least to the fact that these customs had an origin. Of the traditions that go back to these origins, those that are supported by the greatest authorities and that are confirmed by the strongest reasons should pass for the most certain. These are the maxims I have tried to follow in attempting to find out how the freest and most powerful people on earth exercised its supreme power.

After the founding of Rome, the new-born Republic, that is, the army of the founder, composed of Albans, Sabines, and foreigners, was divided into three classes, which took the name *tribus* [tribes] by nature of this division. Each of these tribes was divided into ten curiae, and each curia into decuriae, at the head of which were placed leaders called *curiones* and *decuriones*.

Moreover, from each tribe was drawn a body of one hundred horsemen

3. The name *Rome*, which presumably comes from *Romulus*, is Greek, and means *force*. The name *Numa* is also Greek, and means *law*. What is the likelihood that the first two kings of that town would have borne in advance names so clearly related to what they did?

or knights, called a *century*. It is clear from this that these divisions, being hardly necessary in a market-town, originally were exclusively military. But it appears that an instinct for greatness led the small town of Rome to provide itself in advance with a system of administration suited to the capital of the world.

One disadvantage soon resulted from this initial division. With the tribes of the Albans[4] and the Sabines[5] always remaining constant, while that of the foreigners[6] grew continually, thanks to their perpetual influx, this latter group soon outnumbered the other two. The remedy that Servius found for this dangerous abuse was to change the division and, in place of the division based on race, which he abolished, to substitute another division drawn from the areas of the town occupied by each tribe. In place of the three tribes, he made four. Each of them occupied one of the hills of Rome and bore its name. Thus, in remedying the inequality of the moment, he also prevented it from happening in the future. And in order that this division might not be merely one of localities but of men, he prohibited the inhabitants of one quarter from moving into another, which prevented the races from mingling with one another.

He also doubled the three ancient centuries of horsemen and he added to them twelve others, but always under the old names, a simple and judicious means by which he achieved the differentiation of the body of knights from that of the people, without causing the latter to murmur.

To the four urban tribes, Servius added fifteen others called rural tribes, because they were formed from the inhabitants of the countryside, divided into the same number of cantons. Subsequently, the same number of new ones were brought into being, and the Roman people finally found itself divided into thirty-five tribes, a number at which they remained fixed until the end of the Republic.

There resulted from this distinction between the tribes of the city and those of the countryside an effect worth noting, because there is no other example of it, and because Rome owed it both the preservation of its mores and the growth of its empire. One might have thought that the urban tribes soon would have arrogated to themselves power and honors, and wasted no time in vilifying the rural tribes. What took place was quite the opposite. The early Romans' taste for country life is well known. They inherited this taste from the wise founder who united liberty with rural and military labors, and, so to speak, relegated to the town arts, crafts, intrigue, fortune and slavery.

Thus, since all the illustrious men in Rome lived in the country and tilled the soil, people became accustomed to look only there for the mainstays of the Republic. Since this condition was that of the worthiest patricians, it was honored by everyone. The simple and laborious life of the

4. Ramnenses.

5. Tatienses.

6. Luceres.

townsmen was preferred to the lazy and idle life of the bourgeois of Rome. And someone who would have been merely a miserable proletarian in the town, became a respected citizen as a field worker. It was not without reason, said Varro, that our great-souled ancestors established in the village the nursery of those robust and valiant men who defended them in time of war and nourished them in time of peace. Pliny says positively that the tribes of the fields were honored on account of the men who made them up; on the other hand, cowards whom men wished to vilify were transferred in disgrace to the tribes of the town. When the Sabine Appius Claudius came to settle in Rome, he was decked with honors and inscribed in a rural tribe that later took the name of his family. Finally, freedmen all entered the urban tribes, never the rural ones. And during the entire period of the Republic, there was not a single example of any of these freedmen reaching any magistrature, even if he had become a citizen.

This maxim was excellent, but it was pushed so far that it finally resulted in a change and certainly an abuse in the administration.

First, the censors, after having long arrogated to themselves the right to transfer citizens arbitrarily from one tribe to another, permitted most of them to have themselves inscribed in whatever tribe they pleased. Certainly this permission served no useful purpose and deprived the censorship of one of its greatest resources. Moreover, with the great and powerful having themselves inscribed in the tribes of the countryside, and the freedmen who had become citizens remaining with the populace in the tribes of the town, the tribes in general no longer had either place or territory. On the contrary, they all found themselves so intermixed that the number of each could no longer be identified except by the registers, so that in this way the idea of the word *tribe* passed from being proprietary to personal, or rather, it became almost a chimera.

In addition, it happened that since the tribes of the town were nearer at hand, they were often the strongest in the comitia, and sold the state to those who deigned to buy the votes of the mob that made them up.

Regarding the curiae, since the founder had created ten curiae in each tribe, the entire Roman people, which was then contained within the town walls, was composed of thirty curiae, each of which had its temples, its gods, its officials, its priests and its feasts called *compitalia,* similar to the *paganalia* later held by the rural tribes.

When Servius established this new division, since this number thirty could not be divided equally among his four tribes, and since he did not want to alter it, the curiae became another division of the inhabitants of Rome, independent of the tribes. But there was no question of the curiae either in the rural tribes or among the people that make them up, for since the tribes had become a purely civil establishment and another system of administration had been introduced for the raising of troops, the military divisions of Romulus were found to be superfluous. Thus, even though every citizen was inscribed in a tribe, there were quite a few who were not inscribed in a curia.

Servius established still a third division which bore no relationship to the two preceding ones and which became, in its effects, the most important of all. He divided the entire Roman people into six classes, which he distinguished neither by place nor by person, but by wealth. Thus the first classes were filled by the rich, the last by the poor, and the middle ones by those who enjoyed a moderate fortune. These six classes were subdivided into one hundred ninety-three other bodies called centuries, and these bodies were divided in such wise that the first class alone contained more than half of them, and the last contained only one. Thus it was that the class with the smallest number of men was the one with the greatest number of centuries, and that the entire last class counted only as a subdivision, even though it alone contained more than half the inhabitants of Rome.

In order that the people might have less of a grasp of the consequences of this last form, Servius feigned giving it a military air. He placed in the second class two centuries of armorers, and two instruments of war in the fourth. In each class, with the exception of the last, he made a distinction between the young and the old, that is to say, between those who were obliged to carry arms and those whose age exempted them by law. This distinction, more than that of wealth, produced the necessity for frequently retaking the census or counting. Finally, he wished the assembly to be held in the Campus Martius, and that all those who were of age to serve should come there with their arms.

The reason he did not follow this same division of young and old in the last division is that the populace of which it was composed was not accorded the honor of bearing arms for the homeland. It was necessary to possess a hearth in order to obtain the right to defend it. And of the innumerable troops of beggars who today grace the armies of kings, there is perhaps no one who would not have been disdainfully chased from a Roman cohort, when the soldiers were the defenders of liberty.

There still is a distinction in the last class between the *proletarians* and those that are called *capite censi*. The former, not completely reduced to nothing, at least gave citizens to the state, sometimes even soldiers in times of pressing need. As for those who possessed nothing at all and could be reckoned only by counting heads, they were reckoned to be absolutely worthless, and Marius was the first who deigned to enroll them.

Without deciding here whether this third method of reckoning was good or bad in itself, I believe I can affirm that it could be made practicable only by the simple mores of the early Romans, their disinterestedness, their taste for agriculture, their dislike for commerce and for the passion for profits. Where is the modern people among whom their devouring greed, their unsettled spirit, their intrigue, their continual displacements, their perpetual revolutions of fortunes could allow such an establishment to last twenty years without overturning the entire state? It must also be duly noted that the mores and the censorship, which were stronger than this institution, corrected its defects in Rome, and that a rich man found himself relegated to the class of the poor for having made too much of a show of his wealth.

From all this, it is easy to grasp why mention is almost never made of more than five classes, even though there actually were six. The sixth, since it furnished neither soldiers for the army nor voters for the Campus Martius[7] and was of virtually no use in the Republic, was hardly ever counted for anything.

Such were the various divisions of the Roman people. Let us now look at the effect these divisions had on the assemblies. When legitimately convened, these assemblies were called *comitia*. Ordinarily they were held in the Roman forum or in the Campus Martius, and were distinguished as comitia curiata, comitia centuriata, and comitia tributa, according to which of the three forms was the basis on which they were organized. The comitia curiata were based on the institution of Romulus, the comitia centuriata on that of Servius, and the comitia tributa on that of the tribunes of the people. No law received sanction, no magistrate was elected save in the comitia. And since there was no citizen who was not inscribed in a curia, in a century, or in a tribe, it followed that no citizen was excluded from the right of suffrage, and that the Roman people was truly sovereign both de jure and de facto.

For the comitia to be legitimately assembled and for what took place to have the force of law, three conditions had to be met: first, the body or the magistrate who called these assemblies had to be invested with the necessary authority to do so; second, the assembly had to be held on one of the days permitted by law; third, the auguries had to be favorable.

The reason for the first regulation needs no explanation. The second is an administrative matter. Thus the comitia were not allowed to be held on holidays and market days, when people from the country, coming to Rome on business, did not have time to spend the day in the public forum. By means of the third rule, the senate held in check a proud and restless people, and appropriately tempered the ardor of seditious tribunes. But these latter found more than one way of getting around this constraint.

The laws and the election of leaders were not the only matters submitted to the judgment of the comitia. Since the Roman people had usurped the most important functions of government, it can be said that the fate of Europe was decided in its assemblies. This variety of objects gave rise to the various forms these assemblies took on according to the matters on which they had to pronounce.

In order to judge these various forms, it is enough to compare them. In instituting the curiae, Romulus had intended to contain the senate by means of the people and the people by means of the senate, while he dominated both equally. He therefore gave the people, by means of this form, all the authority of number to balance that of power and wealth which he left to the patricians. But in conformity with the spirit of the monarchy, he nevertheless left a greater advantage to the patricians through their

---

7. I say *Campus Martius* because it was here that the comitia centuriata gathered. In the two other forms of assembly, the people gathered in the *forum* or elsewhere, and then the *capite censi* had as much influence and authority as the first citizens.

clients' influence on the majority of the votes. This admirable institution of patrons and clients was a masterpiece of politics and humanity, without which the patriciate, so contrary to the spirit of the Republic, could not have subsisted. Only Rome had the honor of giving the world this fine example, which never led to any abuse, and which, for all that, has never been followed.

Since this same form of curiae had subsisted under the kings until Servius, and since the reign of the last Tarquin was not considered legitimate, royal laws were generally known by the name *leges curiatae*.

Under the Republic, the curiae, always limited to the four urban tribes and including no more than the populace of Rome, was unable to suit either the senate, which was at the head of the patricians, or the tribunes, who, plebeians though they were, were at the head of the citizens who were in comfortable circumstances. The curiae therefore fell into discredit and their degradation was such that their thirty assembled lictors together did what the comitia curiata should have done.

The division by centuries was so favorable to the aristocracy, that at first difficult it is to see how the senate did not always prevail in the comitia which bears this name, and by which the consuls, the censors, and other crurale magistrates were elected. In fact, of the one hundred ninety-three centuries that formed the six classes of the entire Roman people, the first class contained ninety-eight, and, since the voting was counted by centuries only, this first class alone prevailed in the number of votes over all the rest. When all its centuries were in agreement, they did not even continue to gather the votes. Decisions made by the smallest number passed for a decision of the multitude; and it can be said that in the comitia centuriata business was regulated more by the majority of money than by one of votes.

But this extreme authority was tempered in two ways. First, since ordinarily the tribunes, and always a large number of plebeians, were in the class of the rich, they balanced the credit of the patricians in this first class.

The second way consisted in the following. Instead of at the outset making the centuries vote according to their order, which would have meant always beginning with the first, one century was chosen by lot, and that one[8] alone proceeded to the election. After this, all the centuries were called on another day according to their rank, repeated the same election and usually confirmed it. Thus the authority of example was removed from rank in order to give it to lot, in accordance with the principle of democracy.

There resulted from this custom still another advantage; namely that the citizens from the country had time between the two elections to inform themselves of the merit of the provisionally named candidate, so as to give their votes only on condition of their having knowledge of the issue.

---

8. This century, having been chosen thus by lot, was called *prae rogativa*, on account of the fact that it was the first to be asked for its vote, and it is from this that the word *prerogative* is derived.

But on the pretext of speeding things up, this custom was finally abolished and the two elections were held on the same day.

Strictly speaking, the comitia tributa were the council of the Roman people. They were convened only by the tribunes. The tribunes were elected and passed their plebiscites there. Not only did the senate hold no rank in them, it did not even have the right to be present. And since the senators were forced to obey the laws upon which they could not vote, they were less free in this regard than the humblest citizens. This injustice was altogether ill-conceived, and was by itself enough to invalidate the decrees of a body to which all its members were not admitted. If all the patricians had been present at these comitia in virtue of the right they had as citizens, having then become simple private individuals, they would not have had a great deal of influence on a form of voting that was tallied by counting heads, and where the humblest proletarian had as much clout as the prince of the senate.

Thus it can be seen that besides the order that resulted from these various distributions for gathering the votes of so great a people, these distributions were not reducible to forms indifferent in themselves, but each one had effects relative to the viewpoints that caused it to be preferred.

Without going further into greater detail here, it is a consequence of the preceding clarifications that the comitia tributa were the most favorable to the popular government, and the comitia centuriata more favorable to the aristocracy. Regarding the comitia curiata, in which the populace of Rome alone formed the majority, since these were good only for favoring tyranny and evil designs, they fell of their own weight into disrepute, and even the seditious abstained from using a means that gave too much exposure to their projects. It is certain that all the majesty of the Roman people is found only in the curia centuriata, which alone were complete, for the comitia curiata excluded the rural tribes, and the comitia tributa the senate and the patricians.

As to the manner of counting the votes, among the early Romans it was as simple as their mores, though not so simple as in Sparta. Each gave his vote in a loud voice, and a clerk marked it down accordingly. The majority vote in each tribe determined the tribe's vote; the majority vote of the tribes determined the people's vote; and the same went for the curia and the centuries. This custom was good so long as honesty reigned among the citizens and each was ashamed to give his vote publicly in favor of an unjust proposal or an unworthy subject. But when the people became corrupt and votes were bought, it was fitting that they should give their votes in secret in order to restrain the buyers through distrust and to provide scoundrels the means of not being traitors.

I know that Cicero condemns this change and attributes the ruin of the Republic partly to it. But although I am aware of the weight that Cicero's authority should have here, I cannot agree with him. On the contrary, I think that, by having made not enough of these changes, the fall of the state was accelerated. Just as the regimen of healthy people is not suitable for the sick, one should not want to govern a corrupt people by means of the same laws that are suited to a good people. Nothing proves this maxim better than the long life of the Republic of Venice, whose shadow still exists, solely because its laws are suited only to wicked men.

Tablets were therefore distributed to the citizens by mean of which each man could vote without anyone knowing what his opinion was. New formalities were also established for collecting the tablets, counting the votes, comparing the numbers, and so on. None of this prevented the integrity of the officials in charge of these functions[9] from often being under suspicion. Finally, to prevent intrigue and vote trafficking, edicts were passed whose sheer multiplicity is proof of their uselessness.

Toward the end of the period of the Republic, it was often necessary to have recourse to extraordinary expedients in order to make up for the inadequacy of the law. Sometimes miracles were alleged. But this means, which could deceive the populace, did not deceive those who governed it. Sometimes an assembly was unexpectedly convened before the candidates had time to carry out their intrigues. Sometimes an entire session was spent on talk, when it was clear that the populace was won over and ready to take the wrong side on an issue. But finally ambition eluded everything; and what is unbelievable is that in the midst of so much abuse, this immense people, by virtue of its ancient regulations, did not cease to choose magistrates, pass laws, judge cases, or expedite private and public business, almost as easily as the senate itself could have done.

CHAPTER V
On the Tribunate

When it is not possible to establish an exact proportion between the constitutive parts of the state, or when indestructible causes continually alter the relationships between them, a special magistrature is then established that does not make up a larger body along with them. This magistrature restores each term to its true relationship to the others, and which creates a link or a middle term either between the prince and the people or between the prince and the sovereign, or on both sides at once, if necessary.

This body, which I will call the *tribunate,* is the preserver of the laws and the legislative power. It serves sometimes to protect the sovereign against the government, as the tribunes of the people did in Rome; sometimes to sustain the government against the people, as the Council of Ten now does in Venice; and sometimes to maintain equilibrium between the two, as the ephors did in Sparta.

The tribunate is not a constitutive part of the city and it should have no share in either the legislative or the executive power. But this is precisely what makes its own power the greater. For although it is unable to do anything, it can prevent everything. It is more sacred and more revered as a defender of the laws than the prince who executes them and the

9. Custodes, diribitores, rogatores suffragiorum.

sovereign who gives them. This was very clearly apparent in Rome when the proud patricians, who always scorned the entire populace, were forced to bow before a humble official of the people, who had neither auspices nor jurisdiction.

A well tempered tribunate is the firmest support of a good constitution. But if it has the slightest bit too much force, it undermines everything. As to weakness, there is none in its nature; and provided it is something, it is never less than it ought to be.

It degenerates into tyranny when it usurps the executive power, of which it is merely the moderator, and when it wants to dispense the laws it ought only protect. The enormous power of the ephors, which was without danger so long as Sparta preserved its mores, hastened corruption once it had begun. The blood of Agis, who was slaughtered by these tyrants, was avenged by his successor. The crime and the punishment of the ephors equally hastened the fall of the republic; and after Cleomenes Sparta was no longer anything. Rome also perished in the same way, and the excessive power of the tribunes, which they had gradually usurped, finally served, with the help of the laws that were made to protect liberty, as a safeguard for the emperors who destroyed it. As for the Council of Ten in Venice, it is a tribunal of blood, equally horrible to the patricians and the people, and which, far from proudly protecting the laws, no longer serves any purpose, after their degradation, beyond that of delivering blows in the dark which no one dares notice.

Just like the government, the tribunate weakened as a result of the multiplication of its members. When the tribunes of the Roman people, who at first were two in number, then five, wanted to double this number, the senate let them do so, certain that one part would hold the others in check; and this did not fail to happen.

The best way to prevent usurpations by so formidable a body, one that no government has yet made use of, would be not to make this body permanent, but to regulate the intervals during which it would be suppressed. These intervals, which ought not be so long as to allow abuses time to grow in strength, can be fixed by law in such a way that it is easy to shorten them, as needed, by means of extraordinary commissions.

This way seems to me to have no disadvantage, for since, as I have said, the tribunate is not part of the constitution, it can be set aside without doing the constitution any harm, because a newly established magistrate begins not with the power his predecessor had, but with the power the law gives him.

CHAPTER VI
On Dictatorship

The inflexibility of the laws, which prevents them from adapting to circumstances, can in certain instances make them harmful and render them the instrument of the state's downfall in time of crisis. The order and the slowness of formal procedures require a space of time which circumstances

sometimes do not permit. A thousand circumstances can present themselves which the legislator has not foreseen, and it is a very necessary bit
of foresight to realize that not everything can be foreseen.

It is therefore necessary to avoid the desire to strengthen political institutions to the point of removing the power to suspend their effect. Sparta
itself allowed its laws to lie dormant.

But only the greatest dangers can counterbalance the danger of altering
the public order, and the sacred power of the laws should never be suspended except when it is a question of the safety of the homeland. In these
rare and obvious cases, public safety can be provided for by a special act
which confers the responsibility for it on someone who is most worthy.
This commission can be carried out in two ways, according to the type of
danger.

If increasing the activity of government is enough to remedy the situation, it is concentrated in one or two members. Thus it is not the authority
of the laws that is altered, but merely the form of their administration.
But if the peril is such that the apparatus of the laws is an obstacle to their
being protected, then a supreme leader is named who silences all the laws
and briefly suspends the sovereign authority. In such a case, the general
will is not in doubt, and it is evident that the first intention of the people
is that the state should not perish. In this manner, the suspension of legislative authority does not abolish it. The magistrate who silences it cannot
make it speak; he dominates it without being able to represent it. He can
do anything but make laws.

The first way was used by the Roman senate when, by a sacred formula,
it entrusted the consuls with the responsibility for providing for the safety
of the Republic. The second took place when one of the two consuls
named a dictator,[10] a custom for which Alba had provided Rome the
precedent.

In the beginning days of the Republic, there was frequent recourse to
dictatorship, since the state did not yet have a sufficiently stable basis to
be capable of sustaining itself by the force of its constitution. Since the
mores at that time made many of the precautions superfluous that would
have been necessary in other times, there was no fear either that a dictator
would abuse his authority or that he would try to hold on to it beyond his
term of office. On the contrary, it seemed that such a great power was a
burden to the one in whom it was vested, so quickly did he hasten to rid
himself of it, as if a position that took the place of the laws would have
been too troublesome and dangerous!

Thus it is not so much the danger of its being abused as it is that of its
being degraded which makes one criticize the injudicious use of this
supreme magistrature in the early days of the Republic. For while it was
being wasted on elections, dedications and purely formal proceedings,
there was reason to fear that it would become less formidable in time of

10. This nomination was made at night and in secret, as if it were shameful to
place a man beyond the laws.

need, and that people would become accustomed to regard as empty a title that was used exclusively in empty ceremonies.

Toward the end of the Republic, the Romans, having become more circumspect, were as unreasonably sparing in their use of the dictatorship as they had formerly been lavish. It was easy to see that their fear was ill-founded; that the weakness of the capital then protected it against the magistrates who were in its midst; that a dictator could, under certain circumstances, defend the public liberty without ever being able to make an attack on it; and that Rome's chains would not be forged in Rome itself, but in its armies. The weak resistance that Marius offered Sulla and Pompey offered Caesar clearly demonstrated what could be expected of internal authority in the face of external force.

This error caused them to make huge mistakes; for example, failing to name a dictator in the Catalinian affair. For since this was a question merely of the interior of the town and, at most, of some province in Italy, with the unlimited authority that the laws give the dictator, he would have easily quelled the conspiracy, which was stifled only by a coming together of favor chance happenings, which human prudence has no right to expect.

Instead of that, the senate was content to entrust all its power to the consuls. Whence it happened that, in order to act effectively, Cicero was forced to exceed this power on a crucial point. And although the first transports of joy indicated approval of his conduct, eventually Cicero was justly called to account for the blood of citizens shed against the laws, a reproach that could not have been delivered against a dictator. But the eloquence of the consul carried the day. And since even he, Roman though he was, preferred his own glory to his homeland, he sought not so much the most legitimate and safest way of saving the state as he did the way that would get him all the honor for settling this affair.[11] Thus he was justly honored as the liberator of Rome and justly punished as a law-breaker. However brilliant his recall may have been, it undoubtedly was a pardon.

For the rest, whatever the manner in which this important commission was conferred, it is important to limit a dictatorship's duration to a very short period of time which cannot be prolonged. In the crises that call for its being established, the state is soon either destroyed or saved; and once the pressing need has passed, the dictatorship becomes tyrannical or needless. In Rome, where the dictators had terms of six months only, most of them abdicated before their terms had expired. If the term had been longer, perhaps they would have been tempted to prolong it further, as did the decemvirs with a one year term. The dictator only had time enough to see to the need that got him elected. He did not have time to dream up other projects.

---

11. He could not have been sure of this, had he proposed a dictator, since he did not dare name himself, and he could not be sure that his colleague would name him.

CHAPTER VII
On the Censorship

Just as the declaration of the general will takes place through the law, the declaration of the public judgment takes place through the censorship. Public opinion is the sort of law whose censor is the minister, and which he only applies to particular cases, after the example of the prince.

Thus the censorial tribunal, far from being the arbiter of the people's opinion, is merely its spokesman; and as soon as it deviates from this opinion, its decisions are vain and futile.

It is useless to distinguish the mores of a nation from the objects of its esteem, for all these things derive from the same principle and are necessarily intermixed. Among all the peoples of the world, it is not nature but opinion which decides the choice of their pleasures. Reform men's opinions, and their mores will soon become purified all by themselves. Men always love what is good or what they find to be so; but it is in this judgment that they make mistakes. Hence this is the judgment whose regulation is the point at issue. Whoever judges mores judges honor; and whoever judges honor derives his law from opinion.

The opinions of a people arise from its constitution. Although the law does not regulate mores, legislation is what gives rise to them. When legislation weakens, mores degenerate; but then the judgment of the censors will not do what the force of the laws has not done.

It follows from this that the censorship can be useful for preserving mores, but never for reestablishing them. Establish censors while the laws are vigorous. Once they have lost their vigor, everything is hopeless. Nothing legitimate has any force once the laws no longer have force.

The censorship maintains mores by preventing opinions from becoming corrupt, by preserving their rectitude through wise applications, and sometimes even by making a determination on them when they are still uncertain. The use of seconds in duels, which had been carried to the point of being a craze in the kingdom of France, was abolished by the following few words of the king's edict: *as for those who are cowardly enough to call upon seconds*. This judgment anticipated that of the public and suddenly made a determination. But when the same edicts tried to declare that it was also an act of cowardice to fight duels (which of course is quite true, but contrary to common opinion), the public mocked this decision; it concerned a matter about which its mind was already made up.

I have said elsewhere[12] that since public opinion is not subject to constraint, there should be no vestige of it in the tribunal established to represent it. It is impossible to show too much admiration for the skill with which this device, entirely lost among us moderns, was put into effect among the Romans and even better among the Lacedemonians.

---

12. I merely call attention in this chapter to what I have treated at greater length in my *Letter to D'Alembert*.

When a man of bad mores put forward a good proposal in the council of Sparta, the ephors ignored it and had the same proposal put forward by a virtuous citizen. What honor for the one, what shame for the other; and without having given praise or blame to either of the two! Certain drunkards of Samos[13] defiled the tribunals of the ephors. The next day, a public edict gave the Samians permission to be filthy. A true punishment would have been less severe than impunity such as this. When Sparta made a pronouncement on what was or was not decent, Greece did not appeal its judgments.

CHAPTER VIII
On Civil Religion

At first men had no other kings but the gods, and no other government than a theocratic one. They reasoned like Caligula, and then they reasoned correctly. A lengthy alteration of feelings and ideas is necessary before men can be resolved to accept a fellow man as a master, in the hope that things will turn out well for having done so.

By the mere fact that a god was placed at the head of every political society, it followed that there were as many gods as there were peoples. Two peoples who were alien to one another and nearly always enemies, could not recognize the same master for very long. Two armies in combat with one another could not obey the same leader. Thus national divisions led to polytheism, and this in turn led to theological and civil intolerance which are by nature the same, as will be stated later.

The fanciful notion of the Greeks that they had rediscovered their gods among the beliefs of barbarian peoples arose from another notion they had of regarding themselves as the natural sovereigns of these peoples. But in our day it is a ridiculous bit of erudition which equates the gods of different nations: as if Moloch, Saturn, and Chronos could have been the same god; as if the Phoenicians' Baal, the Greeks' Zeus, and the Romans' Jupiter could have been the same; as if there could be anything in common among chimerical beings having different names!

But if it is asked how in pagan cultures, where each state has its own cult and its own gods, there are no wars of religion, I answer that it was for this very reason that each state, having its own cult as well as its own government, did not distinguish its gods from its laws. Political war was theological as well. The departments of the gods were, so to speak, fixed by national boundaries. The gods of one people had no rights over other peoples. The gods of the pagans were not jealous gods. They divided dominion over the world among themselves. Moses himself and the Hebrew people sometimes countenanced this idea in speaking of the god of Israel. It is true they regarded as nothing the gods of the Canaanites, a proscribed people destined for destruction, and whose land they were to occupy. But

13. [Rousseau adds the following in the 1782 edition: "They are from another island which the delicacy of our language prohibits me from naming at this time."]

note how they spoke of the divinities of neighboring peoples whom they were forbidden to attack! *Is not the possession of what belongs to your god Chamos*, said Jephthah to the Ammonites, *lawfully yours? By the same right we possess the lands our victorious god has acquired for himself.*[14] It appears to me that here was a clear recognition of the parity between the rights of Chamos and those of the god of Israel.

But when the Jews, while in subjection to the kings of Babylon and later to the kings of Syria, wanted to remain steadfast in not giving recognition to any other god but their own, their refusal, seen as rebellion against the victor, brought them the persecutions we read of in their history, and of which there is no other precedent prior to Christianity.[15]

Since, therefore, each religion was uniquely tied to the laws of the state which prescribed it, there was no other way of converting a people except by enslaving it, nor any other missionaries than conquerors. And with the obligation to change cult being the law of the vanquished, it was necessary to begin by conquering before talking about it. Far from men fighting for the gods, it was, as it was in Homer, the gods who fought for men; each asked his own god for victory and paid for it with new altars. Before taking an area, the Romans summoned that area's gods to leave it. And when they allowed the Tarentines to keep their angry gods, it was because at that point they considered these gods to be in subjection to their own and forced to do them homage. They left the vanquished their gods, just as they left them their laws. A wreath to the Capitoline Jupiter was often the only tribute they imposed.

Finally, the Romans having spread this cult and their gods, along with their empire, and having themselves often adopted the gods of the vanquished by granting the right of the city to both alike, the peoples of this vast empire gradually found themselves to have multitudes of gods and cults, which were nearly the same everywhere. And that is how paganism finally became a single, identical religion in the known world.

Such were the circumstances under which Jesus came to establish a spiritual kingdom on earth. In separating the theological system from the political system, this made the state to cease being united and caused internal divisions that never ceased to agitate Christian peoples. But since this new idea of an otherworldly kingdom had never entered the heads of the pagans, they always regarded the Christians as true rebels who, underneath their hypocritical submission, were only waiting for the moment

---

14. *Nonne ea quae possidet Chamos deus tuus, tibi jure debentur?* Such is the text of the Vulgate. Father de Carrières has translated it: *Do you not believe that you have the right to possess what belongs to your god Chamos?* I do not know the force of the Hebrew text; but I see that in the Vulgate Jephthah positively acknowledges the right of the god Chamos, and that the French translator weakened this recognition by adding an *according to you* which is not in the Latin.

15. It is quite clear that the Phocian War, called the Holy War, was not a war of religion at all. It had for its object to punish sacrileges, and not to make unbelievers submit.

when they would become independent and the masters, and adroitly usurp the authority they pretended in their weakness to respect. This is the reason for the persecutions.

What the pagans feared happened. Then everything changed its appearance. The humble Christians changed their language, and soon this so-called otherworldly kingdom became, under a visible leader, the most violent despotism in this world.

However, since there has always been a prince and civil laws, this double power has given rise to a perpetual jurisdictional conflict that has made all good polity impossible in Christian states, and no one has ever been able to know whether it is the priest or the master whom one is obliged to obey.

Nevertheless, several peoples, even in Europe or nearby have wanted to preserve or reestablish the ancient system, but without success. The spirit of Christianity has won everything. The sacred cult has always remained or again become independent of the sovereign and without any necessary link to the state. Mohammed had very sound opinions. He tied his political system together very well, and so long as the form of his government subsisted under his successors, the caliphs, this government was utterly unified, and for that reason it was good. But as the Arabs became prosperous, lettered, polished, soft and cowardly, they were subjugated by barbarians. Then the division between the two powers began again. Although it is less apparent among the Mohammedans than among the Christians, it is there all the same, especially in the sect of Ali; and there are states, such as Persia, where it never ceases to be felt.

Among us, the kings of England have established themselves as heads of the Church, and the czars have done the same. But with this title, they became less its masters than its ministers. They have acquired not so much the right to change it as the power to maintain it. They are not its legislators; they are merely its princes. Wherever the clergy constitutes a body,[16] it is master and legislator in its own realm. Thus there are two powers, two sovereigns, in England and in Russia, just as there are everywhere else.

Of all the Christian writers, the philosopher Hobbes is the only one who clearly saw the evil and the remedy, who dared to propose the reunification of the two heads of the eagle and the complete restoration of political unity, without which no state or government will ever be well constituted. But he should have seen that the dominating spirit of Christianity was incompatible with his system, and that the interest of the priest

---

16. It should be carefully noted that it is not so much the formal assemblies, such as those of France, which bind the clergy together into a body, as it is the communion of the churches. Communion and excommunication are the social compact of the clergy, one with which it will always be the master of the peoples and the kings. All the priests who communicate together are citizens, even if they should be from the opposite ends of the world. This invention is a political masterpiece. There is nothing like this among the pagan priests; thus they never made up a body of clergy.

would always be stronger than that of the state. It is not so much what is horrible and false in his political theory as what is just and true that has caused it to be hated.[17]

I believe that if the facts of history were developed from this point of view, it would be easy to refute the opposing sentiments of Bayle and Warburton, the one holding that no religion is useful to the body politic, while the other maintains, to the contrary, that Christianity is its firmest support. We could prove to the first that no state has ever been founded without religion serving as its base, and to the second that Christian law is at bottom more injurious than it is useful for the strong constitution of the state. To succeed in making myself understood, I need only give a bit more precision to the excessively vague ideas about religion that are pertinent to my subject.

When considered in relation to society, which is either general or particular, religion can also be divided into two kinds, namely the religion of the man and that of the citizen. The first—without temples, altars or rites, and limited to the purely internal cult of the supreme God and to the eternal duties of morality—is the pure and simple religion of the Gospel, the true theism, and what can be called natural divine law [droit]. The other, inscribed in a single country, gives it its gods, its own titulary patrons. It has its dogmas, its rites, its exterior cult prescribed by laws. Outside the nation that practices it, everything is infidel, alien and barbarous to it. It extends the duties and rights of man only as far as its altars. Such were all the religions of the early peoples, to which the name of civil or positive divine law [droit] can be given.

There is a third sort of religion which is more bizarre. In giving men two sets of legislation, two leaders, and two homelands, it subjects them to contradictory duties and prevents them from being simultaneously devout men and citizens. Such is the religion of the Lamas and of the Japanese, and such is Roman Christianity. It can be called the religion of the priest. It leads to a kind of mixed and unsociable law [droit] which has no name.

Considered from a political standpoint, these three types of religion all have their faults. The third is so bad that it is a waste of time to amuse oneself by proving it. Whatever breaks up social unity is worthless. All institutions that place man in contradiction with himself are of no value.

The second is good in that it unites the divine cult with love of the laws, and that, in making the homeland the object of its citizens' admiration, it teaches them that all service to the state is service to its tutelary god. It is a kind of theocracy in which there ought to be no pontiff other than the prince and no priests other than the magistrates. To die for one's country is then to become a martyr; to violate its laws is to be impious. To subject

---

17. Notice, among other things, in Grotius' letter to his brother, dated April 11, 1643, what this learned man approves of and what he criticizes in his book *De Cive.* It is true that, prone to being indulgent, he appears to forgive the author for his good points for the sake of his bad ones. But not everyone is so merciful.

a guilty man to public execration is to deliver him to the wrath of the gods: *sacer estod*.

On the other hand, it is bad in that, being based on error and lies, it deceives men, makes them credulous and superstitious, and drowns the true cult of the divinity in an empty ceremony. It is also bad when, on becoming exclusive and tyrannical, it makes a people bloodthirsty and intolerant, so that men breathe only murder and massacre, and believe they are performing a holy action in killing anyone who does not accept its gods. This places such a people in a natural state of war with all others, which is quite harmful to its own security.

Thus there remains the religion of man or Christianity (not that of today, but that of the Gospel, which is completely different). Through this holy, sublime, true religion, men, in being the children of the same God, all acknowledge one another as brothers, and the society that unites them is not dissolved even at death.

But since this religion has no particular relation to the body politic, it leaves laws with only the force the laws derive from themselves, without adding any other force to them. And thus one of the great bonds of a particular society remains ineffectual. Moreover, far from attaching the hearts of the citizens to the state, it detaches them from it as from all the other earthly things. I know of nothing more contrary to the social spirit.

We are told that a people of true Christians would form the most perfect society imaginable. I see but one major difficulty in this assumption, namely that a society of true Christians would no longer be a society of men.

I even say that this supposed society would not, for all its perfection, be the strongest or the most durable. By dint of being perfect, it would lack a bond of union; its destructive vice would be in its very perfection.

Each man would fulfill his duty; the people would be subject to the laws; the leaders would be just and moderate, the magistrates would be upright and incorruptible; soldiers would scorn death; there would be neither vanity nor luxury. All of this is very fine, but let us look further.

Christianity is a completely spiritual religion, concerned exclusively with things heavenly. The homeland of the Christian is not of this world. He does his duty, it is true, but he does it with a profound indifference toward the success or failure of his efforts. So long as he has nothing to reproach himself for, it matters little to him whether anything is going well or poorly down here. If the state is flourishing, he hardly dares to enjoy the public felicity, for fear of becoming puffed up with his country's glory. If the state is in decline, he blesses the hand of God that weighs heavily on his people.

For the society to be peaceful and for harmony to be maintained, every citizen without exception would have to be an equally good Christian. But if, unhappily, there is a single ambitious man, a single hypocrite, a Cataline, for example, or a Cromwell, he would quite undoubtedly gain the upper hand on his pious compatriots. Christian charity does not readily allow one to think ill of his neighbors. Once he has discovered by some ruse

the art of deceiving them and of laying hold of a part of the public authority, behold a man established in dignity! God wills that he be respected.
Soon, behold a power! God wills that he be obeyed. Does the trustee of
his power abuse it? He is the rod with which God punishes his children.
It would be against one's conscience to expel the usurper. It would be
necessary to disturb the public tranquillity, use violence and shed blood.
All this accords ill with the meekness of a Christian. And after all, what
difference does it make whether one is a free man or a serf in this vale of
tears? The essential thing is getting to heaven, and resignation is but another means to that end.

What if a foreign war breaks out? The citizens march without reservation into combat; none among them dreams of deserting. They do their
duty, but without passion for victory; they know how to die better than
how to be victorious. What difference does it make whether they are the
victors or the vanquished? Does not providence know better than they
what they need? Just imagine the advantage a fierce, impetuous and pas-
sionate enemy could draw from their stoicism! Set them face to face with
those generous peoples who were devoured by an ardent love of glory and
homeland. Suppose your Christian republic is face to face with Sparta or
Rome. The pious Christians will be beaten, crushed and destroyed before
they realize where they are, or else they will owe their safety only to the
scorn their enemies will conceive for them. To my way of thinking, the
oath taken by Fabius' soldiers was a fine one. They did not swear to die
or to win; they swore to return victorious. And they kept their promise.
Christians would never have taken such an oath; they would have believed
they were tempting God.

But I am deceiving myself in talking about a Christian republic; these
terms are mutually exclusive. Christianity preaches only servitude and
dependence. Its spirit is too favorable to tyranny for tyranny not to take
advantage of it at all times. True Christians are made to be slaves. They
know it and are hardly moved by this. This brief life has too little value
in their eyes.

Christian troops, we are told, are excellent. I deny this. Is someone
going to show me some? For my part, I do not know of any Christian
troops. Someone will mention the crusades. Without disputing the valor
of the crusaders, I will point out that quite far from being Christians, they
were soldiers of the priest; they were citizens of the church; they were
fighting for its spiritual country which the church, God knows how, had
made temporal. Properly understood, this is a throwback to paganism.
Since the Gospel does not establish a national religion, no holy war is
possible among Christians.

Under the pagan emperors, Christian soldiers were brave. All the Christian authors affirm this, and I believe it. This was a competition for honor
against the pagan troops. Once the emperors were Christians, this competition ceased. And when the cross expelled the eagle, all Roman valor
disappeared.

But leaving aside political considerations, let us return to right and determine the principles that govern this important point. The right which the social compact gives the sovereign over the subjects does not, as I have said, go beyond the limits of public utility.[18] The subjects, therefore, do not have to account to the sovereign for their opinions, except to the extent that these opinions are of importance to the community. For it is of great importance to the state that each citizen have a religion that causes him to love his duties. But the dogmas of that religion are of no interest either to the state or its members, except to the extent that these dogmas relate to morality and to the duties which the one who professes them is bound to fulfill toward others. Each man can have in addition such opinions as he pleases, without it being any of the sovereign's business to know what they are. For since the other world is outside the province of the sovereign, whatever the fate of subjects in the life to come, it is none of its business, so long as they are good citizens in this life.

There is, therefore, a purely civil profession of faith, the articles of which it belongs to the sovereign to establish, not exactly as dogmas of religion, but as sentiments of sociability, without which it is impossible to be a good citizen or a faithful subject.[19] While not having the ability to obligate anyone to believe them, the sovereign can banish from the state anyone who does not believe them. It can banish him not for being impious but for being unsociable, for being incapable of sincerely loving the laws and justice, and of sacrificing his life, if necessary, for his duty. If, after having publicly acknowledged these same dogmas, a person acts as if he does not believe them, he should be put to death; he has committed the greatest of crimes: he has lied before the laws.

The dogmas of the civil religion ought to be simple, few in number, precisely worded, without explanations or commentaries. The existence of a powerful, intelligent, beneficent divinity that foresees and provides; the life to come; the happiness of the just; the punishment of the wicked; the sanctity of the social contract and of the laws. These are the positive dogmas. As for the negative dogmas, I am limiting them to just one, namely intolerance. It is part of the cults we have excluded.

Those who distinguish between civil and theological intolerance are mistaken, in my opinion. Those two types of intolerance are inseparable. It is impossible to live in peace with those one believes to be damned. To

18. *In the Republic,* says the Marquis d'Argenson, *each man is perfectly free with respect to what does not harm others.* This is the invariable boundary. It cannot be expressed more precisely. I have been unable to deny myself the pleasure of occasionally citing this manuscript, even though it is unknown to the public, in order to pay homage to the memory of a famous and noteworthy man, who, even as a minister, retained the heart of a citizen, along with just and sound opinions on the government of his country.

19. By pleading for Cataline, Caesar tried to establish the dogma of the mortality of the soul. To refute him, Cato and Cicero did not waste time philosophizing. They contented themselves with showing that Caesar spoke like a bad citizen and advanced a doctrine that was injurious to the state. In fact, this was what the Roman senate had to judge, and not a question of theology.

love them would be to hate God who punishes them. It is absolutely necessary either to reclaim them or torment them. Whenever theological intolerance is allowed, it is impossible for it not to have some civil effect;[20] and once it does, the sovereign no longer is sovereign, not even over temporal affairs. Thenceforward, priests are the true masters; kings are simply their officers.

Now that there no longer is and never again can be an exclusive national religion, tolerance should be shown to all those that tolerate others, so long as their dogmas contain nothing contrary to the duties of a citizen. But whoever dares to say *outside the church there is no salvation* ought to be expelled from the state, unless the state is the church and the prince is the pontiff. Such a dogma is good only in a theocratic government; in all other forms of government it is ruinous. The reason why Henry IV is said to have embraced the Roman religion should make every decent man, and above all any prince who knows how to reason, leave it.

CHAPTER IX

Conclusion

After laying down the true principles of political right and attempting to establish the state on this basis, it remains to support the state by means of its external relations, which would include the laws of nations, commerce, the right of war and conquest, public law, leagues, negotiations, treaties, and so on. But all that forms a new subject which is too vast for my nearsightedness. I should always set my sights on things that are nearer at hand to me.

END

20. Marriage, for example, being a civil contract, has civil effects without which it is impossible for a society even to subsist. Suppose then that a clergy reaches the point where it ascribes to itself alone the right to permit this act (a right that must necessarily be usurped in every intolerant religion). In that case, is it not clear that in establishing the authority of the church in this matter, it will render ineffectual that of the prince, who will have no more subjects than those whom the clergy wishes to give him? Is it not also clear that the clergy—if master of whether to marry or not to marry people according to whether or not they accept this or that doctrine, according to whether they accept or reject this or that formula, according to whether they are more or less devout—in behaving prudently and holding firm, will alone dispose of inheritance, offices, the citizens, the state itself, which could not subsist, if composed solely of bastards? But, it will be said, abuses will be appealed; summonses and decrees will be issued; temporal holdings will be seized. What a pity! If it has a little—I will not say courage—but good sense, the clergy will serenely allow the appeals, the summonses, the decrees and the seizures, and it will end up master. It is not, it seems to me, a big sacrifice to abandon a part when one is sure of securing the whole.